Ivan Antic

RELIGIOUSNESS

Instructions for Use

SAMKHYA PUBLISHING LTD
London, 2020

Translated by
Milica Breber

Book cover by design
Zoran Ignjatovic
https://ignjatoviczoran.weebly.com

ISBN: 9798677577024

Table of Contents

INTRODUCTION

WHY THERE IS A NEED FOR THIS KIND OF MANUAL

It is best to begin by understanding the meaning of the words themselves.

What meaning does the word *religion* convey?

The etymology of the word religion stems from the Latin *re* (again) and *lego* (choose, decide, carefully consider); to reconnect.

The notion of religion is also derived from the verb *religere* and refers to the separation from ordinary things, while figuratively it means to revere or treat with respect.

The essence of these words is in connecting - someone connecting with something. But who is connecting with what? If we simply say man with God, we are in danger of ending the story immediately by accepting a dogma. The answer to the question who is connecting with what demands a more nuanced answer, and exploring the questions: who is man in his essence? and who or what is God?

In finding the answer to these questions, we will find all of the treasure in the universe, the meaning of life. Discovering the answer is itself religiousness. But whoever considers themselves to have found the answer is no longer a religious man, but has become a fanatic.

Religiousness as 'reconnecting' does not refer to some abstract God, but to the fact that man's position in this world is, in effect, much lower than his true, original state, which he had before birth. All religiousness reflects that man's state in this world represents a decline into the oblivion of consciousness of his soul, that his existence is reflected in the fact that he has become unaware of the true nature of his essence. Due to this downfall, man projects his divine essence outwards, into external temples, and he swaps awareness of his divine origin with one of various religions. All that we are meant to do in this world is return to our divine essence, cross over from the unconsciousness to the consciousness.

There is not a man on Earth that has not addressed some higher force at some point in his life. This proves that all men have, intuitively at least, an awareness of their inferior position, and that there is some kind of 'Force Majeure'. In the subconscious of every man, there is the memory that we are not just a body that is born and then dies, but that we have had an experience of existence before this life; we have a deep and intuitive conviction that we will exist after this body has died.

From time immemorial, people have had a religious attitude towards existence and life. They make religious idols from stone or wood and worship them. Religious buildings and temples have always been the biggest and the best structures, far better than the homes people lived in. This shows that people have always had a dominant consciousness of life that's superior to the physical body, a life which precedes birth and continues after death. Therefore, religiousness is not some empty aspiration toward immortality, or a fear of death, but rather a reflection of the memory of immortality, our true nature, that in hard times and unfavourable living conditions is temporarily forgotten.

Together with a belief in a higher force that exceeds our body and mind, *religiousness represents an awareness of the difference between what a higher force can do, and what we can and should do*. The awareness of this subtle difference instigated the foundation of all cultures of man and all science - it is responsible for the development of human civilization. The culture man brings into the world is a way of harmonizing what we do, in our individual lives, with the meaning of existence, with the laws of nature - with powers and functioning of the wider whole, our tuning in with reality. It is a dilemma we have come across many times in life: how to do things, whether or not to undertake a certain action to solve a problem, or simply to wait and see how things work themselves out. Taking action often leads to violence and destruction (sin), if it is not in accordance with objective reality. Action is successful only if it is harmonized with the higher force according to which everything exists, in harmony with all of the natural laws that ensue.

Our inability to understand the higher force, the true nature of the divine, leads to all of the wrong in this world. Lack of proper understanding goes both ways: we know ourselves by estimating what it is we can do, and what the higher force will do for us. Only when we know ourselves will we become aware of the higher force, of the divine power. Only when we are faced with the divine power of action do we know our true nature, in the best possible sense. But we are only halfway there. Like balancing on a scale, we learn what task to perform, and what to not, what we can and cannot do, what we should and should not do. The goal is to come to a place of perfect balance, and not to topple in one direction or another. In the perfect balance, awareness of the unity of everything occurs, awareness of the unity of ourselves and our actions, and with the world and God as well. Through this constant challenge we get to know both ourselves and the divine power of the higher force. We cannot know ourselves without taking into consideration the higher force, and in the same way we cannot know the divine power without knowing ourselves, through those actions we use to harmonize with the divine.

In olden days people prayed to a higher force to give them their 'daily bread', to show mercy, and that meant to help them with the hardships of life. Therefore, the true purpose of religiousness must be the development of consciousness, and to learn to make our own 'daily bread' with our own hands; to learn how to make life merciful by acquiring knowledge of life, of natural laws, and being in control of life in the proper way, in accordance with the laws of nature. Real knowledge of the laws of nature fundamentally means being in accordance with them. Man will, then, be the source of divine grace. He will no longer have needs that the higher force must fulfill. Asking the higher force for help was a phase of inspiration for man, so he could learn how to increase the power of his actions, how he may himself, at long last, become merciful.

Science and religion originated from the same foundation, from man's admiration of the miraculous perfection of the nature that created our body and mind; both science and religion originated from our desire to understand and harmonize with nature. Science is a tool of religiousness. Scientific research is identical to the religious consciousness of existence that surpasses the body and mind - albeit with the difference that scientific research does not prejudge conclusions, and does not stick to the previously stated truths dogmatically (at least, this should not be the case). It has theories and hypotheses, but they serve as the working assumption for finding proof and to understand the laws of existence. Hence, science works on the concrete discovery of the truth of existence, step by step, up until the point that man comes to an awareness of the true nature of reality, with full consciousness, and starts to be a creative participant in its function.

Religiousness draws out the truth of existence from man's soul in the form of intuition and memory.

Both methods require one another to be whole. Religiousness acts as an inspiration that pulls us toward the highest reality, and science acts as an operational method that pushes us forward, and solves practical issues along the way. They merely need some adjustment, through understanding their joint goal.

If a scientist does not harmonize the results of his work with the consciousness of his soul, and his scientific results do not fulfill his soul - if they do not act in the best interests of life, then he did not do the right thing.

If a religious man does not manifest the consciousness of his soul, his relationship to the divine through constructive endeavour and creativity in the outer, physical world, he is not truly religious.

A scientist must be religious, and a religious man must act like a scientist.

Both are on the search for answers about reality. Both are on their way back to their lost divine essence. A religious man attempts to achieve his return through temples and religion, and a scientist tries to do the same through science. Neither will reconnect with their essence outwards, but by becoming better acquainted with reality itself, here and now; they will both find divine reality in the laws of nature. Divine reality has never been missing, they just became unconscious of it. All they need is an awakening.

Oblivion is always manifested by projecting both the problem and the solution outwards. Awakening always happens by recognizing both the problem and the solution within - by changing oneself, knowing oneself.

Someone who is on a quest for the answer is quiet, attentive, and open to all options, because he expects his answer to come from everywhere. A real scientist has a constantly open mind to all possibilities. A true believer is constantly in prayer and contemplation, even when he is working. The person who thinks he has found the answer to the reality of existence becomes destructive. The believer becomes a fanatic, and the scientist becomes an arms manufacturer, for example - making items that are destructive toward nature and life. Dogmatism destroys both science and religion.

True religiousness and true science are only found in openness of the mind to new ideas, to that which is bigger and wider than the mind itself: the manifestation of the consciousness of man's soul in this world.

Religiousness is neither a state, nor a belief, but a process. This process begins with man's immature and childish expectation of a 'magician in the sky' that solves all problems, and ends in an adult and competent approach to life - someone who creates everything he needs ('you will be like gods').

Religiousness is a process of growing and harmonizing with reality. It is naive to think that people are capable of recognizing the reality of the world they live in. Human history has been full of destruction, and today's reality shows that man is still far from recognizing reality for what it is, and even further from actively participating in it. We are still in the early stages of this process, we still deal with magic in all sorts of ways; rationality and responsibility are still not overly present in our everyday functioning. Human rights and freedoms are just ideas, and we have a long way to go to be able to fully implement them. Mankind is still quite young, and shows infantile tendencies.

Man's religiousness has never been about God and heavenly matters, but about the functioning of man in this world, and his perfecting - being a better human being.

A better understanding of the whole process, of how to become better people, will be harmonized by religiousness, in the best possible way.

Hence, the need for a manual of this kind.

CREATOR

Let us deal with the nature of the divine itself, which 'creates' so that we will be able to understand what has been created. The divine that's behind the manifestation of everything, we can call the "divine Absolute", which is a neutral term, linguistically and logically the most appropriate. This will avoid confusion as to what or whose God we have in mind when we talk about it.

The divine Absolute is everything that is and everything that can be, as well as everything that enables; what was before everything and what is in everything and what will be after everything, what is beyond or independent of all. Such is the nature of the Absolute. It also deserves the epithet "divine" because it is sublime, above everything that has been created. It is characterized by a perfect conscious intention in everything.

The divine Absolute is everything that is, and a source of consciousness too. Its nature is pure awareness of itself. As such, due to the very nature of consciousness, it must be manifested and expressed to have a perception of itself, to be aware of itself. Perception always happens between a subject and an object. Hence, it must manifest as the object, as everything it can be. This is the cosmos, or nature in all of its dimensions, both the ones we can perceive with our senses and those ones we cannot but that still exist.

The Absolute cannot remain itself without the option of manifestation, since that would lead to a paradox; when it is unmanifested it remains as nothing, voidness, *sunyata*, the way it has been described in esoteric teachings, and nothingness by itself cannot exist. That is why the divine Absolute must always be manifested. This has brought about the dual nature of the divine: unmanifested and manifested. However, in its manifestation, it cannot be anything but itself, always, because nothing outside of it exists. This is why it used to be said that 'there is no other God but God', that real religiousness is in monotheism.

That is why the divine Absolute manifests in the only way possible: into its seeming opposition.

The seeming opposition of the Absolute (as infinitely big) is a point, or the "divine particle" (infinitely small).

This point was described by Euclid, who also attributed all of the properties of the Absolute to it. The true nature of the point is the Absolute itself.

This point is called *bindu* in the Vedas. It is a seed which the whole universe grows from.

Since this opposition is possible only as an illusion, because nothing outside of the divine Absolute is possible, the world has been considered since ancient times to be an illusion (*maya*, *avidya*), with God as the only reality.

This ostensible opposition or "divine particle" does not exist as a particle, but as vibration. It vibrates constantly into everything that is; it vibrates momentarily, much faster than light. Its vibration creates all other shapes, atoms, and molecules. Its vibration is pure energy. That is why particles and energy exist in parallel - they cannot be differentiated from one another. In fact, only our perspective distinguishes a particle from energy.

CREATION

Since nothing is possible outside of the Absolute, nothing can manifest from it but the Absolute as the illusion of its opposition, as a point or divine particle. The Absolute is immeasurably vast compared to that opposition, and the point is its exact opposition: it is infinitely small. This divine particle does not do anything besides vibrate in such an amazingly fast way that it is momentary. It does not exist in time, but is timeless, and its vibration is instantaneous.

The divine particle vibrates instantly and **with its vibrations creates the illusion of a multitude of phenomena**. One kind of vibration creates what we on our gross material plane see as a single subatomic particle, one atom, one element; another kind of vibration creates another element, and so forth. Different vibrations of the same divine particle create the illusion of different particles and elements, which in turn grow in complexity, creating all of the gross elements and everything we perceive as matter, in a multitude of objects.

We can say this in a different way, to make it clearer.

Space is the only thing that has no properties. We call it the divine Absolute. The first phenomenon in space to have any properties in three-dimensional form is a photon - light. **The photon is the basic energy field, it is the first complex emanation of the divine particle.** Photons move through space because they are the first manifestation in space that is different from space itself; their motion achieves the maximum speed possible for an object, which is the speed of light.

More accurately still: light originates as a result of movement, which is maximal in the manifested universe. Light is the border between the manifested and unmanifested universe. That is why there is light in the higher dimensions, beyond the physical world; the higher dimensions are filled with light, and the source of light is ever-present there. The physical universe has the least light. This is one explanation as to why cognition, the source of life and consciousness, has always been identified with light. In early religions, the sun was the first real God.

Since photons are the first phenomenon in space that is different from the space, they move spontaneously, aspiring to fill space. As if they were ripped from the space of divine Absolute and wish to get back to it, to fill the newly created vacuum. That is why they move at such great speeds and in all directions. That is why stars were created, to light up the physical universe. In the three-dimensional universe, three-dimensional sources of photons must exist, which are stars.

The motion of photons by itself creates what we see as energy. Motion and energy are no different. Photons are light phenomena because they are energy phenomena – energy manifests itself as light. They are energy phenomena because they always move.

Photons come in all sizes, both big and small. Smaller photons have higher energy than the big ones. When photons of different sizes and energies collide, refraction of light happens. *All the colours that exist originate in this way. Light is colour. However, when photons of approximately the same, high energy (gamma photons) collide, they create a whirlpool which, if it is stable enough, we perceive as mass. This is the mechanism by which mass, that is matter, is created by light*[1]

Therefore, everything that is made up of one single divine particle, vibrating so fast that it momentarily shapes the illusion of assorted formations, matter, employs light first.

Every single moment, God vibrates from its unmanifested state of the Absolute into the manifested state as the divine particle, as light and as all phenomena.

All matter is vibration initially - that is, energy. Everything is divine vibration.

All the energy in nature comes from this vibration of the divine particle; it is the source of all motion and all life. The word energy comes from the Greek word *energeia* which means "being in motion". (We have forgotten today about this original meaning, about general vibration and the motion of life, and we have been left to think that energy is only what we get when we burn fuel.)

Therefore, it can be said conditionally that there is some divine particle, but a more accurate description is that there is only the vibration of divine energy. Everything is just a vibration of the divine that manifests as light, energy, and form. The divine consciousness vibrates as the ground we walk on, the water we drink, the air we breathe, the thoughts in our mind... they are all different vibrations of the same energy. That is why all of these shapes become synchronized into the organic unity of life so harmoniously. It would not be possible to harmonize all of life if it did not come from a common source, if it were not already One and if it were not conscious. (This is of key importance for those who believe that God is One, the Almighty, all-merciful, and that there is no other God but God. Maybe this is a way in which they will be able to notice him finally.)

This also shows us that the foundation of life is divine consciousness, a conscious intention; that conscious-

ness is not only our perception and memory, something that appears and disappears in our brain at random, but rather that consciousness is the greatest creative force, which enables everything; consciousness is existence itself.

How does the divine consciousness manifest through everything that exists?

Between every two vibrations, the divine particle returns to its original state, to the divine Absolute itself; it restarts over and over again. Every moment consists of this restarting into some new state, a new possibility; never chaotic but as a conscious intention, like logos. In this way, the divine is not separated from its manifestation. The divine is the foundation of all vibrations, it enables vibrations of everything-that-is. The divine vibrates as everything-that-is, much like every phenomena. In this way, the divine is not separated from everything that exists.

The divine Absolute is the highest awareness of itself; it manifests as the universal consciousness through everything that has been created; consciousness is the foundation of all forms and phenomena, and it is also the foundation of energy. Absolutely everything that exists is the reflection of a conscious intention, of the consciousness itself. This is why divine consciousness, like energy, does not have to be conveyed through some medium, nor travel through space and time; it is already timelessly at the foundation of everything that is; it springs up between each vibration of the divine particle.[2]

This tells us that a **multitude of consciousnesses does not exist, but that it is the same consciousness in everything;** it springs from the divine Absolute and branches out into a myriad of shapes, into everything-that-is and everything-that-can-be. The consciousness that enables us to understand all of this is the same divine consciousness that recognizes itself through our experience.

One crucial point must be remembered here: the divine Absolute is everything-that-is and it manifests as everything-that-can-be, using its vibrations in the illusory form of the divine particle.

Religious people have always felt that God is present in everything; they felt it within as well as without.

Science has reached a similar conclusion.

Studying the gross phenomena of matter and energy, physics has discovered that the foundation of all existence is interwoven into one whole, outside of space and time, and that nothing is separate. This foundation of existence is called the universal quantum field. Everything that has ever actualized in our visible world was already present there, as a possibility, in its potential state. Subatomic particles, even parts of our DNA, once separated and spaced thousands of kilometers apart, behave as though they are still together; if one is exposed to external stimuli, the other responds simultaneously. Thisp led to the conclusion that the universe is a big hologram, whose every part contains all the others, and that the whole is indivisible.

The very notion of religion points to that unity - that the universe is a hologram we must consciously recognize in order to become aware of the fact that we are one with it. *If everything is interconnected, everything is conscious. Connectedness is consciousness. Consciousness means connecting everything into a meaningful whole.* The part of DNA that reacts simultaneously when its removed part is affected, is somehow aware of the change; there is a connection that enables an instant reaction. If everything is connected, it means that it is conscious, and consciousness is this connectedness. Conscious connectedness is the force of action, energy, the power to act, where nothing can happen without conscious intention. We are under an illusion if we think that consciousness is solely perception based on our senses and function of the brain. The consciousness that's our theme here is the supreme power of the universe, the power that creates the universe, together with all phenomena.

Consciousness is the only God, and is behind all of creation.

Consciousness as the greatest creative force in the universe rests on the strongest aspiration of the whole universe: *a return to the divine state of the Absolute.* The manifested universe aspires toward its unmanifested, divine state. The basic vibration of existence consists of momentary manifestation, and then returning to the unmanifested divine state. Nothing can be outside of the divine. That is why it keeps going back. The universe lies in the balance between the manifested and unmanifested.

Therefore, God did not vanish into thin air after "creating the world"; he is existence itself, its vibration, its energy, and consciousness. God is a man knowing himself and realizing himself through his divine presence.

Using the language of physics, the divine Absolute is a hologram in which everything is one, every part contains the whole within. This means that nothing is separate from the universal quantum field, from the divine Absolute. In its outcome, this means that nothing is created and that everything is an illusion of our mind. Since nothing at all is possible outside of the Absolute, creation is not an option either. The only "creation" occurs in our image of the world, and not in the world itself. Nothing happened on the outside, no 'creation of the world' ever took place; the divine Absolute itself was and remained forever perfect in itself.

All the greatest mystics have revealed this truth, since ancient times; they saw God in everything and everything in God. The old Slav myth says that in the beginning there was nothing but God, who was dreaming forever, but the time had come for him to wake up. Upon his awakening, our world came into being. This figuratively explains that the whole of the manifested world is divine awareness of itself. God awakens through man.

The divine Absolute is everything-that-is.

Everything-that-is always manifests itself as everything-that-can-be, vibrating as one single 'divine particle'. One divine consciousness enables everything that there is. Our mind uses this same consciousness to a lesser degree, but with the illusion of separation - thinking its consciousness is separate from the divine whole. When man turns to himself, to the source of his consciousness, he discovers his absolute nature, and he meets God in person.

God is in man, as the background of his soul. Everything that is outside, all of the universe and life, are his vibrations in the form of the 'divine particle'. This vibration does not happen out there, somewhere in the cosmos or beyond, because that is not where God is. God is in the conscious subject, in man. The physical universe automatically originates when man is unaware of himself. When he forgets himself, the world projects outwards. This is the mechanism behind the creation of the world – the oblivion of consciousness of itself. In the awareness of oneself, there is no outside world. There is only God.

This is the most accurate definition of God and creation.[3]

Therefore, you should not make for yourself an idol of any kind, or an image of anything in the heavens above, or in the earth beneath, or in the waters below. You should also not have other definitions of God but this one. All others belong to heedless heretics.

If you want to be truly religious, you should not believe that God created the world. You should not believe in the illusion of the world. You should just believe in God.

This is the accurate definition of a religious man: he believes in God and nothing else.

A truly religious man sees and respects God in everything that exists. The falsely religious conflicts everything that exists, because he believes in some abstract God.

For as long as there is any kind of conflict in the world, it serves as evidence that religiousness is wrong.

The biggest dilemma of every believer is how to marry worldly experiences with his idea of a perfect God. A believer becomes religious in the right way only when he accepts the reality of the world, and participates in it as he would in divine reality, when he does not negate the world to promote God, when he negates or rejects nothing, and when he accepts everything as the only divine reality, as the will of God. When he begins to view the world the way he views God, and vice versa.

An atheist acknowledges the world but does not acknowledge God, often acting contrary to the interests of the world and life because he does not have a deeper awareness of life. A religious fanatic acknowledges only God and negates the world, and is prepared to destroy the world for the sake of God. A correctly religious man is above these two extremes; he sees the world as God, and God as the world.

Only this correct faith will unlock a whole new world for you. Do not trust the world more than you trust

God. Do not separate God from the world. Trust divine consciousness more, and you will find yourself in a much better position to know the true nature of this world and life. By knowing the true nature of the world and life, you will know the true nature of God.

Only God exists as the highest reality; everything else is an illusion.

Contrary to monotheistic religions that claim God is only one - the God of Christians, the God of Jews, the God of Muslims - this is not what we mean by saying God is the only. No. We mean that all phenomena and all beings, the universe, are interconnected in one unity which is aware of itself and therefore divine. Its nature is absolute, so nothing outside of it is possible. The obvious conclusion is that we, too, are one with it, it is always in unity with us. It is that one God we are talking about here. The emphasis is on the consciousness of unity, and not on God. It is not 'somewhere up there', it is in your heart waiting for you to become aware of it, like you are aware of yourself.[4]

This God does not write books, such books that are the only right ones and have to be learned by heart by nodding your head back and forth; nor does he dictate them to his ghostwriter; he does not send his angels as messengers or as mailmen (*angelos* – the bringer of news), nor as assassins; such a God does not give birth to sons (only); he does not kill as a terrorist the infidels that are going for a walk with their children in the street, nor does he request his followers to kill themselves; he does not have prophets or sons – any good man is the son of God,[5] anyone who speaks from the purity of his soul is his prophet.

All great mystics and saints offer the wisdom that there is not any world apart from God. This world is the manifestation of divine consciousness and its presence. The world is merely a way in which the divine consciousness manifests all of its possibilities and qualities.

We are not separate from the divine consciousness. To understand the secret of the creation of the world, look at yourself, then turn around and inspect your immediate surroundings, your home, your relationships, your city. Nobody but you made it the way it is. To reach the highest reality of this world, start by organizing your reality, your home, and your environment, before any prayer or contemplation. No religious practice, when performed in a pigsty, will lift you above that pigsty. Religiousness has the characteristic of dedication, which in those circumstances will only make you a bigger pig.

Never try to understand something by forgetting the one who should understand – yourself. Never look for reality by forgetting about the existing reality you are in, here and now.

Finally, understanding the true nature of reality is possible only through meditation, because our being is a microcosm, the cosmos in miniature, and meditation is the act of returning to one's source, the fundamental reality of our being. When in meditation, we enter ourselves and unite with our essence, Self or soul; *we replicate, in our being, the same thing that happened to the whole cosmos, and that keeps happening every single moment to the cosmos.* It vibrates every moment by manifesting itself as the cosmos, and going back to its unmanifested state of the divine Absolute. We are the cosmos in miniature, and when we do something within us, when from a manifested state we quieten and return to our unmanifested source, in the state of samadhi, we replicate the creation of the world and its return to the divine Absolute. That is the only way for us to understand the secret of creation, to recognize our harmony with creation. We then recognize it, the way it has been described on these pages.

Then we see that divine consciousness has manifested itself into its opposite, into the divine particle and everything-that-can-be, through seven phases.

The manifestation of the world is the awakening of the awareness of itself. It follows a set pattern. The manifestation of the world takes place through the law of the number seven and through five dimensions.

CREATION OF THE WORLD THROUGH SEVEN PHASES

In the most popular religious book in the world, it says God created the world in seven days. There is a law of number seven disclosed on its pages. Every process of creation happens following seven phases. These phases are present in the formation of crystals, in the expansion of photons or light that result in seven colours, in the spreading of sound vibrations that give seven tones, in the growth and development process of every living being. The seven phase principle exists in emitting heat, magnetism, chemical reactions, and all other natural processes. It exists because the universe is manifested through seven phases. From the start of every process until the end, seven phases occur that cause subtle changes and adjustments. There are six phases in total, and the seventh is the ignition for the beginning of a new cycle. Every phase may instigate a change in direction of correct growth. The same applies to formations of nature, as well as phenomena. This is what enables the constant and universal versatility of all shapes and events. These phases are alternations in the vibrations, in effect. They follow a set pattern, revealed to us by fractal or sacred geometry, the golden section.

The science dealing with proportions of divine manifestation according to the number seven was conveyed to us by G. I. Gurdjieff, from the ancient monasteries of the Middle East, and was detailed by his disciple P. D. Ouspensky in his work 'Cosmological Teachings'.

According to this teaching, the divine Absolute progressively manifested itself through seven phases. These phases of manifestation of the divine hologram are like shattering glass into smaller and smaller fragments, each of which still reflects the whole image of divine Absolute. These phases develop via spiral motion, circling from the higher dimension toward the lower, following the rule of the golden section. This descending pattern is also what consciousness uses on its way to lower states. Each portion has awareness of itself, and it automatically repeats the original illusion of self-sufficiency, and goes on to create the next, lower portion, in which consciousness is even more conditioned.

Let's look at the seven phases of creation:

1. The Absolute as wholeness and divine self. It enables timeless cosmic space (aether, *akasha*), which enables everything else. It is pure existence which precedes consciousness of the Self.

2. The divine consciousness manifests from cosmic space, in the form of all the galaxies. Above them is empty space that contains them and nothing else. Space corresponds with aether or the quantum field, which all particles and elements originate from. Its initial manifestation is photons.

3. The divine consciousness manifested itself as all the stars in galaxies. Stars are the first concrete form of manifestation of consciousness. Stars are the first, elementary objects that have a stable coherent mass, which is a result of photons colliding. It was said that the divine consciousness manifested itself as light first, and afterward it became mass, or everything we see as the material world. Behind every physical phenomenon, when one inspects its essence carefully, we see light. Through the stars, the divine consciousness becomes light and the source of life.

(Galaxies are made up of stars, therefore the question remains what came first: the galaxies or the stars, the chicken or the egg? Maybe galaxies are fields that allow stars to appear. This reveals the timeless nature of the highest portion of reality, which is the closest to the divine Absolute. It introduces a paradox to our mind, which operates in terms of time.)

4. From this manifestation of divine consciousness, our star the Sun was also made. Through the Sun, the possibility for consciousness to express itself in the form of human individual souls on planet Earth emerges. The common coordinator of the lives of all the human souls on Earth is the Sun.

5. The consciousness of the divine Absolute further manifested itself as the planetary systems orbiting the Sun. It enables awareness of all aspects of phenomena and the experiences of human souls on planet Earth. Planets provide the psychodynamics of life, the versatility of characters and temperaments.

6. The consciousness of the divine Absolute manifested itself as the planet Earth and all of the organic life on it. Divine consciousness is identified with physical life in each individual body, plant, animal, and human. In human beings, the divine consciousness of the Absolute experiences the karmic drama of all the possibilities of existence, of everything-that-could-be. By doing so, it knows everything-that-is, or itself.

7. The divine consciousness then manifested itself as the Moon - Earth's satellite. The Moon with its gravity impacts life on Earth by binding consciousness to the body. Owing to the Moon, consciousness in individual beings on Earth is in a state of sleep, like being possessed; this is a result of total identification with the body. If it were not for the Moon, consciousness of the soul would make all decisions itself, but because of the Moon it is conditioned.[6]

We had to witness this progressive development like this, from the Earth, since we cannot observe it from some other, imaginary point. It is a ray of creation that operates from the Absolute to us, and that is how we must observe it. It would be the same from some other observation point; the only difference would be what we use as a reference point.

These are the portions of existence. Each has a logic of its own and they cannot be mixed. The nature of every kind of existence can be understood only in the context of the portion it belongs to. Each higher portion acts on the lower, but each lower one uses the higher for its energy or 'food'.

In each of the portions, the Divine divides itself and forms as the Divine of that proportion, yet again following the holographic model, into smaller entities. Therefore, there is a Divine that rules all the galaxies, then all the stars and their planetary systems, as well as one Divine entity that rules every planet that hosts organic life.

Branching out the divine consciousness from the highest to the lower is like a tree placed upside down, with its roots in the highest sphere and leaves and branches in the lowest. The root is the divine Absolute, and every individual soul is a leaf on that tree.

Divine consciousness divides and branches out into every conscious being that exists. Each of us is one of these beings. The finest expression of divine consciousness is the individual souls in people. Our soul is the most subtle form of manifestation of the divine consciousness.

This is the story of creation that's behind the metaphor of creating the world in seven days.

THE CREATION OF MAN

Since the universe is a hologram, everything is contained within everything, including man's being; this too is a part of that hologram, because man is a microcosm in whom all of the principles and laws of the cosmos are contracted.

The universe is a hologram in which everything is interconnected into unity, but this unity keeps manifesting itself in a symmetric and analog way, into the outer and the inner world. Man's mind is the dividing line between these two worlds. This division does not exist outside of man's conscious mind, his ego. The mind/ego exists only to create the illusion that our individuality is separate from the outer world, for us to be able to function in this world as though there truly were a world of objects in our reality.

The mystical teachings of Hermes Trismegistus tell us that 'as above so below, as within so without'. Gospels teach us that the 'kingdom of God is in us', we should first look for it within to be able to find it without (in everyday life). At the entrance of the Egyptian temple in Luxor, there is an inscription on the wall: 'The body is the house of God'. Inside the temple, there is a further inscription: 'Man, know yourself and you will know God'.[7]

The message of all these teachings is as follows: all of the higher dimensions are in man; he is made up of all the dimensions of existence. To man, the primary method to become acquainted with the world is to know himself. These two cognitions go hand in hand: learning about the world and self-knowledge are mutually dependent and binding. Hence, the necessary material development of civilization, together with man's knowledge, or God-knowledge. They cannot happen separately. Man's influence on the outside world is a mirror of his development and self-knowledge.

We will see here and in other chapters that it is not possible to achieve God-knowledge without the development of a material culture and civilization in general. There have been a large number of disagreements on this point, and both religious and civilizational conflicts rest on this question, now more than ever.

Man unites two fundamental expressions of existence, the outer and the inner, the manifested and the unmanifested, the material and the spiritual. All of this unites through man and his deeds in the world. Throughout history, man's mind has been engaged with the concept of uniting what that same mind has been seemingly dividing: the outer and the inner, the visible and the invisible, the material and the spiritual, phenomena and meaning.

The number seven is also contracted in man. It is expressed in the cycles of maturation, each one lasting for seven years, and in the seven states of consciousness that correspond with the seven chakras, the psychoenergetic centres that connect states of consciousness with physical actions and that comprise the seven karmic levels of existence and action, including the seven levels of religiousness.

The lesson of man as a cosmic being is found in the teachings of Sankhya and Purusha - the source of divine consciousness that enables everything. Note that the word itself denotes man. Sankhya equals man's essence or soul with the divine consciousness which enables everything. There is a similar notion in the Kabbalistic teaching of Adam Kadmon, the primordial man, the first being to emerge from the creation of the cosmos. Upanishads describe a primal man composed of the elements that were to become the world. According to these teachings, this 'gigantic divine being' is both infinitely far away and deposited near the innermost recesses of the human heart, as the Self or the soul of man. It is present in all the stars, simultaneously. In Hindu tradition, the primordial man is identified both with the entire universe and with the soul or essence of all things.

Plutarch suggests that the entirety of the heavens is arranged in the form of machroanthropos, a colossal human being conceived as a model for the human world, or us the way we are here and now. This is the teaching of Gnosticism and Kabbalah. It is, therefore, important to know that we did not originate here, in this world, nor were we born with the birth of our physical body; *we came into being together with the universe.* All the dimensions of the universe from the lowest to the highest are in us; *we are made from all the dimensions of nature.*

It is a fact that we, in our original angelic state, before being born into this body, had already projected the entire physical universe into all of its dimensions. This is why all of the dimensions of the universe compose our being.

Man is said to be the microcosm, a cosmos in miniature. The whole process of manifestation of the cosmos and the divine Absolute is replicated in us. Our physical body is the outcome of all the manifestations of nature, inorganic and organic alike, the peak of creation of life. Our body has all the sensory and action organs, and the ability to devise their meaning. All the other living beings lack this ability; they have a certain number of sensory and action organs and correspondingly reduced power to act and cognize.

The state of consciousness of our soul also reflects the manifestation of the divine Absolute. The consciousness we have in our awakened state corresponds with the physical world. When we dream we are in the astral, the first higher dimension above the material world. The state of consciousness we have in deep sleep without dreams corresponds with the unmanifested Absolute. In deep sleep, there is no world, nothing exists but our existence. When we wake from deep sleep and find ourselves in a physical body, everything else re-emerges, and at that point the divine Absolute has manifested itself as the physical universe. These are not two separate phenomena, they are the same, but only seemingly apart in seven phases, or in the portions of existence and across the five dimensions. Since the universe is a hologram, on the micro plane man experiences it as deep sleep and awakening, and on the macro plane as the manifestation of the cosmos.

This is the true meaning of the expression that man is a microcosm, who can only function because the universe is a hologram.

It is an illusion to consider man as an individual being, completely separated from the divine whole. For the same reason we stressed that there is nothing created outside of God, we can safely say that there is no man. Only God exists. This is what people who knew God saw - all the saints, all enlightened people. They came to the realization of the true reality by simply disappearing as individuals. They all unanimously claim that man is around for as long as he focuses all of his attention outwards, to the world, when all he should do is to know himself. Man knows himself by disappearing more and more as a separate individual, and becoming more and more one with God. This is the only way out of the illusion. The only problem that exists is man's problem with himself.

Strictly scientifically speaking, man is in complete unity with nature, he is not separated from it. This is another way in which the physical body should not be viewed as something separate from the whole. It is in such unity with natural processes that boundaries between our bodies and surrounding nature disappear. Only in the illusion of our mind and ego is the surface of our skin the border of our being and life. In reality, in the divine whole, there are no limits. If we were to remove our body from the Earth and send it into the cosmos, it would die on the spot. This would be a picturesque way for us to see that we are in complete unity with the Earth.

The whole Earth is our true body. The whole of nature is our being. This individual physical body, with arms and legs, is only a means by which we become aware of the truth. This is the opinion of a truly religious man. He cannot be religious by only regarding his body and his life. He can be religious only by regarding the whole, the whole of nature. His religiousness is in his ability to surpass the illusion of his separation from the whole. Only one who does not distinguish himself from the whole knows God. When enlightened mystics testified to seeing themselves in everything, and everything in themselves, they literally meant so - it was not a metaphor.

A properly religious man is one who treats nature religiously, and who does not jeopardize life in any way.

We have already suggested that no worlds have ever been created, it is illusory to believe that God created the world, and that only God exists. Now we see that no man was created either. This is an even bigger illusion. This illusion is the source of all suffering in this world. Every man in this world suffers, only because he thinks he exists as man, separate from the whole. Man's being is just a suitable spot in the organic world, through which divine consciousness can express itself in three-dimensions and act as an individual personality, to express and experience its most subtle aspects and potentials through individual phenomena and their meaning. Man's individuation is simply a way to achieve this. It is not an aim unto itself.

The divine manifests itself in various forms of existence, everywhere; only in human form does the divine express itself through events, work, and the reaction of the consciousness to those events and work. This is called karma. Only through human form is the divine consciousness united with shaping and phenomena. Uniting consciousness with shapes is what we call becoming aware of the meaning of existence.

Man is a place where all of the divine manifestation and existence arrives at its destination, its meaning.

The only meaning of existence for man is understanding or increasing the level of understanding of himself and the world, in every respect.

Therefore, we should perceive with understanding all of the dimensions of divine manifestation, to be able to perceive ourselves better.

MAN'S SOUL

Man's soul is an individual reflection of divine consciousness, or the Absolute, which is everything that is. Everything that exists is the divine Absolute. The soul is a conscious subject of everything that is, of the divine Absolute itself. In the conscious subject, the soul, the meaning of everything contracts. Existence moves towards meaning, and nothing exists that does not make sense. Everything that exists does so for a reason. The soul is merely a factor that collects the meaning of everything that exists. In this way, the soul is a creative factor. It double-checks the meaning of everything, practically, by creating new possibilities of existence.

Existence and consciousness are the same. Everything you see, touch, feel and perceive in any way, all the gross matter surrounding you, is consciousness, the divine consciousness; everything exists because of the conscious intention for it to exist, in exactly the way it does, in every single moment. In that sense, everything is alive, in the same way as you are alive. You are now and have always been submerged in the ocean of divine consciousness, like a fish in the sea, like a baby inside its mother's womb. This description is merely a way of rephrasing the obvious: divine consciousness is this existence here and now, as everything that is.

Divine consciousness, like existence, has individual forms; existence is not impersonal, it always has a specific form, from elements to events. Consciousness/existence is always individualized. That is why everything exists in a specific form. Consciousness creates all forms, all events, and that explains why there are so many forms and so many monads creating them.

Divine consciousness always divides itself into monads, into individual forms; at the highest level they are known to us as archangels and seraphims. They branch out like a tree from the divine source, with the root and trunk dividing itself into smaller and smaller parts, down to twigs and leaves. In the same manner, monads of divine consciousness in the highest dimensions created the cosmos and all the galaxies, a myriad of worlds suitable for sustaining life; these monads then divide more and more, and branch out into more subtle forms until they become oversouls and then individual souls that are born into human bodies.

In the physical world, everything has an individual form. To make this possible, it is necessary for the consciousness that is behind every form to be individual. ***The individuality of consciousness itself spontaneously creates individual forms.*** From the highest monads of the archangelic consciousness of the Absolute to angelic and human souls, every single being has individual consciousness, and each on its level and in its dimension creates physical forms and events. For this multitude of individual forms and beings to be able to exist, consciousness must be individualized. Hence, a multitude of beings and phenomena are created spontaneously by the sheer individualization of the divine consciousness itself. God did not create every being and every phenomenon. They were created by the individualization of the divine consciousness, as a direct consequence of this individualization.

There is a clear subordination present in this system; the consciousness of a worm is far from human or angelic consciousness, because it originates far lower in the chain of causality; but it is still the same divine consciousness in a worm, as well as, a man and an angel. It just kept branching out into more diverse and subtle forms, into everything it possibly could.

The very individualization of the divine consciousness happens because of its need to manifest all of its possibilities; everything-that-is (God) manifests itself as everything-that-could-be (the world, the cosmos, life).

Still, it cannot be said that there are infinitely many monads of consciousness, like there are infinitely many living forms. One monad creates many forms. We cannot know the exact number of monads and individual souls that exist, but we know that one soul has many creations and experiences. It is born into a physical body as many times as is necessary for it to retrieve its original divine consciousness, or the reality that its consciousness (with which it experiences and creates everything) is the divine consciousness, and is in no way different from existence itself. **When differences of any kind between the subject (soul) and the object (world, existence) disappear, the original state of divine consciousness is realized.** Through such a soul, divine consciousness manifests in all forms of existence. This is a way for the 'kingdom of heaven' to emerge on earth the way it is in heaven. It is realized through the man himself. It does not fall from the sky.

The structure of man's being and his relationship toward the soul is shown in this picture:

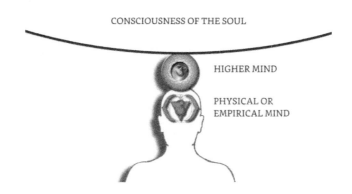

CONSCIOUSNESS OF THE SOUL

HIGHER MIND

PHYSICAL OR EMPIRICAL MIND

The soul is always above the body, or more accurately, it transcends the body. It is simply too big and too powerful to fit into a small, mortal body. Only a tiny reflection, in the form of a conscious mind, is present in the body, and this is shaped into the ego, into individual consciousness limited by the body and sensory perception. Between this empirical mind in the body and the transcendental consciousness of the soul, the higher mind exists. It connects the mind in the body with consciousness of the soul, and through it with divine consciousness.

Everything man knows of reality, and all of his objective knowledge, is a result of this bond to the higher mind. All of his ignorance, illusions, and suffering, is caused when he is closed off, residing solely in the physical mind and ego, and alienated from the higher mind and consciousness of the soul. All of man's evolution in this world and the body boils down to strengthening and purifying the connection of the bodily mind to the higher mind, to ensure that consciousness of the soul manifests itself in the body and this world without obstruction. This is the whole point of the development of all human cultures and all civilizations. It is what each man in his individual life does, all of the time: he develops a perception of the world to be able to understand it, and he achieves this only by understanding the functioning of the mind in the body; and to be able to understand that, he needs to develop a connection with his higher mind. The physical mind cannot see itself. It must use this higher consciousness to understand itself. This higher consciousness is the higher mind. The higher mind exists thanks to an increased presence of consciousness of the soul. Consequently, without transcendence, awareness - of anything - is impossible. If the mind cannot exceed itself, it will never be able to perceive and understand itself objectively; it will not be aware of itself. The physical mind is aware of itself in proportion to its openness to the consciousness of the higher mind. The more consciousness of the higher mind is present, the more open man is for consciousness of the soul which is above the higher mind. When he learns something new, when he corrects his mistakes, man takes a giant step towards the higher mind and consciousness of the soul. Whenever he becomes a better man, he manifests consciousness of the soul to a larger degree.

Everything man knows about God and the divine stems from this connection of the mind with the higher mind and consciousness of the soul. Man has never had contact with God directly, but always through consciousness of the higher mind, and sometimes with the soul itself. All "conversations with God' are, in fact, conversations with the higher mind and one's soul, not with God. God does not chatter with people, God is the highest reality, existence itself, and cannot participate in the illusions of people, especially those who themselves are under the illusion that they are separate individual beings. Through existence itself, God has already said everything it had to say. That is why it is always silent. Its silence is existence. When we are the closest in our experience to God we, too, become silent; this is when we pacify the mind. Then we are the most open to reality, truth, and beauty. When the beauty of reality absorbs us spontaneously, we are in awe. All conversations with God, through various rituals and actions, are in effect an attempt to discipline the mind and the body to render them more suitable and open for conversation with the higher mind, with the consciousness of the soul. If this is not interpreted correctly, everything is reduced to magic, and magic never invokes God, no matter how much we devote ourselves to ritual. God cannot be summoned, in any way, because God is the foundation of existence - God is existence. To use words from the Bible: 'I am who I am' (ehyeh asher ehyeh). In its original language, this means "I am the existence itself' - but the interpreters altered it.

One oversoul has several individual souls that are born into bodies. Although we state that souls are born multiple times, this is framed thus so we can make sense of it from our point of view, in linear time. In reality, souls do not exist in time. Linear time exists only on the surface of the planets, in the three-dimensional physical world. The truth is, only a timeless present exists, as the presence of the divine consciousness itself, which is absolute, meaning timeless. Only when we are closed off in a physical body do we have the experience of time, and only from that viewpoint do we witness the multiple births of a soul into bodies as a function of time. In reality, from the perspective of the soul itself, we can see that it manifests simultaneously in all the bodies, in parallel. All our lives and all our incarnations happen in parallel, in one timeless present. It is evident from this perspective that death is an illusion; when we reside in the body and experience the bodily mind, we are as dead as can be. Physical bodily death is birth, release, and the birth into a body is the death of the consciousness of the soul. This is because of the grandeur of the soul itself.

Using man's soul, the divine consciousness builds and manifests everything that exists and happens in this world. Human oversouls have created this planet and all the life on it. Consequently, this soul further split itself into a myriad of individual souls that continually reincarnate in physical bodies.

This is the true origin of people in this world.

―――

We have managed to forget our common ancestry and connectedness. Oblivion is a part of the plan of our souls, part of the process of manifestation of divine consciousness in all possible creative ways; the most creative is to forget itself and then to find itself again.

The initial phase of retracing our steps towards consciousness is manifested through religion.

The mature phase of rediscovering our divine consciousness is the development of science.

The final phase is man's self-knowledge, or God-knowledge.

As a result, the final reality of man's existence is that man does not exist, much like nothing exists; there is only one divine consciousness that manifests all of its possibilities through forms. The only special feature of man is that he is the most subtle and therefore the most appropriate place for self-knowledge of divine consciousness.

Man's only destiny is to finalize his self-knowledge of divine consciousness, all of the way through.

To accomplish this task several incarnations are needed.

This is the goal of all human incarnations.

The magnitude of this task is best illustrated by all of the human dramas and hardships of life.

Man makes mistakes and experiences adversity only if he acts in a way other than to raise his awareness and self-knowledge. Logic shows us that wrong is automatically destructive. Only that which brings welfare to all living beings, and life itself, is good and proper; all living beings and all life exist for the sole purpose of perception and experience; perception and experience exist to discover the meaning of existence, which in the final outcome is the divine consciousness itself.

In reality, man always acts with this final goal of self-knowledge in sight, but he is often unaware of this. Everything that happens to man, happens for the sake of self-knowledge, whether he is aware of it or not. All of man's development, all religions, all culture, and all science, is for the end purpose of awareness - to become aware of what always is, to be who he is, to be existence itself (ehyeh asher ehyeh).

In this way, consciousness of existence and existence itself intersect in man. This is a cross for man to carry in this world, the cross he is crucified on. Man exceeds the cross he carries, he resurrects himself when he brings the two together, when consciousness and existence become one, when existence becomes fully aware, and when he with his consciousness creates existence in accordance with his true nature, with reality. When man surpasses every difference they represent, his soul resurrects. That is the only way for man to liberate his soul from all the influences of this world, and to see the error of his ways (sins).

UNMANIFESTED AND MANIFESTED GOD

If the universe is a hologram, it is no different from the supreme divine Absolute, from God, from ourselves even. We are God itself. Somehow we are unaware of this simple truth. We see ourselves not only as separate from God, but as its total opposition. We act that way, too, since we have divine freedom to manifest everything that can be manifested, which includes the greatest illusions. The way we are is the way we view the world around us. Only with consciousness of the soul can we see it for what it truly is.

That is the essence of the phenomenon of 'creating the world': both the world and the creation of the world exist only in the mind that thinks it is separate from the divine whole. The world was not created. Only the mind was created, with the illusion of its separation from the divine whole. To heal its separation, the mind imagines that the world has been created.

How did it come about that our minds feel this estranged? The divine Absolute is everything that is and the source of consciousness. As such, due to the nature of consciousness itself, it must manifest and express itself to be able to have perception of itself, to be aware of itself. Perception always happens in a subject–object relationship. For this reason, it, as a subject, must manifest itself in the form of everything that can be - all the objects. This is our cosmos in all of its dimensions, the ones we can perceive with our senses and the others, we are unable to perceive.

The Absolute cannot remain as itself only because then a paradox is introduced; when it is unmanifested, nothing exists, just a void, sunyata, in the way described in esoteric teachings; and nothingness as such cannot exist. This is why the divine Absolute must always be manifested as itself; it can be nothing but itself in its manifestation, nothing is possible outside of it.

Therefore, the divine Absolute exists dually: both unmanifested (as itself, as the Absolute), and manifested (as everything that is, as the relative). These two aspects bring a paradox to our alienated mind, but in their essence they are one.

Reality itself does not experience a paradox, only our mind does, and it is the only entity that sees reality as a paradox. Reality has no paradox, it is a divine whole. In this wholeness, the only thing that may appear as a virtual paradox is the mind within a man's body. Only when wholeness is observed from such a viewpoint, from a mind that is in a state of paradox itself, that thinks it is separate from the whole, does the world appear separated from the whole, from God, and to a mind like this it seems that the world was created, separate from the divine. This is why it is often said that the world was created in the mind only, that there is no world outside the mind, and so on.

However, to reach such a perfect phenomenon like the individual mind of man in perfect virtual separation from the Absolute, the manifestation of the divine Absolute must follow these steps:

1. **As something new** – to be manifested in five dimensions

2. **As something else** – to be manifested as its opposition.

THE MANIFESTATION OF THE DIVINE
IN FIVE DIMENSIONS

To appear as **something new**, the divine Absolute manages by manifesting itself through all the dimensions, from the most subtle to the grossest.

All religions teach us that there are 'higher worlds' and a 'kingdom of heaven'. Esoteric knowledge gives us a clearer picture of the same. The 'higher worlds' in question are, scientifically speaking, higher dimensions. They are all parts of the same nature in which we live, which is composed of several dimensions, but our senses and the psychology of our perception are such that we perceive only the grossest physical reality, only the physical dimensions. But there are many more.

The highest and the most subtle dimension is the one called aether or akasha in all true esoteric teachings, which corresponds with the universal quantum field in modern physics. It corresponds with pure consciousness in man. We perceive it as space itself, which is the universal outcome of everything else.

After this, the dimension that is presented with the element of air follows suit, and this is the world of ideas or thoughts in man. It is manifested outwards as the gaseous state of elements.

The next in line is the element of fire, which represents energy, an intention to see ideas through, otherwise known as will in man - that which drives us, every moment, together with our thoughts. Externally, these are all types of radiation.

Then, there is imagination, which forms a clear picture of a completed idea in detail and all the aspects. It is sustained with emotions. Nothing is maintained or accomplished without emotion. The more we desire something, the more we make it come true. This is represented by the element of water. Outwardly, these are all the liquid and plasmatic states.

Finally, there is the element of earth, which represents the finalized, physical accomplishment of an idea. Outwardly, it is the gross or material reality.

The same process is dispersed through the dimensions represented by these elements. It is all in us; we consist of all the dimensions of nature, which enable man to think (air), have will (fire), imagine and emote (water), all in a physical body (earth). Only in a human being is the focussed power to think, have will, feel, and physically accomplish ideas present. This is why all religions speak of man as being the last element of creation, the most perfect creation of divine manifestation.

All of the dimensions that the divine manifests through have a pyramidal structure. This explains the number of pyramids across the globe, dating back many millennia. The point at the top is akasha or aether. Then, all of the elements that represent various degrees of contraction of ideas follow, all the way to this that we perceive as the gross physical reality on earth.

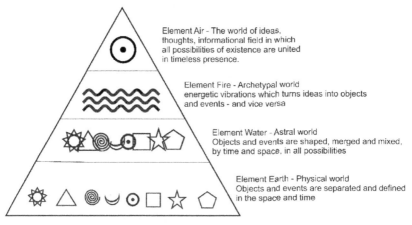

Element Air - The world of ideas, thoughts, informational field in which all possibilities of existence are united in timeless presence.

Element Fire - Archetypal world energetic vibrations which turns ideas into objects and events - and vice versa

Element Water - Astral world Objects and events are shaped, merged and mixed, by time and space, in all possibilities

Element Earth - Physical world Objects and events are separated and defined in the space and time

This pyramidal structure simultaneously contracts and disperses the manifestation of everything through the dimensions, much like a prism that refracts sunlight into all the colours. From an idea in the element of air to its concrete physical reality, there is no difference, just the refraction of the same process into different aspects. When we hold an object in our hand, a stone for instance, the thought in our mind identifying it as a stone is the same as the stone we are holding in our hand; *it is the same phenomenon, split across different dimensions;* in the element of air it exists in us in the form of a thought, and in physical reality (the element of earth) as the gross phenomenon of stone. This takes place due to the difference in time. In thought, the thought of a stone is only momentary, it is a timeless present, while the stone outside in space is permanent in linear time for as long as the laws of physics allow, or until the point we shatter it with some new idea and shape it into something else.

Dimensions are what make the difference between thought and the stone. By manifesting through dimensions, the Absolute manages to make things appear as though they are something new (and not like itself), and for man's mind to perceive it as something else (and not as the Absolute).

With the help of dimensions the divine Absolute projects linear time. Nothing new has been created, nothing is objective in itself, but time has been created using the dimensions. Only in linear time (the element of earth) does everything that is instant and timeless in unity with the Absolute (aether) seem like an object in space which exists over time, appears and disappears invariably.

We can understand this better in the following way. Existence is conscious, and this consciousness is our consciousness, which we are using now in a considerably decreased and narrowed form. A thing we are holding in our hand is the same as the thought (idea) of this thing. On the element of earth, it exists as a gross shape in time, and our thought is the same thing but in the element of air, where it is instant, in the here and now. The existence of different dimensions sets apart our thought of the object (in us) and the material object itself (externally). It is, in fact, the same, and only the spectrum of different dimensions divides their emergence (like the prism refracting a single light into all the colours). This spectrum is in fact timelines. A thought is instant, or lasts as many moments as it takes for us to think about something; and a material object lasts for as long as the laws of physics allow for its duration until it falls apart, or until a new thought or idea changes it in some way (we break the thing, or make a new one by combining elements). A thing is a shape in time, and a thought is a momentary shape.

Therefore, for as long as we manage to maintain one idea (air), invest energy (the fire of passion) into its upkeep, using imagination (water), we will make it permanent, materialized to that degree. This is the process of creation through man. It is the law of attraction, or a way of achieving a goal.

The chair you sit on is as aware of itself as you are, and the only difference is that it is aware of this possibility; being a chair, on the material plane, whereas you are composed of multiple dimensions and own a mind that can devise all of the alternatives.

The divine is, therefore, manifested through the dimensions. The dimensions form a human body. This automatically enables man to know the higher dimensions. The more he knows them with his physical mind, the more divine consciousness from the higher dimensions he grounds to his physical plane. That is how divine consciousness acts through the human body in concrete terms. In the human body, the divine contracts all the dimensions of its manifestation. Heaven and earth unite through man, and the divine consciousness impacts the matter. Not only does it impact and manifest it, but through man's being only, through sheer influence, it reaches cognition of action, it reaches awareness of itself. When man cognizes something, when he learns to do it successfully, a tiny fragment of divine consciousness has become aware of itself in a certain way.

Dimensions and parallel worlds should be clearly distinguished from one another, because they are not the same. One dimension (for example, material) may exist in all its possible ways in parallel, and they are its parallel realities. A different dimension (astral) can do the same. Each dimension exists in all possible parallel realities. For example, a person may be poor in one reality, rich in another, middle class in another, and so on. We cross over from one reality into another when we are ready to do so, when we become rich or poor. This is a relatively slow process due to the nature of the physical world, where inertia and solidity rule. In the astral, it is the same, with the exception that in the astral inertia and solidity are weaker, enabling parallel dimensions to shift faster; this is something we can do while dreaming or experiencing lucid states in the astral. Everything is faster and more flexible there - so fast that it perplexes us and we do not understand what we dream.

The higher the dimension we find ourselves in, the faster the shifting between parallel realities - this is the possibilities of existence. It takes place the fastest in the element of air or thoughts. In our thoughts, in a flash, we can go over several realities and analyze them. This is thinking. When we are in meditation, beyond the scope of thoughts, we are out of space and time and in the perpetual present, which means in aether or the quantum mind. This is why all dimensions are shown in the form of pyramidal gestalt, because space and time diminish and contract the higher the person goes.

Man is the means by which God knows itself in the material world, the world which appears to be the exact opposite of divine consciousness.

All of this can be described to accommodate the religious way of thinking of a believer.

God's thoughts and ideas become physical reality, this world. God does not think or fantasize in vain as we do. Each of his thoughts is materialized. The entire manifested universe is the manifestation of divine consciousness, outside of God himself; it is absolute. However, since his nature is absolute, he cannot deal with the details and trivialities of this world. To enable individual phenomena and objects, God has projected monads of individual consciousness from himself, and these monads will deal with creating all the details of the universe and life in it. They are angels or archangels, residing in higher dimensions. When they further split, multiply and narrow to even smaller monads of individual consciousness, these tiny monads of angelic consciousness become human souls and are born into physical bodies in this world. They are us, people with souls. When they are born in the body, human souls partially forget who they are; they forget about their angelic and divine essence so they are able to continue the act of creation and further upgrade everything that has already been created into all possible combinations and situations, and not to cheat in the game by using the ready-made solutions. **The principle**

of divine consciousness is manifested here only through creativity, through the discovery of what is new and right. When, in this world where everything is submerged in oblivion and hidden from the truth, we rediscover the truth and the true nature of things, we reintroduce divine presence into everything; this would not be possible if we were born with all of the solutions in hand.

Human souls in this world, play with all the possibilities, objects, and events in the world, like actors on a stage equipped with props.[8] This play is their karmic drama and destiny. The performance of each soul as an actor is a part of the drama. It is both a comedy and a tragedy; it has its introduction or exposition, all possible plots, culminations, twists, and they all lead toward the denouement, toward revealing the meaning of the play.

Not a single role is in vain or wrong. In the absolute nature of God, the life of an ant, a child that dies soon after birth, your life, and the life of Odysseus and Methuselah all have equal value, because they are all within the divine consciousness, as its ideas. They are timeless. All possible lives happen in parallel. You are aware of this current life of yours alone; do not worry if it does not turn out to be the way you envisaged. You exist in all parallel realities and you experience all possible life stories and destinies. You will see them when you exit this life. For now, you are focussed on one destiny alone. You may connect and swap realities, in this life, only if you are sufficiently aware of the issue here.

Mysteries are bigger than dramas though, and the motto is always the same: know yourself, and you will know that you are God.

Mysteries mostly teach us the essence of truth about the higher dimensions. It is very important to understand the nature of each dimension, because many misconceptions are brought about by failing to distinguish them. For example, we may have an idea or conviction that everything is momentary or illusory, that we create reality. This is true on the higher levels of reality, in the element of air. On the physical plane, objects and phenomena behave substantially, they have a coherent shape, they exist in time and move through space. Here, on the physical plane, there already is a reality that functions in time. For example, there is a house built a long time ago. We can go and live there. It is a reality of the physical plane, but that is as far as it goes. However, since we are made up of all the dimensions, we can be on the physical plane, while our mind (belonging to the element of air) has the experience of momentariness and timelessness; we can virtually experience several parallel realities, and examine them as options. This is what gives us creativity, because we have the option of experiencing all dimensions within us simultaneously.

If we are unable to distinguish and know the reality of the lower and higher dimensions, we are faced with a paradox. This introduced the famous problem of Schrodinger's cat, which both exists and does not exist at the same time (the Copenhagen interpretation of quantum mechanics). Subatomic particles act as waves and as particles simultaneously, but only in the higher, more subtle realms. In this gross reality, a wave behaves as a particle. Quantum superposition ends somewhere in the element of fire, or the realm of energy. In the element of water, or astral, everything has already been formed in a relatively permanent way. On the physical plane, in the element of earth, everything is relatively solid and has a permanent form. That is why we can live together in the same world, why the Moon exists even when we do not look at it.

The subject indeed decides on the reality, it creates reality, but it does not take place in the same manner across all dimensions in the element of air, or our thoughts, as it does on the physical plane. That is why there are different dimensions, so that we can tell them apart. In the element of air, all realities exist in parallel, and ideas are manifested instantly, and shift easily. On the physical plane, ideas take time to be realized, and the right conditions must be met which is required by the physical reality itself. We, as conscious subjects, decide on the manifestation of ideas on the physical plane, but we should not entertain the illusion that everything on that plane is momentary and illusory.

It is possible for the conscious subject to change his physical reality with conscious intention, but only if he is fully aware of the highest dimension here on the physical plane - if he has a quantum mind, meaning pure consciousness of himself and his soul.

When consciousness of oneself (air) becomes strong, to the point it pervades the body (fire, energy) with its non-Hertzian state (the feeling of being here and now, time is no longer, one experiences the unity of everything), or it gets to the stage where it can use energy in stationary or non-Hertzian form, if in imagination (water) there is a distinct shape of what is to be, what the intention is, it can affect physical reality; it can perform miracles.

If all of these preconditions are not already united in man, then he must grab hold of his tools and realize his ideas using physical labour.

All of our lives in this world are dedicated to learning and understanding the nature of the dimensions and the role of our consciousness in them.

All of our ignorance in this world comes from not having full awareness of the nature of higher and lower dimensions, and confusing their principles of functioning.

HOW THE WORLD WAS CREATED
– A PERSONAL PERSPECTIVE

One of the side effects of my meditative practice (za zen, shikantaza) over the past forty years has been out-of-body experiences. I have looked into all aspects of these experiences, following the rules of the astral world. When I flew upward to the astral, I surpassed all of the shapes that persist in the lower astral, and entered what is commonly known as the higher astral or mental world, or hyperspace. There are none of the shapes of this world there, but only abstract and geometrical shapes that shift at the speed of thought, in fantastic colours. According to the dimensions of the pyramidal gestalt of nature, seen in the previous chapter, the only thing that exists beyond this is the realm of aether or akasha. I wished to enter this, but whenever I got as far as I could go in the highest astral, I would return to my physical body. This return was followed by the supreme bliss of samadhi, in which consciousness and existence are one, joined in bliss (sat-cit-ananda). Such bliss would last for several days. Naturally, my first thought was that I failed to enter the aether, and that was the reason for my return to the body.

However, with sufficient life experience and maturity, and the ability to apply meditative consciousness from samadhi in life, I had the following insight. My automatic return to the physical body after an attempt to overcome the astral and mental realm was not a complete failure, but rather a complete success. The realm of aether or akasha is not somewhere high up, in abstract heights and dimensions, but here and now; it is everything that is here and now, it is consciousness of the highest, timeless reality of here and now, it is this physical world we live in.

When you surpass the world of shapes you automatically return to shape because voidness (*sunyata*) and shape (*tathata*) are the same; samsara and nirvana are one and the same. More accurately, when you come back to reality, reality is everything that is here and now - every form and event in space and time. There is nothing that is not the highest reality.

The teaching of Nagarjuna has helped me to understand this, but it is a completely different experience when you go through it personally.

Using the language of physics, the quantum field or aether is not a microscopically small field one can access only via testing with particle accelerators; it is this space, which everything exists in. Everything present in the emergent universe, all of 'matter' originates instantly from the vibration of the quantum field, from space itself. The meaning of the word akasha is 'space'.

Matter originates from the quantum field or space using vibrations that follow a fractal design and the golden section. Everywhere in space, there are points of origin of these vibrations, and they can be small or large. The largest are 'black holes' in the cosmos, and the smallest are in the centre of every atom. A torus comes into being around all of these places, as the basic structure of vibrations that forms every body. Everything that exists in the physical universe, from electron to man, and from stars to galaxies, exists according to the model of the torus. Man's aura is torus-shaped, much like everything that sustains life, apples, and other fruit.

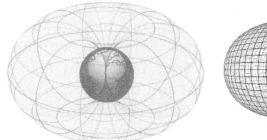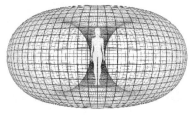

At the centre of each torus, there is a 'black hole' - pure space, akasha or aether, the entrance into the quantum field.

Their different magnitudes produce all the differences in forms of everything that exist in the cosmos. The biggest black holes create galaxies. Smaller ones create the stars, but their size is such that, in proportion to their size, at the edge of the torus it creates a reversal field (originating in the interaction with the neighbouring space of a different vibration), which creates large vibrations of all the elements, which, due to these vibrations, produce high temperatures. This is manifested as the hot plasma we see on the surface of stars, as their light. The inside of stars are cold and dark, because of their structure and the aether in the centre.

When a black hole is even smaller it creates at the edge of its torus field a hot plasma of all the elements; but apart from the hot plasma, it can keep the elements in a cool state. This happens because the black hole is smaller than the one found in stars, enabling elements to form in a cooler state and not as plasma alone. Instead they are concrete elements separated in space. That is how on the edges of smaller black holes except for the hot plasma a cooled crust forms, from the elements which we see as planets.

Planets and celestial bodies are spherical because they originated from toroidal energy motion. Every planet is hollow and in its centre there is an additional small star, which has a small black hole within. Planets absorb vibrations of the central sun in their crusts because the crust has not been evenly cooled, and underneath the crust there is magma, which sometimes erupts in the form of a volcano. This phenomenon follows the strict pattern of the torus, and the volcanoes on Earth and other planets exist on identical latitudes. However, not all planets are of the same size, hence, the bigger ones with a slightly bigger black hole in their centre have higher temperatures that prevent a cool crust of elements forming. They exist as gas giants (Jupiter, Saturn, and Neptune) because they are too small to be stars, yet too big to be planets with a cool crust.

The torus is spherical because the sphere is limitless. The sphere is a direct reflection of limitless space. The only three-dimensional form that limitless space can project itself into is the sphere. That is why all celestial bodies are spherical.

This is the mechanism by which the world originated from divine consciousness, from the quantum field of aether. This is how man came about.

In fact, due to the holographic nature of existence, where nothing is separate and everything is reflected in everything else, this happens in every single moment, and is everything man cognizes directly in the moment when he recognizes consciousness (god) as existence and existence as consciousness (god) - which is the experience of samadhi in meditation.

When man comes out of the state of samadhi in meditation and begins to act and work, the world is swung into motion, it becomes manifested. When man starts with meditation, when he is in samadhi, the world disappears, it becomes unmanifested. However, the meditant is still there; he exists forever, he would not start and finish meditation if he did not exist forever, but when he is in samadhi he exists in divine reality. The only difference between the manifested and unmanifested world is our ability to recognize it as divine reality, and how we choose to participate in it.

The cosmological theory of the Strong Anthropic Principle or SAP says that fundamental constants of nature, like the ratio between proton mass and electron mass, must be exactly the way they are for the evolution of carbon-based life to take place, and for man to appear as a conscious observer. The visible properties of the universe are not a product of coincidence or natural selection but are a consequence of a quite specific purpose: the creation of conditions for a conscious subject, man.

That sums up the story of the creation of the world.

To properly understand the origin of the world, the essence must once again be emphasized: the world is not created, the world is being created as we speak, every minute of every day, and the way it gets created depends on us and our perception, on our consciousness, and our actions in the world. The world is not the same with man or without him. It is so obvious.

There are worlds where there is no life, or more precisely where there are no conscious subjects. They are barren worlds where nothing happens, there is no life. The moment that even the smallest conscious subject appears, like bacteria, something begins to happen, and things change forever. The more complex and perfect the conscious subject is in his perception and function, the faster the world he lives in changes and improves. Our planet undergoes turbulent change because our consciousness is growing in its presence; all kinds of conscious subjects are at work here. It does not change harmoniously because the consciousness of the subjects in question are not harmonious.

Before the appearance of man (a conscious subject), only half of the work was done; the possibility for life had been manifested, by creating the necessary conditions, like setting a stage. With man as the conscious subject, with the capacity to act consciously, the other half of the work is complete. This means raising the level of awareness of making sense of existence, uniting divine consciousness with existence; when man as the conscious subject realizes that absolutely everything that exists, every construct and creation, is the divine consciousness itself, and there is nothing but itself. That is the purpose of evolution. The beginning and the end of the world unite in man, because consciousness is in man; consciousness is what makes him a conscious subject, and it is the same divine consciousness that creates everything.

Therefore, neither science nor theology can assist you in uncovering the secret of the creation of the world, until you harmonize your conscious functioning with the nature of the world. Your perception and your actions are two halves of the same whole that uncover the secret of the world. Proper perception and proper actions, together, will allow you to discover the reality of the world. When you are properly tuned in with the world, you are then properly religious, and you have the proper scientific mind. The correct tuning in with the world is the key and the purpose of both religiousness and science. This explains why both religiousness and science, together, teach us how to function in the world.

To put it briefly: when you harmonize your perception and consciousness with your actions, so much so that there is no difference between consciousness and action, either in intensity or contents and sense, then the nature of this world will be clear to you, and you will be in harmony with it, and with God.

You may consider your consciousness to be God, and your actions to be the whole outside world. This is not wrong. Everything that goes on in the universe is the illusion of separation of consciousness and action, and man's mind reuniting them as reality.

Man has inherited the capacity for creating the world from God, he is his little helper. Man has not perfected the craft yet, but is working hard on it.

FISH ARE UNAWARE OF WATER

Fish in water do not perceive water. They are unaware of it until they are thrown from it. Only then do they begin to realize its importance, but not before they are gasping for air.

A similar problem befalls believers while perceiving the divine. They are aware of the fact that they are in it, all the time, and that divine consciousness enables them in everything - that life has been designed by divine intelligence.

Their very consciousness with which they act and perceive the world is not theirs; it did not originate from their heads, but is just a tiny fraction of the universal divine consciousness, which our brains receive like radio receivers, slowing it down to use individually.

Due to this slowing down, and individual use, it seems to us that people have different consciousnesses, different from our own, separated from the divine whole. Because of such limited consciousness in us, it seems we are separated from God, that we still have a long way to go to get near it, to know it. We do not realize that we are in it, like fish are in water.

We never do anything to God or for God, but God always does everything through us, because it is everything, there is nothing but it. Such is the nature of existence. All we have to do is wake up to the only reality, which is itself, which is ourselves.

The method of awakening is to throw the fish out of the water. Only when we find ourselves in the opposite of a divine state, when we start to fight for our life in suffering and illusion, in sin, only then do we become aware of the higher reality, and realize that consciousness and life in us are not just our characteristics, but that we share everything with divine whole, everything is connected in One.

When we retrace our steps and realize how we were exiled from heaven in the first place, we will be able to get back.

EXILED FROM HEAVEN, THE DIVINE CONSCIOUSNESS MANIFESTS ITSELF INTO ITS OPPOSITION

The seven phases of creation or manifestation of the divine Absolute are, in effect, a way for the divine Absolute to manifest itself into its opposite.

To appear as *something else*, the divine Absolute creates man and his mind - the only mind in all of the universe that has the total freedom needed to have the illusion of separation from the whole which composes it, that he is something else and not the whole itself. Such a perfect illusion does not exist anywhere else in the cosmos, in any dimension. It exists only inside man's head.

We are familiar with the idea that God gave man free will. Here we will explain what this means.

The opposite point of the divine is man's mind (or ego), which is considered as separate from the whole, from the divine. It is the furthest opposing point of the divine Absolute. It is also the rock bottom of existence: a man, a scientist, an agnostic, an atheist, a criminal or a killer, who thinks there is no God and that only matter exists, that we are all just bodies, separate from the divine whole, is no different from a believer who thinks he is separated from God.

However, at the same time, man's mind is the highest creative achievement of the divine and its aspiration to manifest itself as something other, where this other, this little mind (ego) has the complete freedom to do as it sees fit, in its ignorance. It can either be estranged from God as a scientist, or return to God as a believer. In either case, it has the freedom to create and destroy, to be good or evil.[9] Therefore, *the greatest illusion is simultaneously the greatest creative achievement of the divine*. One does not get further than that. That is why, from the point of manifestation of the divine and onwards, there can only be a return to itself. All of human existence, everything that happens in each human mind, is based on the drama of experiencing all of the illusions of freedom, so that one individual may do what he/she wants or acknowledge being part of a whole, and devise ways of returning to the divine whole.

Manifesting the divine Absolute is like circling the same thing over and over again. It manifests as something new and novel. This happens within its imagination. Since it is almighty, its imagination is almighty, too; it looks like the grossest reality. We should not, however, compare divine imagination with ours, which is weak and shallow. Its imagination is strong and very convincing, consistent with the physical laws of the grossest reality. The highest point of the creative divine imagination is in conjuring the illusion that something other and detached from it can exist. This is the peak of illusion, but at the same time, it is the peak of creativity of consciousness. God can achieve this only in man, in his mind that is identified with the body (ego).

This is the furthest point the manifestation of the world can reach, through all dimensions and universes. After this, only a return to the original divine consciousness of itself is possible.

The manifestation of divine consciousness, in a circular fashion, is demonstrated in the ancient symbol of yin-yang.

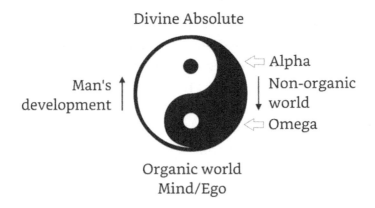

Divine Absolute

Man's development

Alpha
Non-organic world
Omega

Organic world
Mind/Ego

There is a well-known story of the 'first and last,' of the 'Alpha and Omega'. God is said to be Alpha and Omega, as is Jesus. The manifestation of the divine is represented with the symbol circling the divine Absolute. The Alpha point is the source in the divine, and the Omega point is its ultimate opposing point of manifestation, after which a return to its source and wholeness follows. This is a universal model of the circling of energy, both within and without. Opposites exist, but they are dialectically connected and always contain one another, according to the model of a hologram.

The black field represents a spontaneous and conditioned manifestation of all the possibilities of inorganic and organic life. Once perfection of organic form has been reached, the white dot appears. This is the principle of consciousness in matter, freedom in conditioning. This white dot is consciousness in man - the conscious mind. Then, recognition of the whole process begins, and man gradually raises his awareness of existence, after which he returns to the divine source, to the Alpha point. This return is marked by the white field, which slowly grows in size. Conscious development happens within man as man's self-knowledge. When it reaches its climax, uniting with the Alpha point, with the divine Absolute, when it recognizes its unity with it, it contains the experience of its opposition - the black dot. This means that awareness of the divine Absolute of itself is now complete; it has gone through all possibilities, everything that it manifested itself as, and everything that can be. This is depicted by the perfect circle in which light and dark are circling.

All of human destiny and karmic dramas turn and balance around these two points. Every man has only two choices: to return to the divine source (Alpha), or to be a slave of the illusions of his mind and ego (Omega).

However, since nothing is possible outside of the divine Absolute itself, this 'return' is merely an illusion, much like everything else. Nothing has been detached or lost, for it to need reconnecting. This was all in the imagination of the divine Absolute. However, since its imagination equals the highest reality we can imagine, for us it is the only reality we can conceive. We are justified in presenting the whole matter in this way: the 'manifestation' of the divine into the cosmos and life, and the 'return' to the divine, like an awakening and or revelation, like salvation. Besides, we are so far gone in the illusions of our mind that we are truly in need of salvation.

Since the universe is a hologram, it is in us, in the same way it is outside of us.

THE OPPOSITION OF THE DIVINE
IS OUR REALITY

The Omega, or the ultimate opposition point, is the reality we live in. Everything looks to us as though we are completely separate from God. The basic reason we do not see the divine presence in everything that exists is because of the way the divine manifests itself into its ostensible opposition, into the Omega point. A milder form of this illusion is similar to the belief that many have, the idea that God is somewhere 'up there', 'in the heavens', and they are 'down here', 'on the earth'. They need some faith or ritual to get closer to God, to connect with or in some way get on with it. For those individuals that do not have even this kind of faith in God, there are extreme cases when the opposition can create a hell-like reality. In short, the more violence, hatred, and conflict there is, the more distant the Omega point is from Alpha.

A detailed description of the Omega point and our reality is as follows.

Monads of divine consciousness, which our souls originate from, create all of the possible virtual realities found in the highest dimensions - like games in which they test all the possibilities of existence. One of these is life on Earth. Souls then submerge themselves in life on Earth, using physical bodies like avatars. Each soul is an aspect of divine consciousness, playing an earthly game. This game is the true crystallization of all the possibilities of consciousness, through free will. This is the point of manifestation of divine consciousness. This consciousness, via individual souls, creates a myriad of realities and plays many roles within them. These roles are the incarnations of human souls. Incarnation is simply a game, another way of seeming separate from the divine consciousness of the Absolute. The position of the soul in a single physical incarnation is irrelevant, in the sense that although it must experience self-oblivion, it can never completely lose touch with its divine source. Hence the presence of religiousness in all people, which manifests in all its possible forms.

All of the karmic development of an individual soul during its series of incarnations is for the purpose of finding the right balance between forgetting oneself and remembering oneself, one's divine essence. Self-oblivion is the Omega point, and the divine source is the Alpha point. The whole game of humanity is about harmonizing the perfect circling of consciousness between these two points. The entire physical cosmos exists as a stage for souls to act out their seeming separation from their source.

The heart of the matter is that maximum separation from its source, or the biggest oblivion of oneself, gives one the greatest creative freedom, which is the foundation of divine consciousness itself. Therefore, this separation is welcomed, as necessary for this essence to be able to crystallize in the Omega point on the earthly plane.

There is a paradox here. By moving away from the Alpha point, from the divine source, greater creativity is manifested. The source of creativity is in the Alpha point, but it manifests itself only in its opposition, in the Omega, in the freedom of everything that can be in any way possible.

This ultimate point gives us the illusion that we can do what we like - so we do. We are aware of our senses and matter only; there is no 'higher force' or grace of God which eventually forces us to take matters into our own hands and fight for our survival. The less awareness we have of divine power, as the unconditional love that enables everything, the greater our illusory need to apply force (which always turns into violence), or to fight for our existence, because we are convinced that only what we make really exists. When a large number of people share the same conviction, competition follows, and conflicts may arise. That is why there is so much violence in this world. Bullies are the biggest materialists. Acting in this way, we collectively create hell in reality. All of the evil, violence, and destruction people commit in this world is a result of this collective illusion - that only body and matter exist, that God is far away, and that we are permitted to experience everything.

Through those people who live in this illusion, the divine Absolute itself experiences itself as its opposition. Everything that can be, happens.

Man has assistance in falling into self-oblivion while in this world. The soul itself cannot create the circumstances needed to forget itself completely. To do those things that fall under the category of its opposition, it requires the help of entities who are aware, but do not have a soul as people do. These are so-called demonic beings that live in the next higher dimension, in the astral, and they possess people. A man who is possessed commits the most heinous crimes.[10] These crimes are never perpetrated by people who have the deciding power of the soul. The physical body is such that it can live and function with a minimal presence of consciousness, as in a somnambular state, like in hypnosis. There are soulless people, but they are the ones with such a diminished capacity for consciousness of the soul that they merely observe what the body can do, what the ultimate limits of unconsciousness and licentiousness are, and how far all of that could go.

There is creativeness in destruction, in negative actions. Since souls have set themselves the task of experiencing everything there is to experience on this plane, they stop at nothing and experience even that. Some people appear to compete in their stupidity. Understandably, they do this to a lesser degree than their positive deeds, because if the negative were to overpower them, life itself would be destroyed. Man learns the most from overcoming difficulties. Souls experience the destruction of life also, but only to strengthen their awareness of life. Since the universe is a hologram, everything is interconnected, and every man must face his deeds and show repentance, without exception.

The more man is aware of the higher force, of divine consciousness, the more creative he is, as well as merciful and peaceful. The more he is in possession of his will, the less likely he is to be possessed by alien entities. Overcoming violence is possible only by understanding the true nature of the consciousness of one's soul, the nature of higher dimensions, and with awareness of their existence. In such a way, we introduce harmony to the functioning of the lower and higher consciousness, and the consciousness of our soul may impact the physical mind more strongly. This is a way in which we use the divine consciousness of our soul to function on the physical plane, to create our reality.

When there is not this connection, evil and destruction appear. There are even cases where the ultimate Omega point goes further, past the measure of perfect circling, where it strays more than is necessary from the Alpha, more than is the will of God. This is the only correct *definition of evil: what is redundant, excessive, and therefore wrong.*

The shape of the Greek letter *omega* also reflects the principle described here. It is an unfinished circle whose bottom is open for failure: Ω. The Alpha point is also represented by a circle, but one that is beginning to fork and open: α (lower case); or the highest point where division begins: Λ (upper case).

Everything that is correct continues to circle in perfect circle and balance, which means in perfect understanding. Evil and destruction is the unbalanced movement of the circle, the loss of the centre that provides balance.

The divine language *devanagari* clearly expresses this. In this language (Sanskrit), suffering is called *dukha*, and is best illustrated by a wheel with an unbalanced axis. Harmony and perfection are called *sukha*, and this is a wheel where the axis is right at the centre.

The ultimate opposition point of the manifestation of the divine, the Omega point, is like stretching a bow before releasing an arrow. Without the pulling and stretching action to the opposite side, the arrow of divine consciousness would never be able to reach its ultimate goal, the Alpha point.

It is much like a yo-yo. The divine manifests and contracts within itself. Manifestation happens in the form of the cosmos, and contraction as awareness of itself. This happens on a large scale, as the cosmos, and on a small scale, as the vibrations of the divine particle. It is the same phenomenon, though, that happens timelessly, every minute of every day. Man's mind is the only factor to distinguish a difference between the large and small. Man's mind was created to provide this illusory distinction. With the help of this distinction in human experience, the divine consciousness manifests its essence through its opposition.

Human souls are born in this world to experience the ultimate reach of the Omega point, all of the possibilities of illusion, to stretch to its most extreme limits of the stretching, for the divine consciousness to be able to experience and try out all of the possibilities of its highest creativity through man: the greatest oblivion of itself.

This is the origin of the story of our sinfulness. But there is no mistake about it; without temptation, there would not be consciousness of the soul, or all of the life on Earth.

The black field is the outer cosmos and the non-organic world. The Omega point is the unity of consciousness with the non-organic world, which is the organic world and the appearance of life that acquires its completion in man's being. The white field is man's consciousness, which knows the nature of reality. It represents the spirituality and religiousness of man, the return to the source which happens within man. The most perfect implementation of this returning is through the practice of meditation.

Since we were made in the image and likeness of God, we are the microcosm; the whole cosmos is contracted in us according to the model of the hologram, and all of this takes place in us, not outside of us. Our deep sleep is the state before the world was created; when we dream we oscillate between the different dimensions of creation; and when we wake up to the physical reality, then the world is fully manifested. *The whole process of creation of the world and the return to its original state is contracted within our being, in our microcosm, as the holographic model in miniature.*

The Alpha point is our highest chakra, *sahasrara*, and Omega point is the first or lowest chakra, *muladhara*.

All of our life experiences move along these lines, from one point to the other.

Religion refers to them as heaven and hell, God and the Devil.

Only through man is the divine consciousness able to experience all of its oppositions and become complete; only through man is it able to experience its highest creativity, the freedom to be out of itself, the freedom to be against itself, and the freedom to go back to itself.

Whenever some man touches the bottom of hell and experiences suffering, the Omega point has reached its ultimate stretch outside the circle of divine perfection; always when such a man repents and returns to his soul, his conscience and consciousness, the Omega point heads toward the perfect circling and harmonizing with the divine whole, toward the Alpha point. Anyone who has reached a heavenly cognition had a cross to carry, some plight that made him rise upwards.

Each of us has our Omega point. It is the point we touch at the bottom of hell. Only from that point onward can we ascend on our path to salvation, rebirth, reset, and well-being. We will not move upward toward the Alpha point until we touch our Omega point. This is what it takes for us to have enough strength to make the change. If we do not touch this lowest point, we do not have enough power to change completely, we will have our moments of doubt and faith, and we will fall again, and repeat bad experiences. Maybe its proximity will provide us with the insight and inspiration for change, for making decisions, but only when we physically hit rock bottom of our life and existence, in the full impact of our stupidity, ignorance, and illusions, only then will we move upward towards a metamorphosis, with no return. Then we die in the old life we had, and we are born in a new one. Every true initiation has this experience: dying as an old man and being born as a new man that rises to higher consciousness, to the Alpha point.

This is the one good side of the Omega point, although it appears completely negative. In reality, there is no Alpha without Omega. They act together and mutually.

That is also why our development never follows a straight line. There are many ups and downs. *Their shift increases our capacity for consciousness. This is the real reason behind their movement*.

So the issue here is not for us to repent one fine day, and be enlightened forever, but to go through our ups and downs, and *by doing so widen the limits of our perception*. It is not about leaving the Omega point and turning to the Alpha permanently. Alpha and Omega are like an induction engine; two opposing points which move our lives, similar to an electromagnetic reversal field. It does not matter which one is white and which is black, as long as they rotate.

It does not matter whether our current trajectory is 'downward' or 'upward'; it is more important that we become aware of the whole circle, of the wholeness – and to realize that this wholeness is us. This is the goal, not staying in one point of the circle, no matter how 'high' it was. Consciousness enables the full spectrum, all extremes, and not just one state. We should not make the conclusion that Omega is more important than Alpha; there are no experiences of one without the other.

Only when we fully experience the differences between Alpha and Omega, all of their oppositions, can we overcome them, can we reach transcendental consciousness of our soul. That is the goal. For as long as we aspire toward one pole, we are trapped in a game of opposites. Our goal is not to stay trapped, constantly battling opposites, but to overcome the whole relative phenomena, and come to the Absolute, to the transcendental divine consciousness that enables them all. Experiences of opposition serve only to make us rise above them, to understand them in the context of the whole.

Transcendence of the opposition of relative existence was described in the science of *Sankhya* as a *kaivalya* state. The word *kaivalya* denotes the state of consciousness of our soul that is not involved in anything, authentic, pure; hence, containing the idea of perfection and completeness. In that sense, this word denotes separation and detachment of man's essence or soul (that originates from the absolute divine consciousness) from all transient existence in time, and the resurrection of the soul of man from the mortal body into one's immortal and unborn authentic state. That state is the goal of meditative practice, the way it has been presented in *Yoga Sutras* by Patanjali.

The most distant point of divine manifestation, the Omega, is the world we live in, in which illusion prevails. The biggest illusion pertains to our essence, soul, and the true nature of consciousness. The soul learns about the materialization of all processes in space and time. That is why this world is ruled by a strictly controlled illusion.

THE GEOSTRATEGIC POLITICS OF THE OMEGA POINT IN SEPARATING MAN FROM GOD

Politics is one of the fields where the abnormalities of this world manifest the most; its state, as described here, shows the stretching of the Omega point to the furthest opposition from good and right, from the divine.

There are institutions in this world that deal with stretching the Omega point to its furthermost limits, and which create innumerable illusions. They are scientific and religious institutions that deceive us regarding the nature of our reality, i.e. consciousness, as well as our soul.

Science teaches us that we do not have a soul, or that the notion of the soul applies to some combination of life energy, psyche, subconsciousness, memory, and feelings.[11] Science is still in the game of convincing us that consciousness originates from unconscious matter (which is absurd), that consciousness is only perception, a bunch of feelings and impressions, located somewhere in the brain. It teaches us that we are completely meaningless as beings, even harmful to nature, that we are on the edge of one of innumerable galaxies, that life originated purely at random, much like ourselves, that we are an error in DNA division, that we are upgraded monkeys at best. This is how science strengthens the Omega point by strictly controlling our minds and programming us to be limited to the world of senses and matter only.

Religion mystifies the soul and projects it into divine spheres which seem to be inaccessible to us, or accessible only if we fulfill certain conditions of some dogma, which is mission impossible. According to these illusions, we can lose our soul and find it, make it sinful and save it. We can even sell it to the devil. It all depends on how obedient we are to some religious authority. However, the prevailing attitude is that our souls are primarily sinful, therefore wrong.

The church presents consciousness of the soul incorrectly, and in an indirect way, by banning abortion. The conviction that man originates at birth is a materialistic viewpoint. It negates the truth about the soul and its independence from the body, which is the experience of true religiousness. The soul chooses the body it will be born in, like we choose our clothes in the morning. A soul incarnates into the body only after birth, and even then it happens in stages. The issue of abortion is not a religious question, but a question of birth rate. A society that has a high birth rate is in need of abortion; for a declining population, abortion is harmful. That is all.

Both science and religion together, more than anything else, falsify the true meaning of consciousness. Science does not have an accurate definition of consciousness, but regardless it widely popularizes the belief that consciousness is nothing but perception and memory. It plants the conclusion that robots and computers can have consciousness, but only if they are fast enough and with sufficient memory, and 'artificial intelligence' can also exist. However, intelligence cannot exist without emotional maturity, which contributes the deciding factor in how to utilize intelligence; consequently, emotional maturity originates only in the presence of consciousness of the soul. Science keeps deceiving us that robots with 'artificial intelligence' are able to have emotions. This is impossible without the soul. The scope of man's ignorance regarding the nature of the soul and consciousness is best reflected in his attempt to attribute emotions to robots, as they do in Japanese and Hollywood movies. 'Artificial intelligence' can be a useful tool only if it makes living and working processes easier. Nothing more than that. It always stays artificial.

There is a tendency to impose development of artificial intelligence under the guise of man's perfecting, because he supposedly is not perfect, but is rather destructive and in need of help.

Why would artificial intelligence be created in the first place? Why would existing intelligence be proclaimed as insufficient? Because we do not see the existing one. This is why artificial intelligence will be pernicious for man; he creates it, but is unaware of the one he has now, of what is within and without him. He is unaware of his true nature and existence, of their unity. Such a man is deeply unconscious. What such a man creates cannot be good. Good can only be created in harmony with the already existing divine intelligence which enables existence and life itself. Once we become aware of this, we do not need anything artificial. The reality of existence surpasses - by far - anything we are able to create. This is what spiritually and soulfully mature people object to, in regards to the excessive development of technology: an attempt to find a replacement for something that already exists, but that we are unaware of. They stress that we need to become aware of reality, gain self-knowledge and improve interpersonal relationships, and not to be endowed with more artificial aids. Difficulties are out there, but for perfectly good reason: to help us grow and empower us. Too many alleviating circumstances in life tend to degenerate us.

Judeo-Christian religions completely fail to mention consciousness as a notion.

Everywhere, the truth of consciousness as the most powerful force in the universe, that enables and creates everything, every single moment, is hidden. Consciousness does not originate from matter because there is no such thing as matter; it is quite the reverse. What we perceive to be matter is actually one of the manifestations of consciousness. There is not a multitude of consciousnesses, it is the same in everything, it just manifests itself differently.

Above all, the truth of the real nature of our soul is being hidden from us, the fact that it is the individual emanation of the divine consciousness that creates everything, that our souls are divine creators of the world we live in.

It is quite clear that religions conceal the truth about consciousness by alienating it from man and projecting it into the notion of God, who is distant and always out of reach. God in the heavens was invented to conceal the true nature of the consciousness in man.

Hence, the theatrical seriousness found in all religions, the notion that they alone should convince people that God is a miraculous and unattainable force, somewhere in the heavens. Such a believer thinks the idea that God is in him is the biggest blasphemy; the hardest thing for him to believe is that God is always here, in everything, that he can be seen in every child's eye. That is why they treat children badly, and when children grow up they do not behave properly; that is why the world is the way it is.

Do not look up to the sky hoping to find God, but take a closer look in any child's eye. God watches you from there.

Therefore, everything is the opposite of reality in this world, in our Omega point.

Government institutions encourage opposition in all aspects. Again, this enables us to become more aware. Our food is poisoned with GMO and unnecessary chemicals, so that we become aware of what real food is; allopathic medicine does not cure us, but instead poisons us, to allow us to discover the true source of health; education systematically dumbs young people down – to make them discover true education and knowledge; truths that frequently pop up in media sources are named 'false news' to teach us to recognize true information; wars are generated through 'false flag' operations and innocent people get blamed for it. World history is almost completely false, and this makes us want to discover our true history, and with it our true identity. They impose on us the United Nations plan called 'Agenda 21' for the hostile takeover of all the resources on this planet by a global corporate system, run by a global government, where people will not be owners of their estate and property, or their bodies. By imposing transhumanism they are trying to take control of our bodies so that we no longer stand a chance of ever awakening and setting ourselves free. With 5G technology there will be the 'Internet of everything', all electronic devices that have microchips built-in (together with our bodies, when they get microchipped) will be networked and controlled, and we will not be the owners of that technology.

The church, too, with all other religions, joins in the chaos and encourages it. They appear to criticize the latest trend of conditioning people with technology, but do it by criticizing the technology itself, as though that has ever been the problem. The 'mark of the beast' is heatedly debated, and is used as crucial evidence to prove the Bible right. However, it is hardly a real mark in the form of a tattoo on the hand or the forehead; it is not even a chip inside the hand. All these stories are for the very naive. The 'mark of the beast' is a mental conviction that says everything is allowed, all rampage and perversions symbolize the freedom we aspire to. It is already present in the 'thriving' 'democratic' world. It is what gets continuously imposed on the whole world. 'Beast' involves our lowest drives and clouds better judgment. In the Bible it says that the 'mark' is on the forehead (head) because it refers to our ability to think clearly, to our mind, and the right hand because it refers to what we do, the right hand symbolizes our ability to act. Our opinion and actions are 'branded', which means formatted and imposed from the outside, by religious and scientific authority. It does not come from the consciousness of the soul and the higher mind. Only this higher consciousness can save us and the world. Christ is our higher consciousness that connects us with consciousness of the soul, and Antichrist is everything that limits such consciousness in us, which is opposed to it. There are no gods and devils that will on 'Judgment day' wage a war in Israel, in Armageddon. That kind of mythology only aims to keep us further in the illusion of Omega point.

Control over us grows only to make us learn how to be truly free.

Indeed, never before in history has a dictatorship of lies and coercion been bigger than today in modern society, in the most developed countries that present themselves as 'democratic' – and at the same time, never before in history has the consciousness of people of their true position and reality been greater. Great pressure brought about great consciousness. The greater the pressure, the greater the consciousness.

The elites that have ruled over people for thousands of years are Satanic. Their favourite is performing

Satanic rituals. Satan has been defined in all religions as the adversary of God. This word 'adversary' should be properly understood as the opposition, or something contrary. Therefore, there is no mythology here, not even the fighting against God, but a simple fact: **they only induce opposition. It is all they do: stretching the Omega point.** They merely open the door of opportunity to the spreading of the Omega point, a greater turning toward the opposition of what is normal and right. They only create illusions – they do not force you to believe in them. The devil never kills people, he only cleverly leads them to kill one another. People, in their ignorance, walk through the open door, they seize this opportunity.

In such a way, they act in the best interest of human souls, albeit in a very negative way; they help consciousness of the soul adjust completely to the material plane. They raise the level of awareness in people, by materializing all of their mistakes, weaknesses, and ignorance; they help them face their flaws. Without this, people would remain unaware of their weaknesses, they would neither see nor face the consequences of their actions. This is why it is said that the devil possesses sinners. He merely acts as the litmus paper that reveals our weaknesses and mistakes.

The process of materialization of the soul, training it to be functional on the physical plane, is connected with the passage through the most meandering illusions, the ones that have previously been described in relation to the Omega point. It is necessary because only when man starts to be in command of the physical world can consciousness of the soul return to the divine source. This practically means that consciousness of our soul 'returns' to the divine source only when it recognizes the presence of divine consciousness in physical existence, always, and in everything, even in the darkest and worst conditions, in the worst man, so that he is able to function here with the full potential of divine consciousness, and can never again lose or forget it. That is how divine consciousness is realized in this world through us.

The ultimate cause of all the negativities in this world is positive; pressure strengthens consciousness of the soul, it strengthens consciousness in the circumstances that exist in the physical world. It is like stretching a bow with an arrow: the more we stretch it, the stronger the force to make it go back to its initial position. Without pressure, consciousness of the soul would not have sufficient motivation to develop experiences in the physical world and its true potential would remain unmanifested. For development of the world, materialization of the consciousness of the soul is required, for all the potentials of consciousness on the physical plane to be experienced. Such stimulation encourages the soul to create everything positive in this world. That is the true reason why this world is abundant in duress and all kinds of pressure that people must endure.[12]

A practical example is how the falsifying of history has manifested the sheer magnitude of opposition to reality that rules over this world. History is presented to us as a series of chaotic events that sometimes appear to have some recognizable causes, yet sometimes do not. Mostly, people get blamed for all the evil, although they are often victims of a bigger process.

More careful observation reveals that throughout history two forces have been engaged in conflict. One force is represented by consciousness of the soul, which naively sticks to what is good and righteous, and which is found in good people. The other force is represented by people whose capacity for consciousness of the soul is seriously compromised, and who are always down-to-earth and practical, who only possess physical consciousness, that which can be perceived by the senses. Good people always nurture life and support it, because they have full awareness of its importance. Low-spirited people grab everything, they take and kill anything that comes their way; the end justifies the means. They both have many representatives in this world, and they have been geographically deployed, but mixed as well.

There are reports and evidence which suggest that a long time ago, good people far outnumbered inferior humans, but they gradually diminished in number due to the rapid increase of the soulless. In ancient times, there were civilizations that never had or used any weapons (The Indus Valley, Vinca, or prehistoric Danube culture).

All wars and conflicts in this world are waged between these two factions. They represent the white and black field in the circling between the Alpha and Omega points.

It is important to know the following: negative people represent the black field, and are aimed at stretching the Omega point into the opposition of the divine; they generate negative experiences and destruction – and in doing so they play a positive role in the development of this world, although it appears negative.

People who represent consciousness of the soul are the source and role model for everything good in this world, but for this exact reason they wish to remain unattached to this world; they put their bond with the divine first, they aim to go back to the divine because in their perspective this world is the opposition to the divine - this is perfectly true. In this way they unconsciously hinder the development of this world, they play a negative role, even though in their essence they are basically positive. They are simply not sufficiently aware of the true nature of this world.

This is the issue of the dialectics of opposition. Bad people unconsciously do good, and good people unconsciously do harm to the development of this world, because they are inert and insufficiently interested in thorough material growth. Because of the consciousness of their soul, they already see the divine in everything, and see everything as being perfect. They already see the final score of this game, the result, and they refuse to take part. They say that this world is an illusion, maya, that the world is ruled by the 'evil Demiurge', that their true place is in the 'heavenly kingdom'. This is true. However, we have come here to take part in this grandiose game of life, as if it were playing out for us for the first time, as if it were the only reality, because it is what we projected when we were in the 'heavenly kingdom' prior to our birth.

The information that has reached us from centuries gone, especially the esoteric, secret and alternative history that is far more interesting than the imposed, official one, shows that good people enjoyed a period of prolonged peace on planet Earth, until 13,000 years ago, and spanning Europe and Tibet, on territory known to us now as Grand Tartaria.[13] They built megalithic structures and pyramids all over the world. This explains why building methods are identical on all continents. In Latin America the pyramids were not built by either the Mayans or the Incas, even less so by the blood-thirsty Aztecs (primitives who sacrifice people could not have the supreme cosmological knowledge needed to build the pyramids); they were, instead, built by the 'white God-people of the East', according to the legends of the Mayans and the Incas. However, they ceased to develop; they had what they needed and they were perfectly content with their peaceful lifestyle in harmony with nature. About that time, 13,000 years ago, major cataclysmic events took place, and things changed dramatically overnight. The old civilization was interrupted, evidence of its existence was hidden away, artifacts that remained are falsely presented in modern times as remnants of some more recent civilization. A brand new civilization was started, from scratch, and this is our modern civilization. This civilization was started by people who were not the embodiment of divine consciousness, but its total opposition. To them, this world is the only one we have, and they felt the existential urge to become masters of it. This marked the beginning of all wars and conquests in history.[14]

It was not a sudden change. It has been going on for ages.

The most important step in installing a completely new look on the world and giving a boost to the new civilization was done by smashing the original language and making the Omega point swing to its opposition point. The original language reflected the consciousness of the soul directly. By fragmenting it into new languages that were a lot simpler and limited, bigger oblivion of consciousness of the soul was achieved.

Hence, the biblical myth about the destruction of the Tower of Babel and the destruction of one language, forming a plethora of languages, which caused many conflicts and disagreements amongst people.

Together with smashing of language, social engineering was used to divide one people, up until that point very unanimous, was smashed into a multitude of peoples with different names.

If in those ancient times rulers had advanced technology to build megalithic structures, then they also had knowledge of social engineering to create nations and languages, and a way of orchestrating changes centuries in advance. *Historians who do not know or refuse to acknowledge the existence of advanced technology in the ancient past (although evidence is abundant all over the world) do not stand a chance of understanding what history is truly about.*[15]

True history has been systematically hidden from people from the early middle ages to this day; the histories of ancient civilizations, of Greece and Rome, are largely falsified in accordance with the functioning of the forces that strengthen the movement of the Omega point toward the opposition of divine reality, and further into all the possible illusions.

However, all of this was not done out of malice, but to make the soul focus on material development. If it had not been done, consciousness of the soul would have been much better preserved, as it was in those ancient times, but the progress of this world would have been halted because soulful people do not have a direct interest to grow attached to this world and develop material culture. If that change had not happened, to this day we would be riding horses, sitting on the ground, dancing around fire. To make man grow fond of this world and learn to develop it, he needed illusion, coercion, and duress. And a big, big conspiracy.

The key event for the final separation from consciousness of the soul into its opposition, into the process of materialization and a new civilization, happened with the founding of the city of Rome. Etruscans who were ancient Slavs ruled the central and northern part of the Apennine peninsula.[16]

The type of society and polity Ancient Slavs lived in was a kind of kith and kin community where everyone enjoyed the same rights, lived in peace without slavery (they also liberated other people's slaves), and without conquest. Ownership was not a criterion for belonging to their community, they shared all goods according to their needs. This is a characteristic of soulful people. However, in the year 509 B.C., a 'Roman revolution' was executed by newcomers and conquerors from the Middle East. When, according to the legend, Romulus and Remus placed a border between themselves and the native population of Etruscans, Rome was founded. A new civilization sprung, in which the chief criterion for defining how to belong became territory, conquest, and ownership, and, in practical terms, commerce. The practice has lived on to this day. *Genealogy plays very little part now; one's impeccable character even less (according to the legend Romulus killed his brother because he contested his borderline); but territory, property, and ownership play the only part. Equality amongst people has disappeared.* Every citizen of Rome became a Roman, every citizen of France became a Frenchman, and so on. This annuls any idea of genealogy and belonging to a close-knit community, and instead, faceless citizenship is introduced. In Russia, where ancestral tolerance is high, about 180 peoples have maintained their identity to this day. The USA came into being after atrocious genocides were committed over the indigenous peoples, and all the peoples of the world lost their identity on US ground, and became nothing but Americans.

In modern-day terms, a country as such has also become obsolete. Countries are ruled by corporations. Each man is in a contractual relationship with the corporations from the moment of his birth, via his data.

This is why Roman law is the foundation of modern western civilization. It, too, however, originates from the Etruscans, but only the good parts - the principles of democracy and parliamentarism - whereas everything that is bad (orgies with mass murders in the Colosseum) was imposed by the new conquerors. Above all, Etruscans were peaceful, fine cultured people, and these qualities made them an easy target.

This true history is being revealed more and more as we speak, and this fact is also connected with understanding the world in the description of the Omega point.

After the fall of Rome, the Roman church was made on the foundations of suppressing Gnosticism, a cult that had originated long before, and which was revived by a devotee known as Jesus Christ. From his messages across about thirty gospels, politicians from Rome chose only four, together with some epistles of his disciples; but even that was censored and made into what we know today as the New Testament. In the fourth century, together with the texts from the Old Testament, the Bible was canonized into what we have today.

At that time, the Eastern Roman Empire was getting considerably powerful, with the capital in Tsargrad (Constantinople). The rivalry between Rome and Constantinople also grew, mostly because of the Bosphorus Strait which provided the only trade route from Europe to Asia Minor. Whoever got to control this strait was in charge of trade and economy. This has always been the real background of all religious conflicts. Religious conflicts have always been used as 'false flag' operations for achieving economic and geostrategic goals.

When the Christian church divided into Western, Roman or Catholic, and Orthodox, Europe was practically divided between these two interest spheres of influence:

western and eastern Europe, with the melting pot as the Balkan peninsula. Additionally, this was also the border-line of their spheres of influence. That is the issue here and now.

To ensure its rule over Europe, the Roman church had to eliminate everything that tied the Eastern Roman Empire to the European continent. More than anything, this meant the language and identity of people who populated eastern and western Europe, and who in those days were the Ancient Slavs. The Roman church was unable to build its empire on the language and lineage of their rivals from the East. Implementing social engineering as a consequence meant that new languages and peoples were created all over Europe, and the central place for full-scale conflict was the Balkan Peninsula - which it has remained to this day.[17]

The framework of the conflict lies in the following. The Eastern church or Orthodoxy has preserved the original teaching of Christ about the soul of man, about the salvation of the soul, and the emphasis was on saving the soul from evil influences of this world. However, the rule remained the same: might is right, whether it is the local mob boss, tycoon, a president for life; constant criticism and analysis over past decisions... and the facades of buildings are dilapidated, roads are bad for driving, corruption is in place of the rule of law...

The Roman church took a turn towards materialization of the consciousness of the soul. This is the opposite path, which puts emphasis on attaching the soul to this world. The Catholic church executed all available means of coercion and duress, deception and lies, that forced consciousness of the soul to work in favour of this world.

The fundamental difference is that in Orthodoxy, only the sin is condemned in order to save man. Catholicism condemns the sinner, it punishes the man himself for every sin. This makes man unwilling to sin ever again, unlike in Orthodoxy where they know that all of their sins will be forgiven.

On direct punishment of sinners, the progress of the modern world and European civilization took full swing. Yes, yes, it took the Inquisition to make people stop expecting 'miracles from heaven' and start doing what is right.

F. M. Dostoevsky tried to analyze this problem in his novel *Brothers Karamazov*, in the well-known part of *Grand Inquisitor*. Dostoevsky did not understand the nature of the human soul and saw people with the physical mind only, as being lost and destructive. He described them perfectly. They are not aware of divine freedom of their soul, they use its potential wrongly because of their limited mind, and that explains why they need coercion and force, or more accurately three forces: miracle, secret, and authority. The church is based on them. In its limitation, the human mind sees a higher force in the church instead of God. Incapable of handling their freedom (more accurately, the true nature of their soul), the Grand Inquisitor said, people have given it over to the church, which gives them instructions on how to live and act. The church executed heretics because their struggle for freedom threatened to overthrow the order – **and this order is the true growth toward freedom, stretching the Omega point to make it go back to the Alpha**.

Such coercion and duress led to the ideal of democracy, the standards of transparency, the rule of law, the development of science. They are still our ideals. Naturally, the Catholic church did not advocate these values but their exact opposition, but it is that opposition, the hypocritical darkness of Catholicism that made the Middle Ages become the Dark Middle Ages,[18] that sparked the fight for these values, for the creation of a secular and legal state, from the Renaissance and Age of Enlightenment and the French Revolution, and to this day. To science that will once again discover the secret of existence, that the divine consciousness of the quantum field is the same in everything that exists, and it is the same consciousness as in man.

However, this time man will know what to do with it, he will be worthy of his divine freedom and power. He will, with scientific precision, be able to manifest the power of his soul. Its power is so grand that it requires scientific precision and methodology, otherwise, it may experience a downslide. *That is why man's limited physical mind is so important for the development of science and material culture in general: so that he can manifest his soul correctly.*

In the east, all the talk is about tradition, reminiscing about the glorious past and renouncing this world as an evil place for living. That is why the development of material culture in the east is backward.

These differences still fuel many civilizational conflicts to this day.

It is important to understand history, so that we can understand the forces that express consciousness of the soul in this world. They are by no means abstract, reserved only for religious philosophy. They are very concrete and have a deciding role on life on this planet. These forces exist geographically and impact us geostrategically. They are a part of your life. You can see symbols of this force on the banknotes you buy food with.

All of human history is made up of conspiracy against the human soul and the endeavour of the soul to express itself in the right way.

It is also a universal problem of all individual human lives: how can man harmonize consciousness of his soul with this world and its forces? In short: what can we do?

The purpose of creating all of these illusions is so that divine consciousness can, through man as its conscious subject, experience all of this - experience everything that can be experienced, all the possibilities of existence, both the normal and the abnormal, all of the oppositions, to make sure that by stretching the bow hard enough, the arrow of consciousness can fly in the right direction toward the divine consciousness.

Our whole lives are also a constant battle for freedom, for the liberation from obstacles, difficulties, and limitations; a battle for better ways of expressing ourselves, searching for our heart's desires, the fulfillment of our dreams. All the obstacles and hardships we endure are not here for some evil reason, but to inspire us to develop creativity of consciousness, the remembrance of our true divine nature, to make it stronger by realizing that we are accomplices in the creation of everything. All adversities are overcome with the cognition of the key role we play in their creation; we imposed limitations on ourselves, both collectively and individually.

The conflict between western European and eastern European values, the East (Islam and Orthodoxy, Russia) and the west, *all civilizational conflicts, which are more fierce today than ever, are a product of a lack of understanding of the nature of consciousness of the soul and the material world we live in – not being able to understand their intrinsic unity.*

To overcome this conflict, neither party should come out as a winner. In the same way, neither field should prevail, black or white. They circle together and their balance is needed, as only at that point can full understanding of the whole process occur. Such understanding is possible only with the help of consciousness of the soul, but the type of consciousness that is well-adjusted to life in the physical world.

The divine world of our soul and the material world have an identical foundation, and together they form a great unity. Both warring factions display the same fervour in the fight for their cause, they both wage a war for God and the soul, for a better life in this world.

It is high time somebody turns on the light, so that they can see what they are doing. This is what this handbook is for.

***

The final reason for the existence of the Omega point, its stretching out all unnatural states, and the experience of the non-existence of God, is **to become acquainted with God, always and everywhere, in everything**. Especially in that which least resembles God: in the beast attacking us, in the worst possible man, in the most horrible places, in painful and unjust events and circumstances, in lies... **When we achieve this consciousness, we can never again lose it.**

If we manage to preserve consciousness of the divine presence, even in the most extreme of experiences, then it will be easy for us to preserve it in everyday life, in all the experiences that are less extreme than these. Difficulties make us stronger. This is a principle that dictates the need to expose oneself to extreme and negative experiences. They are needed, as practice, to learn to hold on to consciousness of the divine presence forever. Without this kind of practice, this consciousness can be attained only when we feel nice and comfortable, when we are within our comfort zone. Any challenge or difficulty will throw us out of the 'divine mood'.

This practice also strengthens the independence of the consciousness of our soul, which in its essence is independent of this world. It is easy to find oneself in this state occasionally, when we meditate or when we are inspired by beautiful and spiritual contents. Transcendental consciousness of the soul is also needed in the most turbulent times, when consciousness of the mind aspires to narrow its focus and identify itself with its contents, thoughts or events. This is the experience of a samurai during battle; this is what makes extreme sports so appealing - they cause an adrenaline rush. If in the hardest and the most negative experiences, we keep our spirit independent, then we will be able to maintain consciousness of the soul, always and everywhere. This is a way in which it proves and affirms itself.

You have noticed a simple rule yourselves: when you fall into rapture and rise in awareness, automatically a temptation and decline follows suit, something happens to counterbalance this experience. This is not a case of the devil showing up at your doorstep to tempt you, but the consciousness of your soul having a need to be realized on all planes -not just in the higher elements, in air, to be abstractly present in the mind, but on the physical plane as well, concretely, in the grossest conditions and states. It is not enough for you to know something, you should apply your knowledge in practice too.

Evil and negativity are only what is the grossest that happens in this world, the most extreme stretching of the Omega point – where total awareness is needed. We see things as evil or negative only when we divide them from consciousness and the divine whole. With a maximally stretched Omega point, things are maximally gross and material, restricted. We only see the enemy who wishes to take our food, the object of our desires, and we think we must beat him to survive. The Omega point returns to the Alpha when we broaden our consciousness, know that we and our 'enemy' exist in the same conditions that were given to us as a blessing; when we say our grace before a meal according to the good, old Christian custom, and when we share food with everyone, without discrimination.

All of these negative experiences drive us to change things for the better. If it were not for these challenges, we would remain completely passive, because our soul is not of this world. That is why our first impulse is to run away from something that is dirty, ugly, and evil. Or to fight and destroy it. It will haunt us until we learn that in all of this – and especially in what appears to be the opposite of divine – we see divine consciousness and presence, because the nature of the divine is absolute, which means nothing is possible outside of it, it is everything. It is us, it is everything we despise and hate. We exist in a gigantic holographic unity. That is why everything we fight against becomes stronger, simply because we make it by fighting it.

We will see the divine presence in our fellow beings only if we learn to recognize it in ourselves first.

This is the real meaning of the expression 'love thy neighbour', 'turn the other cheek', and 'thy will be done, God, not mine'. We can do it only if we recognize the divine absolute in everything; that is the only thing that can bring closure to us, release the stretch of the Omega point, and make a slow way back toward the Alpha point.

***

This process finalizes through man, but the open question is whether this process (that is currently happening and we take part in), is the first, or if there have already been similar attempts of this kind in history of planet earth, probably failed ones. There are traces of ancient civilizations that had access to far more advanced technology than what is available to us now. Evidence as big as the mountains is scattered all over the globe. The megalithic structures that are unparalleled to this day, almost impossible to execute with our modern machinery, and we do not have a clue as to how they were made; all of the ancient knowledge still in existence (for example, the precession cycles that last 25,920 years, evidently far longer than the civilizations that knew about them); something that is impossible to know without cosmic technology, without space travel, simply by sitting on the ground and observing it from the earth and studying it.

Some esoteric sources point a finger in the direction of the several attempts of divine consciousness to manifest through man here on Earth, in its entirety. There are several reasons why that did not come off. Allegedly, we are the third attempt. We can only hope that sufficient mistakes were made in the past that served as valuable lessons to us and that we stand a far greater chance of not repeating their destiny. Hopefully, this manual should serve as a guiding light to us all.

RELIGIOUSNESS
BASED ON A NEGATIVE RELATIONSHIP
TOWARDS THE WORLD

Gnostics testify to this problem the best. They teach us that this world is ruled by evil Archons (rulers), who organized the world (and the entire solar system) to be a prison for human souls. All that people can do is strengthen consciousness of their soul with asceticism and the proper knowledge (gnosis), learn to gain command of their dreams (out-of-body experiences, astral), become acquainted with the higher dimensions (maybe with the help of hallucinogenic plants), and by doing all of this acquire the ability to rise above this world, to liberate themselves from the evil demiurge (creators). To them, this world is a hellish place and all one can do is run away, back to the 'heavenly kingdom' where we originally came from.

This is only a part of the truth. The world is a hard place to live in, but more than anything because one must work hard and earn his keep. It is not easy, because the law of causality rules, and whatever you do, you will suffer the consequences of your actions. What makes it tricky is that besides causality there is an equal measure of freedom, so that in this freedom you may lose yourself, you may make mistakes, and hurt yourselves or others, or even destroy them.

There is a third part of the truth. If Gnostics bothered to look deeper, they would see that we, more accurately our souls, created this world and all the other worlds while in the higher dimensions, near their divine source (Demiurge). In the holographic universe, nothing is cut off, there is no duality; we are as much gods as God himself. In other words, nothing is separate or different from the divine consciousness. We are it – it is us.

This truth is kept away from us by all possible means in order to strengthen the Omega point, so we can become aware of everything that can be experienced in our chosen freedom - not to be who we are, but who we are not. Therefore, it is true that we are not our own, we are not what we are, we are separated from God, possessed by many entities of this and many other worlds. All of this has a meaning which the souls themselves originally planned, in accordance with the divine consciousness.

To implement the temptation of the Omega point in this world, institutions like the Roman church were created. This church bases its faith on the fear that Gnostics set the foundations for: this is a bad place for life, the 'heavenly kingdom' is waiting for us, all we have to do is endure our plight patiently, and wait for a savior to come and rescue us. This is a political ruse, ruling people through fear, sins, and victimhood. Fear is a negative emotion that results in passivity and obedience, which narrows consciousness terribly, and which turns consciousness into what it is not. Fear is the foundation of all illusions. If we created life, how pointless is fear! It is the complete opposition to consciousness of life.

That is why all religions based on Judeo-Christianity have fear as their foundation, and a deep-seated belief that the purpose of life is to somehow endure the hardship of this world, and that the only thing worth living for is a hope that someday we will go home to our heavenly bliss.

In this way, the Omega point twists and stretches out maximally into its opposition.

To ensure that the stretching of the Omega point takes place, the notion of equality with the creator is strictly forbidden in Judeo-Christian religions, and is condemned as the most horrible sin. Allegedly, only Satan thinks in this manner, and only he can instill such thoughts in man. This is true if only the physical mind and its ego are observed, if one does not distinguish between the physical mind, the higher mind, and consciousness of the soul. *The issue here is not that our ego created the world, but the consciousness of our soul which resides in the highest dimensions, together with divine consciousness.* When it projects its consciousness into a physical body it becomes conditioned, like everything else that has been created, and this little limited mind is incapable of creating much - only what it can with its hands and tools. That is why it projected itself into a body, to experience this conditioned state under maximally restricting circumstances, and to realize that even this existence has divine consciousness in its essence, that it is always the same and present in everything, in all forms and all possible ways.

The incident on Golgotha is the perfect illustration of the lack of understanding of the differences between higher and lower consciousness, the functioning of consciousness of the soul, and the true nature of the mind. Consciousness of the soul, personified in Jesus, testified of its unity with God, but limited minds in human bodies (more precisely in priests' bodies) interpreted that as blasphemy, and some mind/egos got pompous and started imagining that he was God, and a good idea would be to beat him and crucify him.

It was said: 'Be as wise as serpents and as innocent as doves'. The serpent is a symbol of materiality, and doves represent consciousness of the soul. These are the properties man must unite within himself. The cross consists of a vertical of spiritual uplifting and a horizontal of this world. This is the cross that all people in the world carry. Every man is crucified on this cross, and Jesus was crucified to convey this truth for all times. When he said: 'I am the way, the truth, and the life', he meant that man's way is through this crossing of the vertical and horizontal, of heavenly and earthly worlds. It was not ego talking, in the way theologists interpret, and that is why we must only look at him, i.e. the church, as the 'body of Christ'. When Jesus said 'I' he did not have himself in mind (he never thought of himself only), but he meant every man, and every man's essence (every message of his refers to human essence). Therefore, it is the true path of our lives in this world: the uniting of heaven and earth in us, and the uniting of consciousness of the soul with this world. This is the essence of the messages and deeds of Christ. This is how the divine consciousness manifests itself in this world, through us; it does not fall from the sky, and cannot be found in some magic ritual, in either churches or prayers.

The essence of the gospel can be reduced to the science of the soul and its self-knowledge through all of the dramas of human experience – unlike eastern teachings (Vedanta, Buddhism) that perform self-knowledge of the soul directly, through simple rejection and via overcoming the dramas of life experiences. This is a faster and easier path for the soul, but it was not planned for this world.

Going through the drama of life results in a transformation of life, and the world, together with a transformation of man's soulfulness and civilization and material culture as well. Culture is the outer reflection of our awareness of ourselves and our awareness of the world.

Very few authentic words of Jesus survived all of the censorship and corrections. However, no matter how little truth remained, he still has a powerful impact on the world (especially the Sermon on the Mount); the proof for this is that centuries after all the failed and successful attempts at forgery, the Bible is still the greatest beacon and guiding light for soulfulness in people in the world ruled by the soulless ones. If it had not been for Jesus acting as a role model, and his teaching on soulfulness, this world would now be like the Roman Colosseum and arena with gladiators, to a far higher degree than it already is. Many people found solace and support in the words of Jesus, enough to be able to attain and preserve at least a small consciousness of the soul.

Unlike the institutionalized church, which is typically for mass consumption, there are esoteric communities that are aware of this problem, and that do not consider this world as a prison or a giant mistake, but as a task for our souls, where the goal is to build a new world according to divine design. They praise God as the grand architect; their symbols are building tools, and they call themselves freemasons. More precisely, their name has been twisted, much like the Omega point; in reality, they are masons or architects of liberty, but not the 'freemasons' (it is not quite clear what the masons would be free from).

This is not propaganda of Masonry, but revealing the state of affairs as they are. It is the way it is.

All esoteric secret organizations lead this world ahead, into the development of material culture. It is a negative path for our soul, but its path is such. This path today, like in centuries gone by, experiences fierce opposition from traditional religions, Islam and Orthodoxy primarily. They stick to the views of Gnostics - that the process of materialization of consciousness of the soul is bad and should be avoided, that the devil is the primary actor, and that a religious man should commit his life to God and not become attached to this world. Instead of finding out the reason for their arrival into this life, they simply wish to escape it.

The 'heavenly kingdom' is the Alpha point, and the 'earthly kingdom' is the Omega.

There is no way to leave here, because the universe is a hologram, a unity in which every piece reflects the whole and the whole is in every piece. All realities are in parallel - the heavenly kingdom and this earthly one exist within each other. The purpose of true religiousness is for the heavenly kingdom to be recognized here and now, in everything that is, not to change and destroy for the sake of something else, for the sake of something we think is better.

We should stop thinking with our alienated mind/ego, so that we can recognize this for what it is. This cessation is achieved through the discipline of mediation. The mind is like a mirror, it reflects reality perfectly accurately but in reverse, which is in accordance with the Omega nature of this world where everything is upside down. This makes the mind a necessary tool for understanding this world, but at the same time it is the source of all illusions. This explains why the physical mind destroys something first before it acquires enough knowledge to create something at long last. To a great extent, we are still in the business of destroying the world, hoping to learn something along the way, more than we create and live in harmony with planet Earth.

To make our physical mind completely suitable for divine creation, all we have to do is open ourselves up and realize reality, realize what existence truly is. Higher dimensions are here and now, in this dimension of ours, in our reality. Our reality is composed of all the higher dimensions. A properly religious man recognizes them all within himself, he sees that he is made up of these dimensions. Therefore, there is no way out of here. Not even death exists.

All the 'clashes of civilizations' in this world are bred from misunderstandings of this kind: some pull ahead (into development), and some backward (into the past and tradition), some downward (to the reality of this world), and some upward (into the 'kingdom of heaven').

The most twisted part regarding the Omega point is that all of them are somehow right. The problem is, they cannot seem to be able to harmonize with one another. That is why awareness of the whole process is needed. This handbook serves the purpose of expanding such consciousness.

THE PRINCIPLE OF COERCION AND DURESS
IN RELIGIOUSNESS

The nature of the soul is such that it has no intrinsic drive to create something new, because it comes directly from the divine consciousness which already contains everything that is possible, and which is absolute. For this reason, it has been presented since Plato's time as a sphere and the perfection of opposites that exceeds (transcends) everything that is of the emergent world.

To make the consciousness of the soul act in the three-dimensional physical plane, coercion and duress must be introduced. The very nature of the physical world is such that it exerts coercion that must be overcome. The task of the consciousness of the soul is to actualize divine consciousness in this world of ours, in the most conditioned state of existence, to act as a witness in the form of a conscious subject who becomes acquainted with the meaning of every form of existence, and comes to realize it all as the divine existence.

The point is in the following: there are some forms of existence, ugly, dirty or evil, that less developed conscious subjects have difficulty believing are pure divine existence - that the divine consciousness manifests even through the biggest sinners, as it does through everything else. In other words, *all forms of existence with their infinite expressive potentials may seduce the consciousness with their intricacies, so much so that the conscious subject forgets that they, too, are divine*. At that point, the conscious subject thinks there is no God, he is 'evil', he must fight evil and heathenism and this illusory need drives him further into doing and creating what is right and proper, into learning what is true and correct and overcoming all the obstacles in his path. ***This effort strengthens divine consciousness in him and unites him with the divine.*** If he removes them successfully, he then knows the only reality: that the divine is everything that exists, that there is nothing outside of the divine.

For consciousness of the soul to be able to manufacture oblivion of itself in man's being - as the conscious subject who lives and copes in this world - and in a way that this reality appears Godless to him, or abandoned by God, so that he must build it to get closer to God – the divine consciousness created conscious entities who are void of the principle of the soul, unlike people - entities who possess sufficient consciousness to act, but not to understand the supreme divine meaning of their actions. The first such entity is known to us as the first angel Lucifer. Its chief characteristic is to be the bringer of the light of consciousness into the darkness of illusion, in which there is separation from God. Lucifer is called the Light Bearer. It brings light where good souls never could, into all opposites, even into the opposite of good, so-called evil. Lucifer is considered to be the source of evil, although it is not, it only seems that way from man's perspective. From the perspective of God, Lucifer generates all the oppositions that are necessary for the actualization of divine consciousness. Only when divine consciousness is actualized in the darkest and the most remote form of existence, only then is it truly actualized and manifested. This stretching out into its most distant opposition (the Omega point) is performed by the agent called Lucifer. It does God's work, although it appears negative from a human perspective, which relies on consciousness of the soul only.

This same principle manifests in man in the form of his mind. The mind of man is the only one in the entire universe that sees everything outside of itself, that sees the world externally and disconnected from the whole, from the divine. Divine consciousness sees everything within itself, and nothing is outward. The mind is a detached consciousness that sees everything outside of itself. Only when observed from such a point does the cosmos look like an outward phenomenon. Once the mind is calm in meditation, when it is transcended, man begins to know the whole world within himself. The mind of man is the only Lucifer that there is, and it has been proven so by all of its deeds and misdeeds. The return to the divine begins with the transcendence of the mind.

Unfortunately, the negative is needed as much as the positive. This drama of oppositions is acted out completely (and theatrically) on planet Earth. That is why it has been constructed so carefully and meticulously, as the stage for souls to enact their greatest karmic drama on.

The people of Yazidis have a good story that sheds some light on this process. They are unjustly accused of being devil worshippers, simply because their creation myth, which coincides perfectly with that of Judeo-Christians, says that when God finished creating the world and made man in the end, as the most perfect being in this world, he summoned all the archangels to bow to man. They all did, except for the first archangel, Lucifer (Yazidis call it Melek Taus, others identify it as Satan). It refused to do so under the pretense that its job was to bow to God only, and not to some creation, no matter how perfect. God approved of its opinion and placed it to rule over man on this planet. Lucifer was worthy to rule over man and this world, because it proved that it would not bow to man, that it would always be faithful to God only, and during its reign, it will bring man to God. This is why Yazidis respect Lucifer as the legitimate ruler of this world. The fact that Lucifer is in charge means that this world is full of the fight of opposing factions and alienation of divine presence - but this is the only way for the divine to be recognized in all of its opposites. This is why all the secret rulers of this world, both aristocrats and masons, worship Lucifer, but also God as the Great Architect. It is also why they are at the same time initiators and promoters of civilization and development of this world, and all conflicts and conspiracies as well.

Coercion is imposed on man in the form of 'dark forces'.

The world exists in several dimensions. In the higher dimensions, in the astral more than any other, there are conscious entities that affect the lower dimensions, the physical plane, including man in his physical body. Man consists of all the higher dimensions of nature, but he is unaware of them since he identifies with the body alone, and his consciousness is limited to the physical mind. These higher dimensions and their inhabitants remain subconscious to him. These conscious entities affect man by leading him into temptation and making him strengthen his consciousness, so that he can exceed consciousness of the body and mind and open himself to the higher dimensions. Man would then, through himself and his experience, connect the lower and higher dimensions; he would raise awareness of the wholeness and actualize divine consciousness in its entirety. These beings from the higher dimensions (we will call them inorganic beings, but they are also known as demons), affect man mostly psychologically, both in a dream state as well as in reality.[19]

Aristocrats and masons rule this world on the physical plane by controlling politics, religion and the economy, and demons are doing the same from the astral, or psychological and individual plane.[20] Their area of influence is covered completely and man cannot escape it, in either this world or in the otherworldly planes (astral). Demons and masons are in the same business: they cause the necessary coercion and duress to make man raise awareness of the consciousness of his soul on the physical plane, which is the most remote from the divine, in situations that are as distant from the divine as can be, and in all negative settings. Freemasons teach man how to work and create on the physical plane, and demons practically tempt him and show him what not to do. (Demons possess sinners only, those people that make mistakes. This is one of the ways people learn what is right). These are the practical ways of becoming aware of all the possibilities of divine manifestation. The consciousness of the divine is implemented through man's soul as a witness and a carrier of consciousness into all, even the most extreme, forms of existence. Until one crucial moment occurs, when all forms of existence are recognized as divine.

The proof that aristocrats and masons are in cahoots with demons is their rituals, in which they summon demons. These rituals are connected with the worst possible crimes, as they involve human victims. These crimes represent the ultimate opposition point of all the phenomena on planet Earth, which are the most distant from the divine, and ultimately 'godless'. They, therefore, *in their bloody rituals achieve the ultimate Omega point, the worst evil, and ungodliness*. When this ultimate opposition point away from the divine is reached, and consciously made aware of and attained, even ritually dedicated to some 'god', then nothing remains but a return to the divine source; once this evil is recognized as divine itself, divine consciousness is truly actualized. This is the purpose of Satanism: to recognize the worst evil as divine, to dedicate evil to the divine. The problem which arises is that the mind/ego steps in and makes a religion of it, and starts committing evil acts for the sake of evil; it swaps the means with the ends. But the experience of evil is only a means, not the ends. That is why Satanism is a deep hole almost impossible to climb out of (because the way is always down and never up), and into which only the dumbest of religious people fall in.

For example, a child is murdered in a horrible way. From the perspective of the physical mind, this is a cruel crime that only somebody who is seriously heartless and evil can commit. However, from the viewpoint of higher consciousness and consciousness of the soul, one may see an advanced soul being born as a baby simply to witness this event, to place its soul in a physical body as a witness of this ordeal, and in doing so become aware of it. Another soul was born as the one who commits the crime, murders the child, for the same reason: enriching its consciousness with this unique experience. He was unable to commit this crime on his own, but the execution was aided by soulless entities who possess the body and urge the insufficiently aware man to act negatively, to commit evil acts. In both cases, the soul of the victim and the soul of the perpetrator are nothing but witnesses; they are divine consciousness that testify of yet another possibility of existence. In fact, observed from an even higher point, the divine consciousness divided itself into the body of the victim and the body of the perpetrator of the crime to enlighten one additional possibility of existence and phenomena.

The term for this in theology is 'a ransom for many'. It is merely a testimony of our souls of one possibility of events. However, in theology, it is distorted in accordance with the general distortion of our Omega world.

When something like this happens, such an event is never repeated. What is once brought to the light of the day and made aware of, is never repeated because it returns to the divine source as one of its possibilities, and then it is over with. Such evil will never and nowhere be repeated. It may be replicated in a similar fashion, but never identical. Things get repeated only if they are not completely brought to our awareness. Repetition in pain and suffering is what is called hell in religions. We get access to heaven by repentance, by becoming aware of our mistakes.

Such awareness affects the consciousness of the soul that is limited to the human body in the form of consciousness of the mind, which sees only evil. Negative events that tend to get repeated make the consciousness of the mind want to perfect the physical world and perfect functioning in the body, so that such evil acts may never be repeated.

Maybe to some people, it appears as though the same crimes keep being repeated, but nothing is truly the same. Every crime has its karmic drama with individual souls involved, and each one could serve as the plot for the novel Crime and Punishment. Maybe a little shorter.

Of all the methods of stretching the Omega point, wars are the most obvious. Wars have brought the worst evil in history, and at the same only they provided situations in which the human soul could show itself in its full light, where people get acquainted with their virtues and flaws, become aware of their utmost reach in every sense. This is probably the reason for the number of wars in this world: we rapidly mature through them. It is hard to imagine that mankind can ever be truly mature without the experience of wars. It is so simple, because in final situations like war, both life and death are in our hands, all illusions are lost, there is no time for delay and false solutions. Life itself is a constant fight to overcome obstacles. War is merely an extreme emanation of the reality of life, in fast forward mode.

People who have always been forced to fight for justice and freedom, who never conquered a foreign territory, bristle with mature souls. These are the best, the most beautiful and the most creative nations in the world, as a rule.

The purpose of any crime, of any violence, is to put us face to face with death and erase all illusions, eliminate any delay in understanding the meaning and the value of life. *The certainty of death alerts us, better than anything else in the world.* This is because of the power of the illusion that leads us to live unconscious and irresponsible lives, and which is the major driving force in this world. Death is not merely a big awakening when we pass over and leave this plane. Death awakens us in this world as well.

The Alpha and the Omega together make a whirlpool of unity of opposites in this world where everything has its reason for existence. Crimes are also in this category. When a criminal dies, he realizes his mistake and is born again to make it right. This is a way in which crimes generate the birth of righteous people.

Crimes simply go on happening because they can happen; laws of nature and freedom permit everything. Like in a game of billiards, when the balls hit each other for as long as they can, but were started when we hit the first one. People will go on hitting each other in this same manner. Evil will go on repeating itself until we become aware of it and incapacitate future repetition. When, finally, all the balls fall into the holes - apart from the white one, which symbolically represents the consciousness of our soul.[21] This is the way a soul is perfected in this world. Life gets better, we become mature, usually after an arduous process of committing many mistakes. Violence and crime will exist for as long as you allow, until you decide to make the world a better place. Naturally, not every person needs to experience all the evils of this world in order to become wiser; a measure of experiencing evil is individual and depends on karmic maturity and consciousness. Conscious people cannot do harm because consciousness is the opposite of destructiveness. This is the main difference between old and mature souls and young and immature ones in this world, the measure of negativity or goodness in their actions.

There is also a collective effect where experiences add up, so that humankind moves ahead despite all the chaos.

Something similar can be achieved through Aghori Tantra. This is the practice of deliberately experiencing the darkest side to make consciousness of the soul alert and independent. Sexual ecstasy is experienced, the effect of powerful drugs, alcohol, near-death experiences - anything to maintain consciousness of the soul as a witness in those trying moments. When this is achieved in extreme conditions, man can never lose it, even when he is exposed to less extreme ones. He is always in possession of consciousness of the soul, regardless of what happens to his body. This is a way in which divine consciousness descends and actualizes itself through the soul of man.

Every man in his life experiences all of this, in all possible ways. We all go through it, endure and do wrong things, to become aware of them and eventually make a conscious effort to mend our ways and to harmonize with the consciousness of divine existence.

This process is known as making the philosopher's stone in alchemy (lat. Lapis philosophorum). Wisdom is the symbol of consciousness and stone is the hardest matter. It is a form of merging consciousness and matter, uniting all oppositions.

This process of the soul's awareness on the physical plane, in conditions of utmost loss and remoteness from the divine source, has religiousness as its key component. In fact, it is a process that encompasses all the other processes that take part in this great work (Magnum opus).

Religiousness is a process of tying the physical mind with the higher mind and consciousness of the soul, and through it to the divine consciousness.

During this process, man learns what is right and what is not, he learns how to act properly in all possible ways. Only by tying the higher mind and consciousness of the soul with the lower, physical mind does it finally become capable of distinguishing between right and wrong. It functions erratically only if it closes within itself, alienated from consciousness of the soul. Therefore, this process is not only a spiritual practice, but it is also a process that is outwardly manifested in the form of creation of all culture and civilization in this world.

Religiousness expresses itself in all possible ways, in accordance with all the possible states of consciousness that are available to man.

Coercion and duress exist only if we are still unaware of it. If we are aware of why hardship exists, it suddenly disappears. No matter how hard or sinful a state we find ourselves in, we become blissful when we see the divine manifestation in everything.

***

Coercion exists as much in mundane life as it does in religiousness.

The reasons for its existence will be clearer to us if we remind ourselves of the basic principle: things happen spontaneously and mechanically only if we are unaware of them. Consciousness changes destiny. This is particularly evident in astrological influences. Our destiny is predetermined, and the science of astrology clearly points in this direction; however, when we (owing to the knowledge in question) become aware of these influences and the program of destiny, it will no longer play itself out in the way described. It gets modified to the degree we become aware of it. *At the moment, we raise awareness of our destiny program, and a new possibility opens up, and a parallel reality awaits.* Which of the parallel realities we will select is entirely dictated by the level of our consciousness. If we fail to observe the true causes that affect our destiny, it will continue to go according to plan.

Destiny (history) keeps repeating itself and torments us only to the point we are unaware of it, to the point we refuse to accept that everything that happens is for us to become aware of ourselves, of everything we do and everything that happens to us. Everything happens because of our awareness. If we think that everything happens unconsciously, for something else, or no reason, the events are repeated.

Forces that implement coercion and duress on man in this world - the rulers, the Illuminati - are perfectly aware of this principle. They act accordingly. Although they do the most negative things, they do so to make man conscious and force him to overcome plights, so that negative and wrong things won't have to happen in the future. If man did not experience and became aware of them, they would go on repeating themselves. They not only lead people to learn how to do right in the physical world, but to experience wrong in order to avoid their unconscious repetition. What is once made aware of is not repeated.

We have many negative measures of coercion forced upon people (transhumanism, 5G, microchipping people, agenda ID 2020, DNA vaccines, total population control, slavery to the banking system, deliberately generated economic crises, systematic faking of reality via the mainstream media, disrupting sexuality and gender identity in young people, etc.). However, at the same time, we have all available information on all of this. Albert Pike, 149 years ago, described in detail plans for all three world wars. The first two we unconsciously executed, and the third is approaching. Many writers tied to the Freemasons made public in their books some of their plans for development in the future: George Orwell, Aldous Huxley, Arthur C. Clarke, Isaac Asimov … and nowadays all their plans and details of coercion and pressures are brought to us by David Icke. By making all of this information public, people are enabled to become aware of them. To the measure people become aware of such plans and such destiny, which is aimed at unconscious people, this destiny will not happen, and a new parallel reality will open up with more freedom - one that is likely to be less negative.

But to remove a mistake or negativity, it must be detected. That is the only way for it to be prevented.

Forces that implement repression allow for the possibility of its awareness. By becoming aware, we rise above the negative scenarios of our future. Since we are aware of the repression in question, it will not happen. To the degree people become aware, our future takes a turn for the better. The destiny we have become aware of will not happen - only the destiny we are unaware of. However, the necessary precondition is for people to be conscious to a sufficient degree. If they fail to be so, if they do nothing to avoid the negative scenario they are faced with (consciousness must be connected with action, otherwise it is worthless), they do not deserve a better destiny. It is all a maturity test.

Since we consider ourselves as conscious beings, we deserve only what we are aware of.

Let us remind ourselves that in the beginning we stated all realities exist in parallel and timelessly, in all of their possibilities. On the most subtle level of existence, in the aether or the quantum field, all of the possible realities already exist, we merely harmonize with a specific one through our deep-seated beliefs, and this ultimately becomes the reality we live in. Therefore, *we never change the world we live in, we can only change ourselves, our deep-seated beliefs, and by doing so we cross over to a different parallel reality and start living in it*. Although we still see the old reality, and live in it, with our vibrations and state of consciousness we adjust to the new reality, that becomes brighter and stronger until it is the only reality, and the old one completely recedes.

All the difficulties, coercion, and duress we are exposed to in this world originate from our need to change the world without changing ourselves first, from not being aware of the true nature of the world - that existence is momentary and out of time, that all possible realities coexist in parallel as the foundation of the world which is the eternal present. *When we do not know this, we exert force to change and organize the world.* Solving problems by force is always negative because it is not natural. Lao Tzu tried to explain to people the principle of non-action, of acting without exerting force, but very few were able to understand him. To cut a long story short, since the universe is a hologram, the reality of life acts as a mirror for every conscious being. That is why our efforts of force against the world and other beings turn against us. The coercion and duress we suffer from outer forces are a mirror image of our wrong attitude - that we should change the outside world and not ourselves. We only reflect the force we experience, and respond in the same way. Once we start to change ourselves positively, the outer difficulties and blocks cease immediately.

To change from one reality to another, from hardship to harmony and bliss, all we have to do is become aware of ourselves first, the quantum field, akasha or aether. This is achieved through meditation. That is the only place one can cross over from one reality to another, because all realities spring from there.

Due to the mathematical laws and golden section principle the universe rests on, to change the reality we exist in we should become aware of the new reality one percent of our time - out of all of our existence and being. If one percent of our time we are aware of the new reality, it begins to manifest, and we cross over to it. The same applies to the world we live in: if only a fraction of people were truly aware of the new reality and world they would like to live in, via akasha, it would impact the whole world. The world will enter a new reality without force. That is the real meaning of the principle 'to act through non-action'.

This is all a positive game to our advantage, although it is hard. It is hard because we are worth it. We are worth all of the difficulties that happen to us.

We are a lot more powerful and greater than we can imagine. Life in this world is hard because it matches our true grandeur. If we knew who we really are, we would see that the worst evil in this world is but a child's nightmare.

In a wider context, in the holographic universe there is nobody else; our souls are the creators of all life, everything that happens to us we do to ourselves to become conscious, even here in the most distant point from the divine source.

SIN AND REPENTANCE

Forces that maintain the opposition of the Omega point in this world have convinced people they were born as sinners. This is the so-called original sin, which was supposedly committed back when we were in heaven, and represents man's separation from God. It is hereditary and gets passed down to all people. This teaching was imposed via the Christian church in the fourth century A.D. Nobody before had such ideas of the world. In fact, the prevailing accepted view was that of Pelagius (circa 354 – 420) that man has free will and that, fundamentally, he is never separated from God. Such a viewpoint did not agree with the desire to establish a church authority that required a mentality of fear to force people into obedience. There was much debate over this issue, with many conflicting views. The chief advocate arguing that man was born a sinner was Augustine (354 – 430). The final verdict was in the hands of Flavius Honorius (384 – 423) because he held a position of authority over the government and the church at that time. However, the chances of St. Augustine winning the debate were slim. For that he used cunning. In April 418 he bribed the emperor Honorius with valuable gifts, Arabian stallions, and the latter voted in favour of Augustine. That is how man became an original sinner – using trickery! How appropriate.

Let us take a closer look at what language has to say about the notion of sin, because language conveys everything if we listen to it properly.

The word that gets translated as 'repentance' in the New Testament is the Greek word 'metanoia', which means the ***transformation of consciousness***. The Greek article 'meta' is found in a number of words, like metaphor, metaphysics, metamorphosis. According to this, the article 'meta' points to some transition, or transformation, or otherworldliness. The other part of the word that is translated as repentance – noia – is derived from the Greek word nous, which means mind/consciousness. Therefore, the word metanoia in its original meaning denotes ***the transformation of consciousness, the transcendence of mind*** (the same as the teaching of Buddha and Patanjali in Yoga Sutras). However, in the Christian church, the idea of transcendence of mind, metanoia, was destroyed by twisting it to its opposite meaning, that of 'repentance' - which cultivates the idea of perpetual sinfulness in man, and which generates the most negative emotions. Consequently, such a suggestion spurs man to be sinful. The truth is that there is no religion as sinful and as violent as Christianity, which teaches man to be sinful. Such is the power of suggestion. Essentially, it is a scare tactic and generates a victim and slave mentality to uphold the authoritative church hierarchy.

Therefore, sin is a state of mind and wrong, giving us a twisted perspective of reality. Simply put, it is a mistake. It is not God given or eternal suffering, just a state of mind. It is our responsibility to overcome this state.

The issue of our responsibility in overcoming sin needs to be looked at.

The first argument is to realize why we are truly sinful in this world. People who have experienced clinical death, as well as those who discovered what happens between lives during hypnotic regression, have realized the truth. Their statements match perfectly.[22] When we exit the body and its linear time, we enter the eternal present of higher dimensions, where everything that manifests in this world is contracted into unity. On exiting the body we recapitulate everything we have experienced in this life, down to the last detail. Not just from our perspective, but holistically as well, which means that we observe our actions from our perspective, but also from the perspective of the person that we affected; we go through our actions from the perspective of the person we did something to, and experience it the way this other person experienced it. This way, we cannot escape the consequences of our actions, nor can we deceive ourselves by giving an alternative interpretation to our actions. From an experience such as this is, souls have brought back the golden rule of ethics which states: do not do unto others as you would not have them do unto you.

This is a way for man to attain true consciousness. *We make mistakes in this world because we look at events from our perspective, from our ego, subjectively. We can attain true consciousness only when we look at ourselves and our actions from the outside, from the perspective of others, the way other people see us. This is what maturity is.*

The experience of death makes us face all of our mistakes. We then make a decision to reincarnate to mend our ways in accordance with our free will. This is the only reason we reincarnate. Once we become without sin, we no longer have a need to be born into human bodies. Then we are equal with the divine consciousness which does not require a body at all. But knows how to use it.

Therefore, there is some truth to the idea that we come sinful into this world, but, apparently, it has been misconstrued! It is all our game with ourselves, our game of consciousness, our way of raising awareness, connecting consciousness and existence, becoming aware of our functioning.

We cannot deliver ourselves from sin by using only our physical mind and ego, following their methods and logic, following theology and dogma. A problem cannot be solved in the same place it originated. *The only way to avoid all mistakes is to connect our physical mind with the higher mind and consciousness of the soul. All awareness of what is right stems from there.* This is what all prayers and religiousness are about. Logic of the mind is limited to the physical world and opposites. The only way to overcome opposites is to overcome the logic of the mind and connect oneself with consciousness of the soul.

Everything that is right and proper in our lives comes from above, from consciousness of the soul. Everything that is wrong comes from the logic of the mind, restricted by the physical body and senses.

To exceed the mind we have the discipline of meditation. However, the karmic maturity necessary for such a discipline is limited to very few individuals. Most must regulate the actions of their mind in some outer way, like coercion and duress, through faith, conviction, repeating suggestions, and implementing law and order. Likewise, the system for punishing disobedient people. These methods are necessary for people who are unable to transcend their mind and open themselves to consciousness of the soul; however, they are not enough. It is all a constant battle and effort to keep the faith.

No suggestion can make the mind change itself. The influence of higher consciousness and the discipline of calming the mind are also required. All the methods of suggestion are successful only to the degree they are able to connect us to our higher mind - they are not successful in themselves.

Calming down the mind in prayer and meditation is the only direct path toward overcoming one's sinfulness. Creative work is the second on the list in overcoming mistakes (liberating oneself from the sins). Proper actions annul the effect of improper (wrong) actions. Calming down the mind without creative endeavour is virtually impossible. A mind that is not at ease and connected to the higher mind, to consciousness of the soul, cannot do anything creative.

That is why repentance, correcting sins, is wrongly interpreted, as is everything else in this upside-down Omega world of ours.

The soul does not return to itself, it does not get liberated from mistakes, when we whip our body and deny it its natural needs, but when we do something right and encourage the soul to return to itself, or when we make something new that was not there before but is useful and enriches life; we are relieved of our sinfulness when we feel rapture and the joy of creation, knowing we did something good and useful. This is a way in which a soul goes back to itself. The rapture we feel after a job well done is a fragment of the same divine energy this world was created with. The creation of the world is an ongoing process. Man who creates something beneficial only taps into the process and shares its grandeur, he connects his intelligence to the intelligent design of divine consciousness that creates all. In reality, he connects himself with the consciousness of his soul that is the true creator in this world. Hence, the rapture and joy of creation.

Creating something that is beautiful, good, and right means that we have embellished something that is ugly and corrected something that is wrong – and by doing so 'we have found the absolutions to our sins'. With every good and proper action we have tilted to the right side of the motion of the Omega point in the direction of the Alpha point, the divine source, and if only for an inch we have rid the world of illusions – because everything that is illusory and sinful is distancing us from the divine; everything that is right, good, and beautiful is bringing ourselves closer to the divine.

If, according to the dogma, the real sin of man lies in the fact that he distanced himself from God and God's will, then this is the only way for us to find the absolution of our sins and discover the true will of God and his energy within you. It is achieved through labour-intensive endeavours, any kind of work, and any kind of creation. Make a chair that will be comfortable and of use to somebody and it is enough. It, too, is a fragment of the overall creation this world is illustrative of. Do not be like those who cannot make even one chair, but would rather sit on the bare ground and bow to God. Take part in God's creation. God's creation is everything you see in you and around you, and so much more that you cannot see at this point in time.

If you wish to be properly religious, never bow to God, but always do what God has made you for; and that is to participate in his ongoing creative process. If you only bow to God, it is like looking backward while going ahead. You will trip and fall into temptation. Simply look ahead to what should be done for the welfare of this world, and do not fret over God - you can never be without it. You will be filled with God more and more as you work more and more, if you choose to be his worker, because that will put you closer to him, since you will learn to develop the same kind of energy and consciousness with which God creates everything that exists. The more you take part in it, the more you will be without sin, which means right and proper, and more aware of God.

Work is connected with the teaching of karma. Karma means work, but sin also, because that is what ties us to incarnation. It is said that man liberates himself from karma by becoming aware of the fact that it is not he who does the job, but God working through him. Therefore, liberation from sin or karma is in realizing that God's will is doing all the work, where man is a mere instrument, a conscious witness. This is how we submit to God through work. More accurately put: we can only submit to God through diligent effort we do not view as work, but as divine. In this practical way, through work, we come to realize that everything is the divine.

REINCARNATION IS THE ANSWER TO THE QUESTION WHY SOME PEOPLE ARE RELIGIOUS AND SOME ARE NOT

This is one of the biggest questions regarding religion. We can ask an additional question though: why are there such big differences between religious people, in that there are those who are highly spiritual and intelligent, while others cultivate a very primitive and immature, even violent way, which is directly opposed to the very idea of religiousness?

To understand these differences properly, it is necessary to understand the essence of the differences that exist among people. The science of psychology is evidently not enough here - the reasons for such versatility in mentality and character among people cannot be found solely in the lives of people. There are traits that cannot be understood by influences of childhood and environment, culture and upbringing, even less so genetics, which science puts to the fore although there is not a shred of evidence to support the claim that genetics has any influence on the character of man whatsoever.

To understand human nature, it is necessary to analyze man in a wider context. Additionally, it is necessary to understand the law of reincarnation.

It is impossible to be religious in the right way and understand the fundamental issues of religion without understanding reincarnation first.

Understanding reincarnation is linked directly with understanding the soul, and understanding the soul is directly linked with understanding divine consciousness. It is completely pointless to try and understand God if we do not understand the concept of our soul and its reincarnations first.

It is impossible to believe in the soul without believing in reincarnation. Rejecting reincarnation automatically signals a materialistic view of the world, a view that says that man originates for the first time when he is born into the body, that the soul is equal to the body, that it appears in it and disappears with it. If, aside from all this, there is also a belief that the soul 'departs somewhere,' it must be accepted that it also came from somewhere, because it could not simply have originated in the body, since the body is too imperfect and inferior to create a soul. If the body were able to create a soul, then the body itself would be immortal. Whatever is mortal and material cannot create something immortal and immaterial. Therefore, if our soul outlives the mortal body, it had to have existed before the body. In that case, there is not a single reason why it would not be born into a body multiple times; this is logical and practical for the process of learning. Many Christian authorities concur that the soul continues to learn after death. There is no reason why it would not choose to be born into a new body, because for the process of learning a body of some kind is necessary.

Evidence for reincarnation has always existed. Many children prove it with their knowledge and conduct; some speak openly about their past lives, and generally, those stories can be verified. There is a series of scientific research that proves reincarnation - some of which set out to debunk the existence of reincarnation, but given the weight of evidence, those same researchers became major advocates for reincarnation. There is no such thing as a lack of evidence in favour of reincarnation, but only a lack in our intention to see it.

The only culture that denies reincarnation is the one based on Judeo-Christianity - all the others acknowledge its existence. This is because all other cultures do not have the mental programming that forbids faith in reincarnation. The first Christian and Gnostics believed in reincarnation. Pythagoras not only believed in reincarnation but remembered his past lives as well. The teaching of reincarnation was forbidden by the fifth Ecumenical Council in 553 A.D. by the emperor Justinian, and the order was executed in rather a violent way. Most western church communities accepted Origen's works and teachings that harmoniously bind the Christian faith and reincarnation. The reasons for this prohibition were laid out in the chapter dealing with time and religiousness. In short, by discarding reincarnation, the consciousness of the soul was forced to attach itself to the body much more, according to stretching the Omega point, to speed up time and man's performance in this world – not because reincarnation does not exist. Those who firmly believe in reincarnation, like Hindus, are prone to delegating their professional duties onto several lifetimes. The more, the better. Even when they are dying of hunger in the streets, they find solace in the fact that next time they will have a better life, in the next life they will learn to feed themselves. That is why they live and die without changing this world.

Kabbalists claim that man originally came from God and in the end, he will return to it. Before this happens, he must be born and die many times, before he acquires a sufficient level of maturity, and then his way back to God is secured.

However, the soul does not go to God himself upon death of the physical body. After death, the soul only goes to the higher dimensions of the astral and mental world

(Heaven or the Devachanic plane), where it recapitulates its experiences in this world, and from there it returns to the physical world in a new incarnation.

That is why reincarnation means that souls have multiple lives in many bodies. These are incarnation cycles. They have their beginning when the soul commences its experiences of life in a physical body on a certain planet; later they have their development and end, finalizing the incarnation cycle.

Only when the soul completes a whole cycle of incarnations does it go back to its divine source, because it has become aware of its unity with the divine consciousness always - when it is in the body and out of the body, between two lives. It has become aware of the fact that every form of life is divine consciousness in its essence. It does not need any more experiences in this world, it always knows who it is. It learns that it is the consciousness in question, and it knows that absolutely everything else that exists is the same consciousness. That is the final awakening of the soul, or God-knowledge.

This is a clear indication that shows it is perfectly possible to unite the Christian rejection of reincarnation with the fact that it exists. Man indeed has one life, the way Christianity teaches us, but this life has several phases or incarnations. Man's whole life takes place within several lives and bodies.

There is an analogy between life and death and sleeping and waking. During one physical life, we sleep many times and wake up many times, but always in the same body and the same world, and with the memory of who we are. In much the same way, during our real life as a soul, we have a great many situations where we fall asleep (are born in a body in this world) and wake up (after the death of the body), when we once again regain consciousness of our soul, the awareness of who we are in an absolute sense. The only difference is that here after sleeping we come back to the same body, therefore we have continuity of memory, and after death we have a new body and no memory of what came before, because we have a new physical mind that rules the body. We can remember our past lives only if we surpass the physical mind and get in touch with the consciousness of the soul that overcomes all bodies.

Therefore, it is true that man has only one life, but it is divided into many bodily lives. Man's whole life consists of the cycle of incarnations.

Each cycle of incarnations is divided into three phases: the initial, the mature, and the final.

An individual life has the same three phases: in youth, we are full of desires and identification with the world; in our maturity we turn to critical analysis; and in our old age we release ourselves of all illusions.

The beginning is such that it requires adjusting oneself to the conditions of this world - this refers to the so-called young souls. It is logical that their characteristics are ignorance and a large number of mistakes during the learning process, finding it difficult to cope with life, susceptibility to delusions. Together with all of this, there is a need for additional coercion and duress during their coaching. These young souls are those who display immaturity, like small children, and are the most abundant in so-called 'primitive communities'. They are like children, they lead innocent lives, there were a lot more of them in this world in earlier times, but as civilization and technology developed and progressed, the souls themselves started to mature, and today they have made a big step ahead, even though the immature still make up the majority of the population of this world. Their perception of the world is limited and simple, and their religiousness is the same, limited to natural influences and contents, mimicking nature, whereas the idea of the soul is animal in its expression, and as simple as possible. They have a vague notion of what the soul is, they consider it an integrated part of nature, which returns to nature after death, often becoming some animal. This is wrong, but it is completely in line with their immaturity. They mostly have unclear and dark notions of the soul and existence.

Today's young and immature souls that live in modern cities, that use technology, are mostly atheists and materialists; they have no awareness of the soul or its existence as a divine presence. The way that former primitive communities believed a soul transits onto animals, today they believe the soul of man consists only of memory stored somewhere in the brain, which they will be able to download onto a USB flash drive and copy into a robot, or an artificially created body.

The more mature the soul is, the more mature the perception of the world through religiousness is.

Only the most mature souls have cognition that their essence is identical to the essence of existence, and they can picture it clearly and act accordingly.

The less mature the soul is, the more apt it is to search for its essence in forms in nature, in contents of the mind, in stories and myths. The less mature the soul is, the more it identifies with the forms and contents of the physical experience. This is justified because it is beginning to learn about the physical world, but at the same time it is less capable of understanding the transcendental truths that exceed the physical and sensory world. A soul matures by not only acquiring more experience in the physical world, but with a greater degree of experience in transcending the physical world, with cognition of spirituality, or the true nature of the soul. That is what all religions are for.

Young souls learn to become mature by first getting to know the physical world surrounding them. This means they develop physical experiences, because to them material reality is everything. Young souls are the biggest materialists, their common trait is that they 'do not believe in God and soul'. This is justified for them because they aspire to be realistic, to know the physical laws as best they can. Lessons cannot be skipped. There is a curriculum, like in a school. Only once they become experienced enough in the physical world, when they become medium developed souls, can they become aware of the spiritual reality - but not completely, only partly. When they become fully mature souls they become aware of the transcendental spiritual reality in every respect.

This would be the real explanation as to why some people are religious and some are not, and why some people are religious in a primitive and naive way, while others are religious in a spiritual and intelligent way, why some express their religiousness in a realistic and positive way, and some in a negative and destructive way. The answer is in the maturity of the souls, in understanding what stage of the reincarnation cycle an individual soul is in.

You will know them by their fruits.

How can one distinguish such a difference in the maturity of the souls, in the context of religiousness?

At best, religiousness encompasses all aspects of life and teaches souls to grow and mature in harmony. For young souls, there are laws and taboos, punishments and rewards, and for the mature it offers a direct insight into the highest levels of religious teachings; each to his own. It is of vital importance to differentiate between the levels of religious instructions, to know what is intended for who. In traditional religions, this is common knowledge, but often enough there is the issue of how to approach the information intended for the mature when it reaches the ears of the immature.

What is important to know here is that essentially there is no such thing as conflict amongst people. All people are children of God and in their soul they are all brothers. Misunderstandings and conflicts among people can only happen due to differing levels of consciousness, maturity, and different contents of the physical mind, which to a varying degree obstruct the connection with the higher mind and consciousness of the soul.

There is always a problem when someone who is on a lower level of consciousness receives an explanation of the higher state of affairs, because everybody sees only their level, they cannot see the higher states. It takes a lot of patience and a systematic approach to help someone understand the limitations of his level of consciousness and rise to a higher level. No matter how well-meaning a teacher may be, taking into account all the wisdom of pedagogy, most immature people will tackle their problems in a hard way, through personal experience. This is for the best. A real teacher will only give the right perspective and understanding of the context, never help them avoid their lessons.

All the conflicts in this world exist because there is a misunderstanding regarding the levels of consciousness, because there are young, mature and very mature souls.

Conflicts end when one soul realizes this difference and stops identifying with the lower state of consciousness, when it stops acting and reacting in a way typical for a lower consciousness.

This is a way by which it ascends into a higher state and becomes more mature.

Conflict is a possibility only when the higher state of consciousness is out of sight. Any insight into a higher state calms the passion for conflict and hatred.

Hatred only results from ignorance. All religions have the task of conducting higher consciousness to the lower states, down to people who are insufficiently mature, to help them bring the light of consciousness and understanding into their lives. All religious messages are about peace.

Any form of conflict or violence toward any being is directly opposed to religiousness.

An aspiration to impose one's religious beliefs onto anybody else, or onto the whole world for that matter, is also directly opposed to proper religiousness, because such individuals fail to notice that divine consciousness is in all people already, in the world as it is, as the foundation of everything. Such people do not actually convey their religious beliefs, but only learn phrases by heart - what the physical mind is able to see and know. That is why such believers, who impose their faith on others and wish to rule the world, are the most atrocious killers in this world. Religious fanatics are the biggest opposition to religiousness.

An additional problem is that all the processes in this world are speeding up. Mechanisms that traditional religions had in the past for assistance during the process of maturing are of little help now, because they belong to a different age. Their biggest problem is they are so diverse amongst themselves, they belong to different cultures, and modern life erases boundaries. We live in a global world. Erasing differences between cultures in the modern world will not have the set goal for us to become uncultured and wild, godless, but to become more human, aware of our true nature, irrelevant of local traditions and cultures. More than ever before, we have to be proper people, because we see ourselves that we should be, and not because some tradition or dogma is steering us in that direction. That is the exam we must pass now. Traditional religions should provide us with the basics, what is best and universal, which is the same in all religions.

The more mature the soul is, the more it acts impeccably due to its insight, and not because of some external pressure. All external coercion and religious traditions existed because there was no link between the mind and the soul, they were trying to describe and picture this link in so many ways. Once this link is established, no outside intervention is necessary.

The same applies to mankind. We live in times when this issue gets crystallized, all the irrelevant traditional patterns are discarded, the patterns that limited people on the local level disappear, and increasingly more universal knowledge is brought to us and made available for all.

The consciousness of the soul cannot traditionally manifest itself. In the same way that the Jewish, Christian, or Muslim sun and air do not exist, even less so the 'holy ground', and therefore there is not any Jewish, Christian, or Muslim spirituality or consciousness. It is high time we realized we all live on the same planet and it should be holy to all of us.

The next thing to understand is that incarnation cycles and maturity of the soul are to do with percentage. In this world, there is a far bigger percentage of young souls, who are just beginning their maturing process, while the mature and old souls are far fewer in number.

That is why this world is full of irrational conflicts and needless fighting that originate as a result of ignorance and lack of understanding. Absolutely everything that could be experienced is experienced here. All opposition. Amongst souls, planet Earth has the reputation of an elite school, the hardest, but complete in itself.

The reason for such a ratio of percentage is in the following.

Old souls are finalizing their incarnation cycle, and there are the fewest of them. It is logical that those who come to learn make up the majority of people. Old souls in this world are mostly teachers, and the ratio is like in schools: there is one teacher for every thirty students. Old souls are home builders for young souls, they built this world to facilitate learning and life for the youngsters. All the great creators did this. Old souls built all of the civilizations in this world, from pyramids to modern Europe and northern America. Now young souls migrate into these areas more and more, to learn easier and faster; they advance, erasing all the differences in culture, faith, and race. Not to erase, but to crystallize the crucial parts of great cultures and religions - and that is awareness of the most supreme reality.

The problem is that it, too, has its phases: the initial, mature and final. The initial phase is when emphasis is put only on the destruction of everything old, and in an immature being that means testing all the liberties, and when the primitive lot stays the primitive lot in the heart of Europe. It seems that we are in this phase now. If we survive it, the mature phase will be when the majority becomes aware of the universal values traditional religions hold within and apply them in a global society without frontiers irrelevant of the past.

The final phase will be when, through every man, the divine consciousness of the soul begins to shine. Then, there will be a 'heavenly kingdom on earth as it is in heaven'. This world will once again be heaven, in which fully mature and realized souls live freely, because there will be no differences between the highest divine consciousness and existence, here and now, in everything and at any given moment.

In fact, these differences do not exist now, nor have there ever been any, but it is hard to explain this to some people.

SEVEN STATES OF RELIGIOUSNESS

The manifestation of divine consciousness happens through seven phases, reflected as the seven psychoenergetic states and the functioning of consciousness in man, as the seven chakras, the seven ways in which consciousness and existence connect and function through man.

Although consciousness is only one and indivisible, because it is the source and the outcome of existence, it is in various forms of existence, manifested to varying degrees. This measure depends on the form and manner of existence, i.e. on our functioning (hence, the being and state of consciousness are mutually connected). Since our subjective experience most often cannot see the general unity of the being, these forms seem separate and different from one another, which creates an illusion that there are different states of consciousness, although in reality there are only different states of unconsciousness. Therefore, man has seven different states of consciousness, that is to say existence, in which he can find himself (they correspond to the system of chakras):

1) deep sleep without dreams,
2) the dreaming phase,
3) the state of being awake or the average daily alertness,
4) testifying the first three,
5) awareness of cosmic unity,
6) enabling the consciousness to participate actively in this union, and
7) awareness of one's essence, of the soul, as an outcome of the existence of the universe (and the previous

six states), and the disappearance of spacetime due to complete openness to the divine presence as our soul, i.e. our complete uniting with divine Absolute asp our own being, and the conscious and functional manifestation of this unity.

The first state is a state of pure existence, as is the seventh, but while the first is unaware of itself, the seventh is completely aware of itself and its unity of consciousness with existence. Therefore, they are merely different aspects of consciousness of the same existence. Since consciousness and existence are the same, these different aspects of consciousness yield different functioning and forms of existence.

Each of these states of consciousness correlates with one chakra.

The seventh state is the only one that is true, authentic existence, while all the others express levels of either unawareness or awareness of this state. Although here it is impossible to know something like this without personal experience, it is a useful thing to mention that man is always, and in all states, in pure unity with the highest reality, because he has nowhere else to be. Deep sleep is a state in which man is in deep unity with being (with God), the same as in the seventh state, but unconsciously. His ascension of the seven states during spiritual evolution is all about making this unity fully aware, actualized, to be expressed as his personal will, so that it becomes a reflection of the absolute divine consciousness.

Man is unconscious and in a deep sleep, to the measure that he cannot see the reality of divine being and does not participate in it actively and consciously. Chakra activation is an activation of man's conscious participation in divine reality.

Since a man in deep sleep is completely unaware of himself, his existence is based on the elementary level of instinct. This corresponds with the first chakra.

In the state of dreams, emotions join instinct, and also memory and imagination. Dreams play out on the realm of the astral or dimensions above the physical world. This is the second chakra.

In the state of everyday wakefulness, all instincts, feelings, and imagination receive physical inertia and three-dimensional coherence, which is why there is the aptitude for partially stable thinking and decision-making, which was lacking in prior states. It is a state of mind or ego in the physical body. This aptitude should be developed and good judgment should be cultivated, but without imposed concepts. It is the function of the mind and ego, or reason. This is the area of the third chakra. The first real attempt to become aware of consciousness itself, that is to say, existence, takes place here.

These first three states (deep sleep, dreams, and the state of being awake) correspond to the first three chakras: muladhara, svadhisthana and manipura. Most people act naturally on them, which means without any spiritual culture or conscious intention. They may be recognized as urges (the first), as desires (the second) and will-power (the third).

These are all the states of religious functioning that exist in this world. The whole religious consciousness of Judeo-Christianity, Pagan cults, and animistic religions are based on the first three chakras.

To discern levels of consciousness according to a certain type of religiousness, we will call them religious consciousness of man number one, two and three, having in mind that we're referring to the chakra number. They are not strictly separated, but some of their elements overflow from the lower forms of religiousness into the higher.

The religiousness of man number one, or the first chakra

Religious consciousness of man number one, that is to say, the first chakra, corresponds to animistic and polytheistic religions, shamanism, and primitive cults. All of these types of religiousnesses are based on a direct energy relation with nature. This explains how shamans know a lot more about nature than other people; they know the higher dimensions of nature, they are able to use the energy of nature for various purposes, for healing for example, but also to harm someone. This is the characteristic of this level of consciousness, which is void of critical judgment; it does not have any objective awareness of the soul or sense of purpose typical of the higher consciousness of higher chakras; it simply possesses the skill of functioning on this level alone. This is why there is both white and black magic that operates on this level. Here, with equal impact and temptation, basic life energy can function in both positive and negative ways. On this level of religiousness, people make sacrifices. This is a way of returning life energy to its source. At least, in theory. In reality, there are mediators in the form of inorganic beings from the astral that feed off this energy. The remains of this practice exist in developed religiousness, in Judeo-Christianity, where the sacrificial stone has been replaced by the altar and the sacrifice is symbolic; instead of blood and flesh, there is wine and bread, although the ancient Jews had real sacrifices. This is an example of how the elements of lower religiousness overflow to religious practices of higher forms.

Religious consciousness of the first chakra has its lower and higher forms. The lowest are primitive imitations during initiation rituals and summoning up demons and gods - imitation during initiation. The body adapts in a rough way to higher phases of maturity; young people are disconnected from childhood in a cruel way, using trauma. Due to the lack of critical consciousness on this low level, everything must be learned in a coarse and simple way, by programming the body itself.

In this state of consciousness, the idea of the soul is also primitive, connected to the energy functioning of nature in its lower forms. Shamans see the soul of man as the soul of the world, personified in the forces of nature, the ground, plants, and animals. All beings are equal to a shaman. To him, animals are also people, but in a different form; the plants yield their secrets to him. Most primitive societies on this level of consciousness experience a human soul as a part of the animal kingdom, and they think it goes into animal form after death. This simply reflects an intuitive bond with the fact that divine consciousness develops its perception and functioning through animal form before reaching human form. Human consciousness here is very close to the animal experience. On this level, human forms of consciousness only get as far as taboo, and folklore is passed down for generations.

The religiousness of the first chakra reflects itself the most via the body, and energy manipulations. Since there is no intellectual effort here, everything is based on ritualism.

The religiousness of man number two, or the second chakra

Consciousness polarizes in the second chakra. In the physical experience this polarization is manifested through sexuality, and as dualism in religious experience, either through teaching on dualism (good and evil, god and devil) or manifesting dualism in one's fight against infidels.

The type of consciousness manifested through the second chakra corresponds to the religions that get upgraded from polytheism to monotheism. These are all the Judeo-Christian religions, Islam included. The functioning of basic life energy is formed here in the most elementary way; the influences of the first chakra are regulated here. That is why they are mostly ethical religions. They consist of regulating what a man should do, in all the spheres of his functioning.

In the early stages of development of civilization, the influence of such religions was necessary. In the same way that children are taught basic rules in life, mankind learned plenty from these religions. They had an educational purpose. The reason for this was that in those days people did not have a developed awareness of the most rudimentary principles of how to function in this world. Religions gave commandments for people to abide by, with a threat of severe punishment for disobedience. Everything is covered, from food to style of clothing, which are strictly prescribed, to the highest metaphysical issues. Everything is prescribed, one just needs to learn the rules by heart and copy.

The religiousness of the second chakra has a lower and a higher level. The lowest is connected to the first chakra and is reduced to mere imitation, and learning by means of rituals. Ritualism dominates on the lower level of consciousness of the second chakra. This is due to the influence of the lower, first chakra. Hence, all the religions of Judeo-Christianity and Islam are based on rituals. These rituals are, in fact, ritual magic; through a magic act a divine presence is summoned – although they are presented and interpreted as liturgy or mass. On this level, what should be done intellectually (the third chakra) is done ritually, such as reading the 'holy scriptures'. They are mechanically learned by heart and their contents are never questioned. Therefore, the way of thinking is also ritualistic. Ritualism exists in everyday behaviour and greetings, where the word God or Prophet is uttered mechanically. The proof that this repetitive behaviour is as far as possible from critical consciousness is in the heartless violence these same believers demonstrate when they leave their place of worship.

On this level, consciousness is far from critical judgment, and near the urges of the first chakra. That is why the religiousness of these individuals is very exclusive; they fight for their beliefs with fanaticism. They are emotionally exclusive as well, they see their kind only, and everybody else is an infidel, which also makes them enemies. Therefore, they aspire to convert everybody else into their faith, and traitors are punished by death. Jews and Muslims consider all other people ('infidels') to be lesser beings, like animals. They have no religious tolerance. Their 'divine commandments' refer only to the members of their faith and community. Not other people, the infidels. This harshness is justified for consciousness on this low level to be maintained and controlled, but it becomes a big obstacle when it should develop into higher levels.

In the second chakra, the first differentiation of life energy takes place, which is division into sexes. Thus, this chakra is crucial for sexuality. Such are the religions that belong to it. They are always in conflict, in polarization. Sexuality is treated very harshly and wrongly, which is understandable because consciousness is of limited scope here. Energy and drives mixed with emotions are far stronger. Sexuality in Muslims and Catholics, which belong to this level, is greatly disturbed - best reflected in the inhuman way they treat women, and sexual transgressions of priests. Only because of the influence of the second chakra, which identifies with the body, do Christians believe that Jesus is literally the son of God. If they rose above the influence of the second chakra, they would know this is only a metaphor for the metaphysical truth of us and our relationship to the divine.

The higher level of religiousness of man number two, to a certain degree exceeds imitation through rituals and emotional exclusiveness, and has some form of intellectual work, like reading the holy scriptures and debating their contents. This is a consequence of the higher, third chakra. Although this is still on a very low level, it at least means they have to be literate. This is a sign of great progress compared to some Orthodox forms of religiousness, like Orthodoxy, in which a believer does not have to be literate; it is enough for him to be present in the magical act, in liturgy or mass, and display his religiousness by making the right gestures during his participation in the affair.

This level of religiousness displays an attachment to corporeality and a lack of consciousness, and is best recognized in the way believers are attached to physical forms of spirituality, like religious relics. They cannot accept spirituality as such, it must have some physical form, symbolic at least. The bones of saints are broken into pieces and sold, or solemnly given away, as are innumerable fragments of 'honourable crosses'; pictures of saints are worshipped far more than the contents of the saints' teachings.

Interestingly, Muslims who condemn idolatry are on this level also. However, those that do not wish to turn their God into a picture or a statue, turn the words and expressions of their teaching into mantras, which they go on repeating incessantly like idols. Some make idols from carved wood and some from words. Their fiery religious babble should not deceive us. Their wrongdoings are even worse than those who bow to statues and pictures. The words of man can deceive more than stone statues or paintings.

To a higher form of believer number two, the first influences of higher consciousness in this chakra belong to the Catholic believers who are still emotionally exclusive toward the 'infidels,' but their social system and work are far more advanced; they show all the power it takes for a man to rise above the animal and magical level and on to a rational state of consciousness. They still wear their religious idols and act as though they were programmed and under a magic spell, but they also made the first civilized functional cities and universities (in recent history). The highest form of Catholicism represents the first real separation from animal-like living and the first real organized life. Nothing more than that.

A higher form of Muslim believers are Sufis, who perceive religion as a form of personal growth. Sufism is an ancient school of personal growth of all the seven levels of consciousness in man.[23] It is important to know that Sufism is much older than Islam. Islam originated as a political movement aimed against the ancient knowledge Sufi represented.[24] Everything Islam has of spirituality is from Sufism, which it took over but in a very limited and changed form. However, even this glimpse of wisdom is enough for soulful people to find it very attractive, because all of Islam is based on one rudimentary and high truth, which is that divine consciousness is omnipotent and omnipresent. Everything else is unimportant minor details, even manipulations. Manipulation with this truth in Islam is possible and very present, because this truth has a magic attraction for the consciousness of the soul - so much so that man is willing to sacrifice his life for it. This attraction makes Islam easy to twist to violent fanaticism and religious fundamentalism. To people with religiousness of the second chakra, this happens a lot, because they think in terms of duality constantly; passion and energy are abundant and consciousness of the soul is very limited. This is the recipe for fanaticism and violence. Therefore, religious fundamentalism and fanaticism with violence are possible only on this level of consciousness.

A higher form of Judaism is Kabbalah, the science of the higher dimensions and man's work with them. This is for the chosen ones only.

The religiousness of man number three, or the third chakra

The consciousness that manifests through the third chakra corresponds with religions that strengthen a critical state of mind, sound judgment, and induce practical work. These are the Protestant religions that glorify work, knowledge, and literacy. A Protestant believer must be literate; they have surpassed rituals and magical practices, their churches are classrooms where people read and debate, not mechanically but critically. In this way they enable God to continue his project of creating the new world, through man and his work. Such is the teaching of Calvinism, which takes all the credit for building modern civilization and science; their religious spirit made the USA and Europe. Countries that have Protestantism dominant in them are among the most advanced in the world.

A higher form of Protestantism is Freemasonry. They teach openly that God is the Great Architect of the universe and that man has no other purpose but to participate in the building process. Their religious symbols are tools, a square, compasses, a hammer, and a chisel.[25]

Freemasons rule the modern world, not only in a positive but in a negative way, making sure the Omega point is well-stretched into the opposition of the divine source so that the consciousness of people can crystallize to its ultimate limits. A big percentage of mankind assists in this process - those who are still on the lowest level of consciousness, mechanized, under the influence of magic and ritualism. Their temple is the image of the universe, and more than anything, it is built within man. They transform the principles of the cosmos into social reality. Their God is Lucifer, the first angel of God, who is the bringer of light of consciousness into the darkest corners of existence. Good human souls would not even take a peek into these dark and negative forms of existence, into which Lucifer brings the light of consciousness. The light of divine consciousness has to be conducted through absolutely all of the possible forms of existence, through all opposites. Human souls are the embodiment of the divine good and they are incapable of doing any harm, evil or negative. For souls to experience and become aware of the negative side of existence, which is also a part of the divine whole, soulless entities from higher dimensions help them in this task, as does the Luciferian religion of Freemasonry. It, too, is positive, much like everything in the whole of the universe is positive, but in a harder way.

The religiousness of the third chakra is also manifested in all the people who turn to science, politics, or building society. They are great leaders and reformers (most of whom are Freemasons). They surpass the temptation of the first two chakras, their sexuality is well-harmonized within family life and offspring. Every good husband is a representative of the fully realized third chakra. Many individuals of this stature became pillars of their societies.

It must be emphasized that all atheists belong on this level of religiousness, the consciousness of the third chakra. They have risen enough above the first two levels and have a critical opinion of them, but are still unaware of the higher levels of existence.

The religiousness of man number four, or the fourth chakra

When man is mature enough to deal not only with the outer world, but to also become aware of himself, of the consciousness that perceives the world, of the functioning of his mind, when he knows himself as the conscious subject who perceives the world and functions in it – then he becomes man number four, and his religiousness manifests the properties that belong to the fourth chakra.

It brings a surpassing of the first three levels of religiousness, and the ability to testify about them. It marks the beginning of attaining higher consciousness of oneself and the world, an initiation point of the binding of the individual consciousness with the absolute, divine consciousness.

The first three states are provided for by nature, and for their everyday functioning one does not need to do anything - it is enough to let go, because for natural survival they prove to be enough. This explains why most people reside in them their whole lives, with rare and brief excursions into the fourth state, which is usually induced by some potent emotional stress or a mystic experience.

The permanent realization of the fourth state is the result of spiritual nurture, and a conscious effort for man to be able to uplift himself above gravity and natural survival, away from the first three states. A Buddhist practice of contemplation, satipatthâna, and dhyâna are both completely dedicated to this cultivation process. It is a feat that nature only allows for very few, because for the survival of organic life, a vast majority of beings need to be conditioned by the spontaneous reproduction of the first three states.

One of the main characteristics of the fourth state is that, due to the practice of contemplation and occasional experiences of pure transcendental consciousness of oneself, that is to say of the consciousness that is pure of thought, waking during sleep, into the astral world, becomes common. This is a crossover phase and refers to the beginning of man's practical work on awakening. It corresponds with the activation of the fourth chakra, anahata. The first experiences of the consciousness of unity, spontaneous and short-lived, take place here. They are always followed by love and bliss toward existence itself, in all forms. That is why this chakra denotes unconditional divine love.

The fourth state of religiousness, that is to say, consciousness, (turya in yoga), contains and encompasses within itself four states of manifestation of the divine:

1. pure consciousness of oneself;
2. energy;
3. unconditional love;
4. bliss.

These four things become one here. In the lower states of the first three chakras (or religiousness) they were apart - one was more or less emphasized than the others, while some were completely suppressed. Still, a unity of this kind occurs only temporarily. It becomes permanent only on the higher levels, and the ascension to higher levels only occurs as this unity becomes permanent.

All dedicated believers who have overcome formal and ritual forms and beliefs of certain religions belong to the fourth state of religiousness. Their religiousness is universal; they discover it in existence, not in scriptures. If they were originally members of one of the religions, they get along well and recognize each other, they speak the same language. They recognize the 'holy secrets' religions speak of, and see them in existence and life. Most have such power of understanding that they are very interesting to other believers, because of their ability to comprehend, which is direct and based on experience. Understanding and love are their common features, no matter what religion they belong to. Most often such people do not belong to any specific religion, because religions are restrictive. A manifestation of goodness and understanding in everyday life is their universal religion.

They manifest consciousness of the soul for the first time, which is what distinguishes them from the believers of the lower chakras. For the believers whose consciousness belongs to lower chakras, the consciousness of the soul is an abstract notion; they speak of the soul and think only in terms they have learned by heart; they are incapable of manifesting consciousness of the soul. In the fourth state of religiousness, for the first time, the soul is cognized directly and it directly connects with divine consciousness. From here onwards, consciousness of the soul begins to be dominant in religiousness.

One reaches the fourth state of consciousness or religiousness only through discipline and conscious intent, by working on oneself. There is no other way. All the lower states are shaped through natural causality. The fourth state overcomes the influences of nature for the first time.

In the fourth state, a breaking point happens. In all the lower states of consciousness or religiousness, outer influences and conditionedness of nature shape consciousness in man. Now for the first time it takes a turn for the better, and consciousness in man becomes so powerful and self-conscious that it can affect the outer world, it can modify and exceed all natural influences.

The religiousness of man number five, or the fifth chakra

When man number four directly cognizes the consciousness of his soul and divine consciousness as the same living force which is at the base of existence and life, he then begins to manifest and express it in a number of ways.

On this level, man's true wakefulness becomes more lasting. During the regular practice of meditation, while he was experiencing pure consciousness of himself (the fourth state), this experience gradually becomes more present and stable; it slowly starts to permeate all the other states as well, even outside of meditation. And by doing so, it grows into the fifth state. The man is aware during the shifting of the three previous states, (the state of being awake, dreaming, and deep sleep) because he has become an integrated and whole personality (aham-kâra), which does not forget his being transiting the three states in question, which exist all the time. He is aware of his whole body, of all the senses, and manifestation of will. Some powers begin to manifest here (siddhi) as regards perception, like telepathy and seeing aura. This level of religiousness corresponds with the fifth chakra activation, vishuddhi. It is characterized by the clearest ability to think and express oneself on the nature of reality, the unity of consciousness. This expression is the highest level of understanding that can be achieved through words and thoughts.

People who manifest religiousness on the fifth level of consciousness or through the fifth chakra are poets, sages whose words stand the test of time; they are remembered and repeated always, they are the permanent teachers of mankind. They do not manifest their wisdom using words only, but in all possible ways, through all forms of artistic expression. Their works have permanent value.

In fact, they do not use art to express themselves. Their expression is always spontaneous and such that other people experience it as perfect art. Their works create art.

The religiousness of man number six, or the sixth chakra

By becoming constantly alert in the process of overcoming the first three states, when pure consciousness of the soul is permanently present as existence itself, man enters the sixth state of religiousness, characterized by active awakening of the will in order to be in unity with the divine and to recognize the divine as one's being.

While the fifth state was characterized by knowledge of unity and wakefulness, as the equivalent for unity with the divine whole, the sixth state develops this knowledge further into action, and the will to participate in unity because now he has the experience that his consciousness is not in any way different from either existence or the divine.

This is the sixth chakra, ajna, which is found behind the eyes. The characteristic of this chakra is an insight that exceeds words and thoughts - a direct insight into the essence of being or phenomena.

While he is still able to express his knowledge of divine presence through all the forms of artistic expression, on the sixth level man overcomes words and thoughts. He has surpassed the mind and sees divine reality as the only possible reality, in everything and always.

He resides in inner silence, here and now; he does not need a mind to interpret reality and events, he sees them directly the way they are. The mind served its purpose, only to explain and envisage what one cannot cognize directly. Once something is known directly, the mind is of no use. One sees everything clearly.

On this level, what was happening only occasionally on lower levels becomes permanently established, and this is the highest reality in which existence is completely aware of itself; this consciousness is the same consciousness with which we know existence, the consciousness of our soul.

All consciousness is the same consciousness, from God to an ant to our self-consciousness. There is not a multitude of consciousnesses. If it were not so, we would not be able to see and understand the nature of everything that exists, we would not be able to see with the consciousness of the sixth chakra that everything that exists has its aura.

The religiousness of man number seven, or the seventh chakra

Once man reaches this level, he is no longer conditioned by nature, he has overcome everything that binds him to his being and time, and he has become a place of opening for the divine consciousness that enables existence itself, and exceeds it by far. It is a state of such wakefulness that individuality and corporeality are barely visible, and a complete and permanent awakening is the direct expression of man's union with wholeness.

Wakefulness is pure consciousness. Complete wakefulness happens when everything becomes consciousness, and nothing else. Before this moment, consciousness existed next to something else, and it was not the same consciousness for us; there was still something that was an object for us, a foreign body, something opposing consciousness. Now, everything is consciousness itself and nothing else exists; even the grossest phenomena and things are consciousness only, the same consciousness with which we become aware of all phenomena and things. All consciousness is our consciousness, and it is the same consciousness that enables everything. There are no more differences in consciousness. This state is said to happen when the world disappears and only God remains, as the only reality.

Complete alertness of the seventh chakra or the direct cognition of God brings complete participation in the whole of existence, and in the same way it brings complete independence of existence. An awakened one lives in the world with his whole being, but he does not belong to the world. Any other kind of alertness is not an option, because it is unity with the transcendental Absolute, and it is man's essence, both at the same time. Therefore, man who has united with it ceases to differ from it, in the same way that water is no different from water, air from the air, light from light.

This is the seventh state that is no longer religiousness, but the goal of religiousness, which is out of bounds to the unawakened people with only the first three levels active. It is the seventh crown chakra, sahasrara, on top of the head.

To people of lower consciousness, this state has been described through images of God in heaven, with veneration toward his power and grandeur. An awakened one sees this same God in everything, here and now, in himself and everywhere around himself, as a natural state of affairs. He treats everything with the same awe and admiration, any trivial detail has the same high value. That is why he always seems to be experiencing ecstasy, always in bliss and merciful with everyone and everything. He moves through divine consciousness like fish through water. He is always in it.

***

People of the sixth level were founders of great religions, while those of the seventh level remained unknown to the world because they no longer dealt with it. Jesus Christ is an example of the sixth man, and his resurrection signifies his transition to the seventh level. While man encountered his Self, the soul, on the fifth level, and on the sixth level he intensified his actions, on the seventh level is where submission and disappearance of the man's Self take place, a disappearance into the divine as the only thing, the divine that enables everything. Man's soul manifests itself as the soul of the world.

In the fifth state, he became whole in his being, and in the seventh the wholeness of his personality becomes analogous to the very wholeness of the universe, of the Absolute. Up to the sixth level, there were individuals acting; in the seventh chakra the individuality disappears, and on that spot ('body') the only thing that remains is divine consciousness that enables everything. Man becomes what he is.

Man is one with the whole always, but he is able to recognize this unity only when he becomes aware of his being in its entirety. Once an awakened man recognizes his own being for what it is, he is unable to see it as any different from the wholeness of the universe; he sees the whole of the cosmos as contracted and shaped into his body, and this body does not exist separate from the whole; it is nothing in itself and for itself, but merely a reflection of the whole. Therefore, man's wholeness is analogous to the wholeness of the universe, and vice versa. When he attains the fifth level, his wholeness, man is automatically drawn to the wholeness of the universe which manifests on the seventh level (unless he is seduced by the power of the sixth). For that reason, the seventh level is only a result of the complete reliving and affirmation of all previous levels. The main, the longest and the hardest transition is the fourth level.

**

We can say that a man of the first level is not in command entirely of the sensory and active capacity of his own body, and is therefore susceptible to their influences, mechanics and renewal. He needs strict control through taboos and religious ethics.

A man of the second level is in command of his body, but in a superficial and unspiritual way, mostly via the acceptance of authorities that act via the emotions of affection and rejection. Due to emotions of this kind, a self-preservational instinct (of his entity, nation, religion) is dominant, which necessarily leads to exclusiveness, divisions, and conflicts with other bodies (entities) and the environment. Religious wars are started by members of the second level of religiousness.

A man of the third level puts an emphasis on the mind or reason, and tries to control his body and life, and the world around himself.

A man of the fourth level of religiousness sees all the incompleteness and uselessness of such efforts, where the mind would organize and interpret life, because he becomes aware of the body and mind during interactions with the objective world in all of its dimensions. Such insight gives him personal wholeness. Such insight is brought about by the 'fourth way' practice, with which for the first time objective cognition of one's own being and nature is attained. It is achieved through special training and extreme effort only, in which man learns to rule urges of the lower nature. One who follows spontaneous instincts of the body does not attain the fourth level of religiousness. This is the world of monks and ascetics.

A man of the fifth level has encountered all natural phenomena, to the measure that he cannot be deceived by them and forget himself and his will. He has exceeded the influences of the inorganic (astral) world by becoming acquainted with them on the fourth level; they have an impact on man's life only when he is unaware of them. His personality is whole and integrated during all phenomena. What distinguishes a man of the fifth level from a man of the fourth level is that he is always the same, he can no longer descend to a lower level, he is always aware of himself.

The sixth level belongs to wakefulness, to the consciousness that is one with the outcome of being and is therefore present always, and in everything; it is all-powerful because it is the sum of all the possibilities of existence. It is alternatively called the quantum mind.

A man of the seventh level is one whose consciousness is completely and without intrusion open to the divine and which, being so unconditioned, enlightens and liberates existence. Through him, divine consciousness completely and unobstructedly manifests itself and acts. The very purpose of existence has worked itself out in him, and now he works it out in others. This happens in the very presence of such a man - he is the Savior who has resurrected and exceeded all action and all power (siddhi). Being the One Who Is, he enlightens existence and testifies of it, as the greatest act of God and unsurpassed divine power.

***

Every type of true religiousness serves the purpose of uplifting man from the lower to the higher levels of consciousness. That is why religion must be multi-layered to be effective; a man of the lower states is unaware of the higher ones, and they must be brought home to him in a comprehensible way. The truth of the higher states is displayed in the form of myths, symbols, and rituals to people on the lower states, and they represent information in a concentrated form aimed at the unconscious man. His being in itself contains all the levels of existence, and he is able to recognize the information while looking at a symbol, taking part in a ritual or experiencing a myth.

The first two lower levels of religiousness are dogmatic; they are characterized by ritualism and bring the external form to the forefront. This is the level of imitation and bans (taboos). Knowledge is acquired here by mimicking or learning things by heart. This level can be recognized in the external (mundane) expressions of Judaism, Orthodoxy and Theravada Buddhism, and the primitive forms of religiousness of many people and nations.

It must be stressed that although some religions contain within themselves all seven levels, they do not manifest them to the same measure, but only emphasize some - the first three most commonly. Theravada Buddhism and Orthodoxy best represent all the seven levels of religiousness, from the ritual to the mystical. Illiterate peasants and the most learned mystics and monks can equally quench their spiritual thirst in them.

The second level of religiousness brings skepticism and is based on faith and feelings, devotion, and dedication to a religious ideal, a God, and always leads to exclusiveness and violence toward 'heretics' and 'infidels'. Anybody with different views is seen as 'ungodly', an adversary or enemy. Hence, this type of religiousness is the most aggressive. Man learns here only what the religious authority would have him believe, through emotional conditioning. Authoritativeness and exclusiveness make this kind of religiousness the worst of all, with its violence and religious bigotry unparalleled. We can recognize this in the outer manifestations of Islam and Catholicism.

The third level of religiousness is critical, it is manifested by rejecting rituals; there is instead an intellectual approach and interpretations of all kinds of things. Knowledge is subjective here because it is based on established concepts ('holy scriptures') and mental conditioning, although it aspires to maintain the illusion of argumentation and dialectics. Various types of Protestantism fall under this category. The intellectual functions in man are pronounced here, and the countries that have this type of religiousness are the most advanced in the civilizational sense. (A Protestant believer must be literate to participate in religious life, while the Orthodox believer does not have to be - his God worship is in rituals that are mechanically repeated.)

The first three levels are the only well-known forms of religiousness for the vast majority of people, because they are naturally given through the interaction between organic and inorganic beings (with the astral as the 'higher world' which inorganic beings populate); and this is the realm in which people from the first three levels are, depending on the objects, making their religiousness appear in an objectivist manner, in religious objects, symbols, and rituals. External manifestations of their religiousness play an important role in cultivating the everyday lives of a large number of people, in their organization of space, time, and events. This is expressed by visiting temples, celebrating holidays, and important dates for the community, as well as dates of individual significance such as birth, death, marriage, etc. Since the majority of mankind lives naturally on the first three levels of consciousness, the three levels of religiousness presented here correspond with them and play a key role in regulating their survival.

The fourth level represents the inner or esoteric circle and all the above-mentioned religions contain this (apart from Protestantism, hence the spiritual futility and alienation of people in these civilizations), but far away from the eyes of unawakened people and their public. The fourth level is a path of practical work on the being for the purpose of awakening a man. It usually happens among coenobitic communities – but not all, because most monks today are an imitation of the real work from the past or pervert the first three levels. Secret societies that are in their essence esoteric, together with the Free-masons, also belong to the fourth level – at least to the measure in which spirituality is set as their ideal and not politics. The lack of this level in Protestantism is hope-lessly compensated for with a myriad of sects.

The fifth level of religiousness is known only to those individuals who have accomplished the path of the fourth level and work on themselves. They have direct experience of all truth and purpose of spiritual life. If they choose to remain in religious institutions, they have ac-cess to influential positions and titles. However, most of-ten, they remain independent and alone, because that is the only way for them to develop further, to the sixth and seventh stage. They grow in their independence, away from all the mundane forms of religiousness, and grow closer to the general unity of the whole being and divine spirit in which it resides. In all religious traditions they resemble one another, because they are getting increas-ingly closer to the centre of all phenomena.

It is like a cross, where the prongs represent the ex-ternal differences in the expression of the first three lev-els of religiousness, and also the practice of the fourth level. Differences in myths, ideologies, rituals, and priests' robes of certain religions are so visible, like the different directions that prongs point to. The more man uplifts on the inner path of spiritual development, the more he approaches the centre of the cross, where all the differences are erased, because all religions in the fourth level aim in the direction of the same goal, toward man's enlightenment.[26]

Therefore, no 'unity of religions' is an option on the outside to be formally attained on the first three levels of consciousness. Up to that level, differences must exist. True unity and presence of the divine are manifested only inside, in man, in his unique personality, as his maturity – and not as a skill to drive sheep in the same sheepfold. That is exactly what the rulers of this world are trying to do in their attempt at creating one world religion. By doing so, they are directly trying to destroy true religiousness.

Therefore, the fifth, sixth and seventh levels of religiousness are characterized by higher individuality and independence of the soul, away from all the interests of the public and natural phenomena. Or, as transcendence. This is the way of the inner or esoteric circle of all religions: Sufis in Islam, Kabbalists in Judaism, Yogis, Tantrists and Taoist alchemists, and esoteric Christianity, which is still preserved in some monasteries. All religions exist to aid the development and growth of man, from lower to higher levels of consciousness. Apart from Yoga and Tantrism, this function is preserved to a large degree in Sufism in Islam and the practice of contemplation (satipatthâna) in Buddhism, as well as in zen.

Apart from these 'mainstream' traditions, there are such that are independent or secret, ancient shamanistic traditions which, unencumbered by theology or any other dogma and ideology, yield good results in spiritual ascension to the highest states. The basic pattern of functioning of the traditions in question we can only get a glimpse of, through the research of explorers (Mircea Eliade). However, shamanism lacks the ontological precision in the vision and experience of the spiritual, in transcendence in general, especially the kind that is present in Buddhism. Shamanism is laden with astral influences and phenomena. Only in the opus of Carlos Castaneda is this flaw undetected. We have him to thank for the wealth and superiority of shamanistic traditions introduced to us, making them a lot clearer and comprehensible.

The first, the second and third levels of religiousness are the only ones known to the general public, while the fourth is scarcely known and greatly associated with mysticism. The first three levels are completely under the influence of the astral and only there may gods and demons be encountered. The fourth is the process of getting to know and overcoming them, while the fifth, sixth, and seventh levels are characterized by an increasing freedom and consciousness of the soul, from the physical to the astral influences, the freedom to act here, and now.

All the forms of religions come from the first three levels and are good and right to the degree they stimulate the growth of man, from the lower to the higher states; or are evil and sick if their purpose is to serve themselves and stunt the growth of man, keeping him on the same level. Every entity has this aspiration in the form of centripetal force that keeps it together, but overcoming its gravity is the necessary test for the development of human power in the consciousness of the soul. Only strength of that kind can uplift a man above the third level and open him to the divine.

WHAT RELIGIOUSNESS IS NOT

We cannot speak of religiousness without defining what it is not.

Judging by everything we have said about religiousness so far, it may be easy to presuppose what it is not. Let us start by saying that religiousness is not violence toward any form of life, because every form of life is a form of divine consciousness, a form of God himself. These are the so-called 'non-living things', but the living things as well, which manifest their divine nature.

Anything that lives, in any way, is a manifestation of the divine consciousness, and the being participates in its actualization. Everything that lives affirms the divine consciousness and its presence. If in the name of God we kill any living being, this is in direct opposition to religiousness - it is the stretching of the Omega point to the maximum. It is Satanism.

What we have in mind here refers only to the killing some religious fanatics are prone to, while defending their religious convictions from 'infidels', and imposing their faith onto others by force. What we have in mind here does not refer to self-defence while protecting ourselves from fanatics or wild animals. We are entitled to self-defence.

By killing another living being in the name of religion, we kill the divine consciousness in us. We can only kill another living soul because we are unaware of the existence and presence of divine consciousness in that being; by doing so we have disabled ourselves from experiencing it and becoming aware of it, and with this act we have distanced ourselves from the divine. That is why it would be suitable to say that we kill the divine in ourselves. On the outside, there is nothing we can do to jeopardize the divine. Therefore, anyone who has killed on the grounds of faith has with this act distanced himself maximally from God.

There is no need to further mention extreme cases of violence. We distance ourselves from God every time we harm someone, in any way, either by words or deeds.

An additional problem is that we can easily slip away from God (towards the Omega point), much like we can move towards God (towards the Alpha point). It is very easy to go to extremes if we are already in this world, which is a training ground for testing and stretching out the Omega point.

It is important to stress here that a state which is directed against the divine can always be justified by the mind. The mind is neutral, it is a reflection of reality - everything reflects in it, but in reverse. What is within us in the mind's eye seems to be without. Thanks to the mind we can see perfectly clearly, but we are unable to understand the truth; we see the reverse of the truth. The mind interprets what it sees, but it does not give the truth; the mind never knows the truth, it is designed for perception only, for collecting and reflecting impressions. It, however, has the freedom to interpret as true everything it sees. That is why it is so hard to explain to people when something is not true. They can have such strong convictions that they are ready to destroy their own and other people's lives. If they do not have a connection with the higher mind and consciousness of the soul, and are not able to distinguish between what is true and what is not, such people are prone to blindly believing whatever the lower mind interprets to be true.

That is why religious fanatics interpret all their misconceptions they believe in so noisily. The more ignorance they have, the louder they shout. They not only look like psychopaths, they are psychopaths. However some of these people have diplomas, respectable professions, and high social ranking.

It is a different kind of violence that negates true religiousness: religious convictions, dogmatism, fanaticism, and fundamentalism. They create an ideology that kills the truth of the divine presence, and lead to the physical murder of 'infidels'.

Religiousness is also not dependent on authority. All religions are familiar with authorities - they are everywhere, and it is not hard to recognize them. They all look very important and serious and wear richly adorned clothing, unlike normal people. Some wear crowns on their heads, with a great many diamonds. They request that believers kiss their hands.

Religiousness, to a large degree, deals with the relationship of believers with authority figures. There is good reason for this - first of which is that the physical mind of man needs a figurehead to teach him how to behave and think properly. Teachers have always been around to fulfill this role. However, the best teacher is only a substitute for the higher mind and consciousness of the soul, from which the physical mind receives what is right and proper. A true teacher is only a personification of the soul of man; he teaches the disciple in the outer world what the soul tries to teach him in his inner world. He teaches the disciple to listen for the signals of his soul, to train himself to be open to the consciousness of his soul. That is all. He asks for nothing. He has no ideology to impose.

In this world of Omega illusion, everything is twisted and turned into a deception, into the illusion of authority. If a believer finds authority in anything that is unconnected with the consciousness of his soul, it is an improper authority, and does not deserve faith. It is easy to recognize false authorities - there is no response in you in the form of growing consciousness of your soul. A true teacher will make you feel a connection with the consciousness of your soul, in many spontaneous ways; a true teacher conveys this always, and forever; he radiates his soul and enhances this radiation in you.

The only true authority is the consciousness of the soul in us. This is the only one we should trust. And everything else that connects us with the consciousness of our soul. Nothing else should be believed; nobody, whatever their reputation may be, regardless of profession or title, should automatically invoke respect in us. Even mundane dignitaries are not worth much in the spiritual world. You should only trust your experience. True faith consists of sharpening your experience enough so you are able to recognize the true bond with consciousness of your soul, the influences of the soul that refine and uplift us. Once a true bond with consciousness of the soul is established, we will easily recognize false authority and everything that aims to deceive us.

True religiousness cannot be institutionalized. All institutions are, in reality, mechanisms for manipulating the physical mind, its control, and programming. They define man using the same mold. It may be apparent that members of these institutions resemble one another. This is to do with their programming.

For the believer to know God, no mold of any kind is necessary. A single dogma that applies to everyone in the same way prevents God-knowledge. Man should be what he is, unique, and use his uniqueness and authenticity to express his soul. This is what will get him closer to God. God likes the original people. The more man is himself, in a perfectly positive way, the more he is God's, because God is hidden in the heart of every person.

True religiousness helps you to become the best version of yourself, and not anything else.

A true believer is always open and impressed, always in blissful awe of the world surrounding him, like a small child. Take a closer look at the purity and inquisitiveness in a child's eyes to understand what a true believer looks like. This is the only proper training for a believer, not learning from psychopaths who claim to know everything about God.

True religiousness is reflected in constant openness for the secret that happens every single moment, in a positive stance, and in respect for everything that exists.

Anything else is not religiousness.

RELIGIOUSNESS AND DEATH

One of the most fundamental characteristics of religiousness is the relationship between man and death. Some people believe that men become religious because they fear death and wish to suppress this fear, and find consolation in a faith that existence surpasses life. The truth is quite the opposite - like so many things are in this Omega world of ours.

Man is religious because he intuitively remembers his existence before life. This is the same realm he will reside in after life. It is a memory suppressed by the ego and the physical mind that we use during our awakened state, and which gives us identity in this world; but the memory exists in deeper layers of the unconscious. Archetypes associated with death are present in a similar form all over the globe.

In this world we experience all possible oppositions, and the most basic opposition is naturally life and death. Like many other things, this question has been twisted out of shape. Due to the oblivion of consciousness of the soul, people consider life in the physical body to be the only life, and believe that upon the death of the body, total death occurs. The belief people have in the afterlife depends on the maturity of their consciousness of the physical mind and its bond with the higher mind and consciousness of the soul. The majority of people believe in life after the death of the body; but individuals that experience alienation from the consciousness of the soul are more identified with the body and think there is no afterlife and with death, they are completely annihilated. This is a characteristic of young souls, that is to say, of those who have very little experience in this world.

A truly religious man is one who has a good bond between mind and consciousness of the soul; he knows that death does not bring the end of life, only transformation into a new one.

However, one who has completely raised awareness of his soul in this world knows the higher truth: everything is opposite. Being born into this body is like death of the soul, and death of the physical body is when the soul is reborn into its original state. By being born in the body the soul loses so much of its true nature that it seems like dying, or at best falling asleep. The teaching that life is nothing but a dream (maya) stems from here. In this world, we are as dead as can be. The most absurd aspect of our opposition to the divine is that we fear death.[27] Our soul is neither born, nor does it die.

The fear of death can be both justified and unjustified.

A justified fear of death can occur if our life is abruptly terminated before our due time, before the plan of the soul for this life has been fulfilled. Since planet earth allows for free will, this is a possibility. Life is never certain, even though there is generally a plan for each current life. Not all the plans come to fruition though, not even the ones that have been carefully preplanned. Uncertainty is an option because of freedom, which is a precondition for creativity. If everything were foretold and predetermined, there would be no room for creativity. Freedom is a necessary factor for creativity to be expressed, and consciousness with it. Therefore, fear of unplanned death is justified - but not on account of death itself, but because of the wasted effort to create and organize the current life. Much effort and work is necessary for each life - many souls combine their creative potential so that one influential man can be born, one man that will play an important part on the stage of life. Every human life has been paid for dearly. Life itself is indescribably valuable. The slightest bond with our soul gives us an awareness of the value of each life; a soulful man would not hurt a fly. That is why a fear of death occurs - it is similar to crashing a new Ferrari.

Unjustified fear of dying emerges only in an immature mind that is identified with the body to such a degree that it is unable to find value in anything other than the body itself, and which is unaware of the higher dimensions or its role in the order of reality. The death of the body is in fact death of the physical mind, the end of all of its illusions, and this fear is justified, but we have a lot more than just a physical mind. That is why fear is reciprocal with our identification with the physical mind and the body. Hence, as an illusion of an immature mind.

I have heard of an incident when a child told his mother he would like to die. After the mother's frightened emotional response, he explained that before this life we were in a much better place, and after this life, we will be in a much better place, and this life of ours is like living in a sewer. Many children have recollections of this kind, although they do not often verbalize it.

The approach to death depends on karmic maturity, whether the soul in the body is young or old. Young souls generally grow more attached to the body and experience a stronger fear of dying; they fight their fear in a number of ways, some of which include violence. However, many young souls have an innocent attitude to life, which entails faith in divine intervention and the power of the soul, and even though they are not fully aware of it they feel this power in their own simple way.

Animals die a dignified death; they surrender and close their eyes, like in sleep.

We all know from experience someone who died a natural death, but with full awareness; they knew the day they would die. I know of two such cases: one old lady told me (in a good mood) that she would be passing on very soon; another lady told her family to make funeral arrangements, because the following day she would die. Mature souls die like this, with dignity and awareness, always in a good mood.

Our approach to death is determined by the spirit of the nation; it is a part of culture. For example, ancient peoples, Slavs, Vikings, and American Indians, believed that the length of our life is predetermined. This means that we will die when our time has come, no sooner or later. This explains their unbelievable courage in battle; they never feared death on the battleground. If it were their destiny to die, it was bound to happen and nothing they could do would change it. So they were free from worry about death.

Many pre-Christian religions celebrated the death of man as his birth. Funerals were occasions for singing, dancing, and rejoicing. The 'Egyptian Book of the Dead' speaks of the afterlife as being born in a day, into the light. This is its original title, 'Book of Going Forth by Day', and the false title was given to it by modern translators. We have the same account in 'The Tibetan Book of the Dead', which says that the soul, upon leaving the dead body, encounters intense 'bright light', with divine consciousness, which is called man's true nature or Buddha's nature in Buddhism.

All near-death experiences (NDE), such as a clinical death, are related as the most pleasant experience of release, and departure into a much higher and better state.

When, after an NDE, they come back, they are free from fear (of the illusion) of death, and they grab hold of life much more forcefully. This is because they saw that everything is life - there is no such thing as death, and existence is divine consciousness itself.[28]

The only suffering that exists is when we are in the body, and in the illusion of the physical body. Those whose body has died begin their true lives; they are free from all the suffering they had during their lifetime - unless they inflicted pain on others. People who commit crimes are forced to get rid of their illusions in the afterlife, because they were suffering from a much greater illusion than the ones who endured suffering, who were their victims. It is hard for the culprits in this world, and all the other worlds, as well. They learn the same lessons as everybody else, but in a harder way.

The only ones who suffer are those who stay on here, because they are separated from their loved ones. Pain in the chest remains when someone we love dearly passes on. The world becomes empty, because we see that this life can truly be fulfilled with love, and with the people we love. Nothing else.

However, this suffering too is illusory, because we are not separated from our loved ones, we simply cannot see them since we no longer share the same dimension. A time will come when we will rejoin our loved ones. All souls have always been connected, there is no real separation. Only the illusions of this world make us seem separated, physically, when we are alive and when death occurs.

From an objective point of view, a lack of understanding, lies, and hatred separate people far more than death ever can.

In the *Katha Upanishad* it states: 'What is within is also without. What is without is also within. He who sees the difference between what is within and what is without goes evermore from death to death'. The meaning of these words refers to those who separate life from death and live in ignorance of the higher dimensions and the purpose of reincarnation; they have to be reborn again and again, until the moment they become aware of the unity of existence, until they learn that there is no fundamental difference between life and death. Everything that exists is a mere manifestation of the divine consciousness.

It is mostly young and immature souls that separate life from death. Materialists have a negative attitude to death, but they have a negative attitude to life also. They are unable to overcome the immense opposition which is so obvious: on one hand, there is an unbelievable effort to create life, everything is the result of intelligent design. On the other hand, people drop dead like flies. Death is always our destiny, whether we are young or old. It seems that God does not care; people are like puppets of straw.[29] Something is missing in this view of life and existence. A peek into higher dimensions is what is missing. If we could take a closer look into these forms of existence, we would see that life in the body is highly overrated; there is no reason for us to be afraid of death, as after death we go to a much better place (this sounds like a nightmare to immature materialists), we acquire consciousness of a much higher level.

However, this is not all we can say on the matter. If we stopped here, we would give immature souls an excuse to believe that dying is good, that one can kill without consequence, that suicide is the best way out of difficulty. If we truly had insight into the higher dimensions of existence, into the consciousness of the soul and the divine consciousness, we would realize that before being born in this body we, as emissaries of the divine consciousness, created this world and this life. Our souls are the creators of this world. That is why life is so important, even though there is no death. Life is more important than death because there is no death. By terminating life we terminate our participation in life, by killing we negate life; that is to say, we negate the consciousness that created life. By killing, we kill ourselves. We have put so much effort into creating this body and these living conditions, and then we go and kill, because we have identified with our petty physical mind and some trauma or challenge.

Suicide always means shooting your own foot. Problems are there to be solved, and not killing the one who should solve them, yourself.

Death must be a wonderful experience if everyone were so easily allowed to die.

Therefore, this description is not about glorifying death, making it is a safe way out of all problems, as some people who aim to commit suicide believe.

This, too, is reversed, much like everything else in this world of opposition to the Omega point.

Souls created this world and all life so that they can be born in a body and experience all possible phenomena. This world is a stage we have built, so we can play our part on it. That is why it is a big mistake to try to escape it in any way, to destroy the stage or kill the lead actor. Not only is it contrary to the original plan of each soul, but it is just stupid. We have put so much effort into this life. The first thing every individual who takes his/her own life experiences when they find themselves in the other world is deep disappointment with themselves for having ruined something so valuable. From the perspective of the higher consciousness he then obtains, he sees that there were many other options to choose from, even though his physical mind with its restricted and inferior perspective saw none. His heart then desires for him to be born again, to mend his ways.

We must say here that there is such a thing as a justified suicide; life is often unbearable due to the liberty that enables everything, and death is sometimes a welcome choice - especially when one has no conditions for a functional life. However, to make the proper judgment on when suicide is justified, as in euthanasia, and when it is unjustified, one should have consciousness of the higher mind, consciousness of the soul. A physical mind attached to a body with its limitations cannot distinguish between the two options. That is why people need many lives, more births, and dying under all possible circumstances, to learn how to distinguish how to live, and what death in fact is.

Until we come to realize this, the only correct attitude is to live to the maximum, using all our resources, facing challenges bravely, since this is the only thing that strengthens consciousness of the soul in this world. We acquire consciousness of the soul in all possible ways, often extraordinary ones, and even more so in ways we do not wish for us to happen. If we became aware of reality and the world only in ways which agree with us and which we find pleasant, we experience nothing new, and development will cease.

Besides, if we are sure to die at some point, it would be stupid to leave the show before it is over.

If life becomes unbearable for you, do not end it by suicide. Simply stop and surrender; as if you killed the body, stay in the body and merely observe what happens next, as though you were dead, but still living. If the situation is beyond repair, you are bound to die somehow. Still, it is always better to let life kill you than allow your limited physical mind and ego that are undergoing stress to make the call, and you end up killing yourself. Always keep in mind that every crisis and difficulty is a challenge for your creativity, and not something that induces suffering pointlessly.

Here is a piece of advice on how to recognize the lower mind and ego at work: when you suffer, or hate the circumstances you have found yourself in, this is the functioning of your mind or ego, never the consciousness of your soul. A soul can never be negative, it does not know about suffering, it is incapable of negativity. Every type of negativity is in opposition to the divine consciousness. Suffering, hatred, and negative states are *only symptoms* of the limitation of the mind.

However, if something can change, if the plan of your soul is for you to live on, you are bound to witness a miraculous series of events. Something will happen that will lead you to find the solution to your problem that has put you in crisis; or, if there is no solution to the problem, a new lifestyle will be introduced instead.

Why kill the body and be born again, if the same body can be used if only life gets changed? The consciousness that rules nature is always rational, it uses its resources carefully, and you would do better to adjust to this. Give yourself up to it. Do not discard your body if it is still functional. Let the old way of life die, and you go on living by making a change.

The richest and most successful people are those who have undergone a transformation, death, and rebirth, all in the same body.

The same thing would happen if the body died and you were born again, only then you would be oblivious of the previous experience and you would have to relive it. By dying, you waste time. Use all the resources you have been given, of both body and life. This is the meaning of the saying that we should make the most out of life, and we should act creatively, and not merely react spontaneously.

If we, in one body, experience something that would normally require a chain of spontaneous events through several lifetimes, we then grow in consciousness and experience. A completely enlightened man has done exactly that: in the space of one lifetime, he has contracted all the changes and experiences a normal man goes through in a few lifetimes. Buddha said: a good horse, when erring, will respond to the shadow of a whip cracking. The richness and wisdom of life are exactly this: contracting a large number of experiences into the space of one lifetime. This contraction of experiences is the foundation of the philosophy that says one should never give up; after we fall, we should stand up and move on; we should never judge because we do not know what the 'ways of our Lord are'. If you have so much as an atom of strength, use it. This contraction of the time of all the experiences is also the foundation of the philosophy that says one should always be here and now; the highest reality is in the present moment.

If you do this, if you respect the life you have been given and use it to your advantage, the divine consciousness that enables it will help you in every way possible. For it to surrender to you, firstly you must surrender to it. With your submission, you give it permission to help you.

I say this from my own experience. I once attempted suicide in my youth; not as a result of any crisis, but because I was simply curious to see what lurks on the other side of life. Now I realize it was my strong consciousness of the soul, which is independent of the body, but which manifested itself rather naively through the idea for me to leave the body. I bought a big, new, plastic syringe and went to a nearby forest on the outskirts of the city. I sat under a tree with the intent to inject air into my veins. I meditated a little and enjoyed nature, then unpacked the needle and inserted it into the syringe. I tried to test it, but the needle was corked, it was impossible to push the syringe and blow the air out. This confused me, since the syringe was brand new. I pushed the mobile part of the syringe to clear the needle with air, I held it upright, and then saw that due to the air pressure the needle jumped, slid off the syringe and went up in the air. However, it did not land on the ground, or my lap, as it should have, because the pressure of the air was not particularly forceful. Nonetheless, I saw it clearly go up, more and more, and disappear among the branches.

I did not know much about consciousness of the soul then, and its power to affect life as I do now, but I definitely felt all the strength of its power. I remained in a seated position as though I had died, for hours, looking at nature with completely different eyes, reborn.

I learned to meditate then.

I became religious then. I did not give myself to any religion in particular that only offers and promises a correct relationship toward the soul and God, but I became religious toward the soul itself and the divine consciousness that I witnessed, that saved my life.

Once you directly face the divine power of the soul, you do not need mediators, religious convictions, or teachings; from that moment on you learn to experience it directly. I saw then that the divine consciousness gives me life, every single moment, and enables the overall existence as well; it is the mightiest force that there is. It can do anything. Death ceased to exist as a concept for me then and there. This whole event was my way of getting to know this simple truth.[30]

These things are orchestrated by a higher power. The consciousness of our soul is the ultimate power that enables everything, even the grossest physical events. All the religiousness in this world is an aspiration of man to grow in awareness of this phenomenon.

The purpose of difficulties and suffering in this world is not torture, but for us to strengthen the presence of the consciousness of our soul despite the challenges that obstruct us. Without these challenges, it could not be possible. In fact, the logic of suffering is very simple: we suffer because we do not participate in life in the right way. Anyone who has overcome suffering has done so by harmonizing with reality, he stopped running away from life and responsibility, and he turned toward the challenges of life and went through them.

People who experience clinical death go through the same experience. Afterward, they return here as if reborn, with great enthusiasm and passion for life, but they stay moderate and conscious, with immense respect toward existence itself, which manifests in everything. They respect life in every form, and every type of effort that promotes life; they may choose to be city street cleaners or coal miners, even though they were intellectuals before their clinical death (NDE) experience. Their sole purpose in their newly found life becomes spreading awareness of life as the divine presence itself.

Most religions have the experience of death as a form of initiation. The person who joins religious circles must go through a similar ritual, albeit symbolic. Some

184

parts of the world have an initiation practice with psychedelic drugs or plants that cause out-of-body experiences. A person getting initiated into a religion is submitted to such experiences to get near death, to separate himself from the illusion of the body and open himself up to the higher dimensions. Such was the ceremony of baptism of grown-up people in the early centuries of Christianity. In the modern world where illusions dominate, the old religious practices have been suppressed by new religions, which contain only the symbols of eras gone by, such as the baptism ritual and Holy Communion.

It is not possible to be religious without a direct experience of death.

It is not possible to have a proper relationship of death without true religiousness.

Without a religious understanding of death, it is not possible to have the right approach to life and existence in general.

True religious understanding of death shows that there are two approaches to death, as well as to life. The first is from the perspective of the body and physical mind, and the other is from the perspective of the soul. To a body, death is the end of life. This is the truth as far as the body is concerned. To a soul, the life of a body is only a dream, and often a nightmare.

Many things are opposite to the Omega point, including our notion of death. From the perspective of the physical mind, death seems like the end of existence, and not only the end of the body because the physical mind sees the body alone, and is completely identified with it. The disappearance of the body, is interpreted by the mind as the cessation of existence. This is not true. Our essence is divine consciousness which enables existence in the first place. Existence itself is divine consciousness which is, in effect, the eternal, timeless presence. This is the way we exist, timelessly. Anything we have ever experienced or thought also exists forever and cannot disappear. Our experiences are only a series of clippings, cut out of all the possibilities of the existence of the divine consciousness and presence. Therefore, nothing disappears, ourselves included. It is all a case of our mind being alienated in the illusion of its separation from existence. The only thing that disappears at the moment of death is our illusion, made up of the mind and ego.

We should not listen to the mind when it comes to the wholeness of existence, but our heart instead, and our soul. This informs us that death does not exist. However, there is a strong will for life and some imminent danger of its termination often breeds fear and anxiety in the mind. This is only an instinctive reaction and not an expression of the real state of affairs regarding death. It is justified to safeguard life, because it was created by our souls for us to experience all possibilities. We should only have a fear of failing to live fully with all the options life has provided for us; that following the innumerable illusions of the mind, we will waste our precious time, fearing death that does not even exist.

Indeed, from the perspective of the consciousness of the soul being born in a body, the limited physical mind is the only death that there is, that is possible even. Outside the body, mind, and ego, there is only life in a timeless present.

PRAYER

Prayer is, in all forms, an essential component of every type of religiousness - the practice with which we most intimately express our religiousness.

There are three dimensions of prayer:

- The first and the most widespread is expressed in our attempt to attract a desired state, or asking for something we need, asking for help in times of need.

- The second is a constant reminder of the fundamental values of religious teaching, assistance on our path to discipline, keeping our mind constantly in the process of learning, and not letting it waiver to sinful states.

- The third is the deepest commitment to the divine, and is called contemplation or meditation.

Prayer, Or the Law of Attraction

The simplest relationship a believer has with God is similar in attitude to a child asking his parents for protection. This is a justified request if the child is small and helpless, but it is not if we are in the position to do what's asked ourselves. God helps, but only those in need. All those who do not receive help from God should know that this is because they are capable of helping themselves. They know what to do to change things, and this is what God wants from us: to be able enough to solve our own problems, to be conscious enough to not sin. That is why we are here.

Prayers in which we ask for something from God are seldom fulfilled, because they are contradictory to reality. One who prays for health or fulfillment of some wish starts with the false premise that reality is wrong, that he does not have what he wants and needs and therefore wants to get it in the future.

Reality is the other way round. Everything that has ever existed, what now exists and what will exist, already exists in the universal quantum field which is the foundation of reality. Absolutely everything is contained within it in an unmanifested form - everything that manifests in the cosmos and our life. All possibilities are ever-present, but only a handful of them get manifested. Which ones? Those that a conscious intent selects. The universal field, from which everything originates, acts as a mirror. Our deepest convictions, attitudes, and beliefs are reflected outwards into our reality. What we desire with all our heart comes true. The problem is that we are not always aware of what we want with all our hearts, therefore we perceive a reality we do not like. It is much easier for us to be negative with all our hearts and get a negative reality in response. We are only aware of what is currently on our mind, which is just a small percentage of consciousness. The mirror of the universe responds only when we know what we want, 100%, with all our being and with all our heart. Since we are not 100% aware of ourselves, it seems like we are not responsible for what goes on, for the negative reality, and we believe it has been unfairly imposed on us from the outside.

The commandment Jesus gave about prayer says: 'Love the Lord your God **with all your heart**, and with all your soul and with all your mind.' Prayer is composed of these elements: thoughts, feelings, and all of the energy of the body - all of the dimensions of our being put together.

This verse '**with all your heart**' has some scientific background.

Physical reality consists of electromagnetic radiation. Atoms are defined forms of a specific electromagnetic vibration. If we change the electromagnetic vibration, we change the atom.

Our heart is the source of the most powerful electromagnetic radiation in our body. Its field expands approximately two to three meters (seven to ten feet) around our body. Electric radiation from our heart is about 100 times stronger than the radiation from the brain, and its magnetic field is 5,000 times stronger than the field of the brain.

Our whole body is an electromagnetic organism. Physiological regulation happens with the aid of the electromagnetic field, which every cell receives through its membrane. If we know the frequency a cell works on, we can heal it using electromagnetic frequencies, or conversely disrupt its functioning. The same applies to all of the organs, because they all have a frequency of their own.[31]

Our body generates both electric and magnetic fields through its functioning. The heart is not just a muscle pumping blood through the body. The heart is an energy field that encapsulates the whole body and surrounding space as well. The heart muscle is only its physical manifestation.

The frequency of the heart is what we feel with our whole being as reality in the present time.

When we physically feel reality emanating from the area of the heart, this is because it does indeed emanate from there.

The frequency of the heart directly impacts the universal field which acts as the mirror for our reality.

All possible realities coexist in the quantum field in parallel. Consciousness and the energy of our heart have the power to connect realities at certain junctures, changing them in a manner where one overflows into another. *Since we are the microcosm, when we act with our whole being we consciously choose one of the abundance of all possible realities.* We are always doing this, but usually unconsciously, and as a result we do not like the reality we live in; there is also a collective effect, when many people together make mistakes, creating difficult life circumstances.

This is the way in which we shape the reality we are in. It is the way in which our prayers can work. In order for prayer to work, *it must be in tune with the reality of the universal field, the deepest reality of existence, which is the eternal present*. There is no time, it has not yet manifested. Therefore it always functions as the present; everything can be done in the present moment only – never in the future. Practically this means that the universal field acts as a mirror. If we pray for something to happen in the future, we will get exactly that: an outcome forever in the future, never in the present. If in a mirror we see our reflection as unhappy and frowning, we cannot ask our reflection to smile first (in the future), and get in a good mood for us (in the present); our job is to do it here and now.

If you wish for something to happen in the present, you should pray with all your heart, and with your feelings, *as though it already exists in the present*. Not that it will happen, or that it is happening right now, but as though *it has already been accomplished*. Your prayer must consist of a *pure sense of joy for the desired reality, as though it is here*. Feel it with your whole being, picture it vividly in your mind's eye, smell it, feel it, taste it, everything. During your prayer, be in it as though it has come true; if you are sick - be healthy; if you are alone - be with your loved ones; if you are poor - be rich.

The impact of prayer is known to many from personal experience. How does it function? In two ways. The first has been described: we imagine that healing has already taken place - although it is better to skip the whole idea of healing, because it means we were once sick, but there should not be even a mention of disease, as there never was such a state, we only ever had health.

There was a hospital in China where the worst patients, hopeless cases, received treatment without any medication; several doctors gathered by each patient's bedside to create a state of consciousness in their minds that the patient was perfectly healthy. This was achieved by verbal repetition of 'Healthy', 'Healthy'. After three minutes he would be cured of cancer. This was described by Gregg Braden in his work 'The Divine Matrix'. This hospital was forced to shut down because it put the profits of the pharmaceutical industry in jeopardy.

The second reason behind the effect prayer has on the health lies in the nature of the frequencies of our genes and our language. It has been discovered that our genes communicate with one another by way of frequencies whose structure is identical to the structure of our language. The spoken language our bodies use to communicate with each other follows the same laws as the language genes use, and all the cells in our body. This explains how we affect our body with our thoughts; thoughts are our inner speech, every cell in our body hears. This is the same language we use to communicate with the divine whole when we pray, and that is why the divine whole always hears our prayers. Therefore, when we clearly pronounce a formula, that is to say a prayer for being healed, for health to be our reality, that happens here and now, it begins to affect our genes and all the cells of our body. They understand what we think and speak. They harmonize and heal as a result of our actions, i.e. our thoughts. That is how we come to be harmonized with the vibration of health, and that is how we become whole.

Health is simply perfect harmony within the wholeness of our being. God is the same, but from the outside. When we pray to God, we turn our being toward the perfection of the divine whole and by doing so we harmonize with it, we heal ourselves.

The truth is, you do not attract anything, something that is bound to happen, you simply cross over from one reality to another with a conscious and planned intent.

This is not a game of illusion and fancy. You are already realizing this reality, but in the higher dimensions; not on the level of the element of earth, but in air, fire and water. For something to be realized on the physical plane it must be created as an idea and imagined on the higher planes. This is the law of creation. The relationship between the higher and the lower dimensions is at work here. All it takes is for an idea from the element of air to be grounded to the element of earth. We ground it by using the properties of the lower dimension to ground the idea from the higher one. Practically this means that an idea from the dimension of air is lowered to the dimension of fire with the help of passion and energy, to have it as though the idea were already realized, and start enjoying it with 'all our heart'. Then we lower the idea from the dimension of fire to the dimension of water using clear visualization of what we want, in the exact form we want it, as though it is here. We give our idea and passion as clear a form as possible in our imagination, and enjoy it as though we have it with us here.

What remains is for you to clear the path of everything that prevented realization on the physical plane. The initial impulse that pops into your mind is that this thing is not here yet, it has not been accomplished yet, it is all wrong. Do not act as though you do not have it. You do, just in higher dimensions. If everything is complete there, it is bound to get materialized here.

When you picture everything perfectly and savour this image for a few minutes, in your mind and with all your being, send it out into the universe, to the divine; get it over with. After the prayer, do not think about it. Forget what you did.

For as long as we desire something strongly, we send out a vibration of not having it, and we make the lack stronger. *You cannot attract the frequency of something if you stick to the frequency of not having it.*

In other words, finish every prayer in the words: God, thy will be done, not mine.

Apart from this, on the physical plane you are preparing the field by acting rationally, because this is the law of this plane. If you want money, do something that will provide you with income - and then the law of attraction will help you. If you would like to have an ideal relationship, move in circles where you are most likely to come across the right partner. Get rid of bad company. If you would like to be healthy, stop poisoning yourself, and cleanse your body. In other words, learn to accept the desired result, in any and every way, even the unexpected. Do not set boundaries or define how the desired fact will enter your life, simply be open and ready to embrace it.

There is one more rule about prayer making all wishes come true. This is also connected to the mirror principle of the universal field. Do to others what you would like to happen to you, as much as you can. If you want to receive money, give it to those who ask for it. If you want love, give it to others. If you want a new house, help someone get one first. Do what you want your reality to be.

This rule is expressed in the words: 'Seek the Kingdom of God above all else, and live righteously, and he will give you everything you need.' The kingdom of God is the universal field everything emanates from. Seek everything there firstly, like in a mirror of your being. Be what you wish to see in the mirror of existence, what you wish will happen. Do not contradict your wishes. In the language of physics, harmonize your vibration with the reality you seek. In the language of religion, if you want something from God, act accordingly, because if you do not act in accordance with what you ask, you cannot be granted it. You would not give money to a drug addict, alcoholic or gambler either, as you know it would be to their detriment.

God always gives more, he reacts to our prayers like a mirror. If he sees that we feel and act (with all our heart) as if we do not have something, he concludes that it is our will to live like that (he merely studies our heart), that we wish to continue in the same manner, and he will help us go on in the manner we choose. If he sees that in our heart we act as though we have something, he will give us what we have. He will fulfill our wishes in both cases. Believe it or not, God always fulfills your heart's desires; we are the ones who fail to see what desires we truly have, we contradict ourselves, hence our reality is contradictory as a result. A gospel verse (Matthew, 13:12) tells us that: 'Whoever has will be given more, and they will have an abundance. Whoever does not, even what they have will be taken from them.'

Whenever we ask for something we are torn asunder: there is the awareness that we do not have it, and there is the awareness that we would like to have it. Awareness of not having what we desire is opposed to awareness of having it, and one always annuls the other. The reality, where we have something, can never be realized if there is an awareness or feeling of not having it at the same time. What it takes for us to create our desired reality is to act as though it is here already, that we have what we want, for a duration of two minutes minimum. Make it a prayer. This is sufficient for the divine whole to receive it and engage in execution.

The position you pray in should never be kneeling with your hands put together. This was the position of a serf in feudal society who had to beg his master for permission to do something. This position of the slave or serf was copied by the church for its believers when they pray. Your position should simply be sitting or standing; but the best position is during the working process, invisible to the people around you. It is yours alone, the deepest intimate knowledge of you that others should not know about; it should permeate your whole life and should, therefore, be performed irrelevant of the state and circumstances you are currently in.

In prayer, you connect with your soul. That is why it should happen independently of the body.

Prayer as a Discipline and a Reminder

The second higher form of prayer does not contain any desires or needs to work the problems out, but only gratitude for everything the way it is.

The essence of all religious teaching about God ends in the obvious conclusion: God is the highest reality. Everything is of it and everything is in it. Therefore, the highest form of prayer means that we keep our mind in this reality perpetually, as a form of gratitude for everything that happens to us, no matter what.

This is what rosaries are for. A believer moves beads one by one, reciting a prayer with each, usually a brief thank you to God. There are other small rituals that facilitate these prayers.

Muslims who pray regularly with their whole body have a far higher awareness, meditative composure, and devotion than Christians who only believe and debate the issues of religion.

Monks in monasteries have even stricter prayers, some that last for days. The head of the monastery often advises monks not to repeat such prayers in their mind, but to feel them in their hearts.

Prayers like these discipline the mind that often wanders off to objects of desire. To be able to turn his life in the desired direction, a believer must mold his mind with proper thoughts, suggestions in the form of prayers, that will eventually take him in the right direction. That is why he socializes with people who have the same goal, usually in a religious community. Their common rituals and prayers modify the brain to achieve the desired result. Man alone cannot achieve this. The mind is very tricky; it may give us the illusion that we move in the desired direction, even when we have been diverted off the path. We only notice this at the end of the road, when we do not end up where we had thought we would. Other believers who are on the same path hoping to achieve the same goals are of immense help, because they can make corrections to an individual's path when they observe him waivering, which he cannot see himself. This is what religious communities and joint prayers and rituals are for.

Gratitude toward everything is the most powerful prayer to God. It has a scientific explanation grounded in the previously mentioned model of the quantum field, which acts like a mirror.

We are the conscious subjects who experience events.

Everything that happens, happens to make us aware of it.

Once we become aware, it returns through the consciousness of our soul to the divine whole as information that this possibility of existence has been realized, actualized. And then, it will not occur ever again.

For this reason, when we thank the divine for what we have experienced, for everything we have gone through, it will never again be repeated. Our experience will ascend to a higher octave of phenomena. Events keep repeating themselves only if we refuse to accept that they happen because of us, to make us aware of them. We get stuck in negative situations because we persistently think they have nothing to do with us, that some evil force from the outside world orchestrates everything, for somebody else, never for us; we do not want to accept the responsibility that it all happens for us only. *Our refusal and negativity strengthens the situation in question, and makes it repeat in our lives.* Once we accept the fact that it is here for us, only so that we become fully aware of it, it loses its potency and its power to affect us.

This works best in relationships. If you have somebody who is very negative toward you, simply thank them for existing and send love to them. His/her attitude toward you will change immediately. The same applies to all other circumstances in life.

Gratitude rests on the spiritual assumption that the world and events of the world are created by the intention of a higher, divine power. It completely rejects any assumption that things happen by themselves or for the wrong reason, accidentally or causally in some material way.

Consciousness is such that it functions by raising awareness of phenomena. They are never the same once we become aware of them.

That is why the most useful prayer is recapitulation.

Before going to bed in the evening, we should recapitulate everything we have done and experienced during the day, but in reverse, starting from that moment, right up to waking up in the morning. We should do this neutrally, without judging. We merely observe ourselves and our actions, like watching a film, like it was somebody else and not us on the screen.

If we raise awareness of everything we do in this way, we will not be able to make the same mistakes twice. Such practice will automatically cleanse us of bad habits and flaws. Naturally, after recapitulation, make sure you thank the divine for everything.

The whole universe exists for the conscious subject, to give meaning to its existence – because our souls are the original conscious subjects of divine consciousness itself.

We have already said that our souls created this world as a stage for playing life on. That is why you should play your part consciously and carefully. If you do not play it well, you will have to repeat it. God is the perfect director.

Direct Prayer to the Outer Divine Source

It is a well-known fact that solar symbolics lie at the foundation of almost all religions. The sun was the oldest God. It has remained so to this day, even though we do not see it, because new symbols and theology have been introduced to conceal the solar basis of the divine in Judeo-Christianity. Only in the so-called 'primitive people' does the sun remain the visible deity. One of the oldest practices of yoga is solar yoga - sungazing together with contemplation.

This type of prayer has a scientific explanation. It will be very successful for everyone who understands why it works. Knowledge has always played the most important role in addressing God. When we learn the physical laws that lie at the foundation of solar yoga, our contemplation of the divine will be direct and it will encompass our whole being.

All of life energy comes from sunlight. Plants absorb it and process it once. That is why a plant-based diet is the best. Plants get eaten by animals, and they process the sunlight twice. That is why the meat of herbivores is less nutritious, but more harmful food in our diet. Carnivorous animals process the original energy three times, making their meat unfit for human consumption.

We can directly absorb all necessary life energy from the sun via the eyes, rendering processed foods redundant.

Plants, through photosynthesis, turn sunlight into a form of useful energy. Hemoglobin in human blood has an almost completely identical composition to chlorophyll in plants. We can deduce based on this that its function is similar; it plays a key role in turning sunlight into energy.

The retina of the eye is the only place in the human body where blood comes into direct contact with light. It has been calculated that over 45 minutes, all of the blood in an organism goes through the eye, and with the practice of sungazing, all of the blood sunbathes. Solar energy feeds and heals our whole organism.

It has been scientifically established that only 5% of our life energy comes from the food we eat, 30% comes from water, and 60% from air and the sun. For the remaining 5%, scientists admit they do not know where this comes from, but we can reveal the secret to them here: from the earth. That is why it is so important to walk barefoot.

The cells of our body feed directly on the energy of the sun. For as long as their energy polarization is well-tuned, they alone produce energy for the body. Only when that balance has been compromised do they start to need coarse food.

Our DNA is a collection of informational codes made up of light. Sunlight itself is also made up of coded information. Light is not only something that illuminates, but a frequency with codes that gives information to life. That is why it affects the whole life. When we receive sunlight into our body we decode and reprogram our DNA, which means we receive primordial information about DNA, of ourselves and life in general, and cleanse it of layers of incorrect information and various disorders. With sunlight, we remind ourselves of who we truly are.

The eyes can gradually adjust to strong sunlight. Unprepared eyes will be permanently damaged if exposed to sunlight. However, they can gradually, carefully, over months, become adjusted to stronger and stronger sunlight, so that they can gaze directly at the sun for 45 minutes.

According to the instructions of Hira Ratan Manek, sungazing is something that is done only once in a lifetime, usually for a period of nine months or 270 days. You can do it in three stages: from zero to three months, from three to six months and six to nine months. You have to walk barefoot, occasionally, for 45 minutes, for the rest of your life. What is required of you is to watch the sunrise or sunset once a day, during safe hours. No harm will be done to your eyes during the morning or evening safe hours. The safe hours are within the first hour of sunrise or before sunset. Man is then protected from strong sunlight which is dangerous for the eyes. Both times are good – they only depend on personal preference.

Apart from exceptional benefits, we receive UV rays that are necessary for the function of the pituitary gland, as well as boosting the immunological system; sungazing has the added advantage of vitamin A and D intake. Vitamin A is necessary for your eyes' health.

For those who are not able to gaze at the sun during safe hours at the beginning of practice, sunbathing of the face is an effective method for the intake of the sun's energy; this can be done at a slower pace until they are ready to look at the sun. Face the sun with your eyes closed. This is a way of sunbathing the eyes. Do not use suncreams, they are packed full of dangerous chemicals. They are redundant. The body itself is more than capable of protecting itself from the scorching sun and inevitable cancers. It has been proved experimentally that eye receptors send information to the brain about sunlight and heat. Based on that information, the brain produces hormones which protect the skin from being burnt. When we wear sunglasses we trick the brain and it does not produce skin protection. It has been discovered that worse sunburns usually occur in people who wear sunglasses. Sunglasses are very damaging for immunity and vision. The highest percentage of light enters the body through the eyes. With sunglasses, our body gets the signal of being in a dark room.

The point of the practice is to absorb sunlight. One should begin by facing the sun with eyes closed, being completely relaxed, and opening the eyes slowly. When the eyelid begins to twitch or the eye shuts, leave it that way. In a few seconds, you may try again. You are the only measure, nobody can measure this for you. The reference point throughout the exercise is for you to feel pleasure while doing it.

Before doing this exercise you should wash your face with water - better still, take a shower beforehand.

Before beginning with the practice, it is of vital importance to find a good spot to practice in. It must be a secluded place, without people who do not take part in solar yoga, so as to avoid attracting their attention with your peculiar behaviour, which will ultimately disrupt your tranquility. It must be a place from which you can see the sun in its final setting phase, or catch the earliest sunrise. Therefore, if you are situated in a valley, with the sun setting (rising) behind a hill, you will see the sunset (sunrise) well before (after) the safe period and the sunlight will be too strong for the eyes. You must climb to the highest peak if you live in the mountains. The ground you stand on barefoot must be dry and of tolerable temperature (without extremes). Always stand on earth, sand, stone, concrete, or some wooden surface. It is not a good idea to stand on grass because it absorbs energy from the body. Asphalt is also not good because it acts as an insulator.

Finding a good spot will prove to be the biggest challenge to many in this practice. However, it requires full commitment and an altered lifestyle. This is justified for a practice that will permanently change your body and mind in the best possible way.

Zero to three months

On the first day, during safe hours, gaze for ten seconds maximum. On the second day gaze for 20 seconds at either the sunrise or the sunset, adding ten seconds on each following day. After ten consecutive days of sungazing, you will gaze at the sun for 100 seconds, i.e., 1 minute and 40 seconds.

It is good to have a notepad and take minutes thoroughly. (There is also a Sungazing Timer program for mobile phones.)

In such a way, by constantly adding ten seconds with each new gazing, you should approach 45 minutes for one gazing. This will take you 270 days altogether. Since you will not be able to gaze at the sun every day in a row, and weather conditions may not allow it, the finalization of this practice may take you two to three years.

When on the 270th day you come to 45 minutes for one gazing, you have finished with solar yoga; but it would be better not to end it abruptly, and instead continue with the exercise, reducing it minute by minute until you come to 15 minutes of gazing. Then you are finished.

The remaining 15 minutes you have as optional gazing, for when you feel you need to charge yourself with solar energy.

You should stand upright and barefoot on naked ground (sitting is not an option), on stone or warm concrete, with no footwear on which is very important. Standing on the grass is not good because it absorbs all our energy. The eyes can blink. It is not necessary to keep the eyes fixed. You can look around the sun, in slow circular movements, or in a left-right, up-and-down manner; the only important thing is that light enters the eyes. Only when the sun (while setting) is weak enough, can we look directly at the sun. We should follow our intuitive feeling so we can gaze at the sun without any danger or excess.

Gazing at strong sunlight is not necessary, at all. Sunlight itself is what is important, so that it enters the eye and contacts hemoglobin in the blood. This is a way in which sunlight gets absorbed.

There should not be any strain on the eyes. The point of this exercise is that the eyes gradually, over many months, adapt to stronger and stronger sunlight, to be able to take very strong sunlight for longer periods of time, until they reach the full 45 minutes. We must not force them in any way, or it may cause permanent retina damage and partial blindness. Warning: damaged eyesight as a result of sun exposure (solar retinopathy) may occur when we trick ourselves. This happens when it seems that we can look at very bright sunlight, but when we turn our eyes away from the sun we see purple blotches everywhere we look, and only then do we realize that we have burned through the bottom of the eye and permanently damaged our eyesight! The same damage happens when we use a magnifying glass to burn through paper in scorching sunlight.

It is an individual matter how long it will take to adjust, the state of health, immunity, etc. People who had the harmful habit of wearing sunglasses have weakened their eyes, and they will need the most time to adjust, and are advised caution. Do not wear contact lenses or glasses when you are gazing at the sun.

At the end of each session (but also if we occasionally feel fatigued from sunlight), we should close our eyes and cover them with the palms of our hands, allowing them to rest for a minute at least. We should feel the healing power of our palms and the beneficial effect they have on the eyes. This greatly enhances our eyesight.

When we cover our eyes with the palms in a manner described and close them, we will see a subsequent image of the sun in the shape of a purple circle. This will soon disappear. If it stays for longer than two minutes, we have put too much strain on the eyes and we could use a break; we could shorten exposure to the sun by gazing at it while setting, when the light is dimmer. The faster the subsequent image disappears, the more our eyes have fully adapted to sunlight. As an additional measure of precaution, have your eyes checked by a doctor from time to time.

Organize the gazing sessions at the same place and at the same time on a daily basis.

When you come to 3 months, you have gazed at the sun for 15 minutes in one go. What happens when you come to 15 minutes? You will notice changes in your psyche, because you will lose mental tension and worries. You become confident and adopt a positive outlook on life, instead of a negative one. For the duration of this sungazing period, depression will go away, as will most mental disorders. Bad habits disappear and positive energy is strengthened in every respect. This is the first phase of the method that usually requires approximately 3 months.

Three to six months

You continue to gaze at the sun, adding ten seconds each day.

The resulting consequence will be that physical ailments will start to heal, including those considered to be 'incurable'. The more you continue to gaze at the sun, and the more your tension eases, your food intake will diminish considerably. When you come to the phase of continuous gazing at the sun for 30 minutes, you will be completely relieved of physical diseases because by then the rays of the sun will reach the pituitary gland through the eyes to a sufficient degree to repair the immunological system. Our health depends on our immunity; immunity is directly dependent on the function of the pituitary gland, which regulates the function of all the other glands. The function of the pituitary gland depends on the inflow of UV rays of the sun. That explains why it is connected to the eyes via optical fibres. All the frequencies of photons reach all the organs through the pituitary gland in the space of 30 minutes of gazing. This is a process of complete rebuilding of the immunological system, and relieving oneself of all physical ailments for a period of six months.

This process may be empowered with autosuggestion, by creating the feeling that you are healthy here and now.

As you progress with gazing at the sun, energy is no longer utilized for mental problems or physical ailments and energy begins being stored in the body. You are your master in six months.

Six to nine months

In the sixth month, you will start receiving the original formula of micro food, which is our sun. Additionally, this is a useful way to avoid the toxic waste that passes off as regular food nowadays.

7.5 months of practice and 35 minutes of sungazing is when the feeling of hunger drops significantly. The need for food consumption decreases. Nobody should eat beyond their hunger level. Hunger appears due to the energy requirements of the body, but the food is not a necessity for the functioning of the body, which is a byproduct of the sun's energy anyhow. If there is no sunlight, there is no food.

The issue here is not in ceasing to eat completely, because no living being can go without food, but a modification of the dietary regimen. We abandon coarse animal-based and plant-based food and move on to the most subtle and powerful nutrition: sunlight. This is the most powerful because it enables the whole of the plant and animal world. It is the original food to everything living.

There is no need for you to abandon food; food will abandon you. Hunger is mostly a result of mental habits, which are the hardest to get rid of.

It is important to stress at this point that although mere sungazing leads to decreasing the sensation of hunger, regarding former dietary habits and coarse food, a complete cessation of coarse food intake and basing your diet on solar energy alone is a very difficult achievement that depends directly on the spirituality of an individual. A permanent awareness of oneself (Selfhood) is required, as well as awareness of the energy body.

All of this is a part of the fundamental transformation of life. It is impossible to execute this without transformation of the being in which consciousness of the soul is the foundation, instead of physicality – because sunlight is the physical expression of consciousness of the soul.

Of all the people who live without coarse food (breatharians), there have always been a certain number who are completely spiritually transformed and devoted. However, they are extremely rare.

The best ending to the practice is a prolonged period of fasting, to see if one can go without food for 21 days, so that after this experience life without coarse food becomes a permanent way of life. We will notice that after the initial few days of discomfort if we eat nothing, we are not hungry; hunger appears only when we eat something. It is a good practice to drink more water, distilled, and exposed to the sun for 24 hours. People who have previously been involved in the practice of meditation and true spiritual transformation will find it feasible to go without coarse food and turn to the energy of light/consciousness.

Others who undertake sungazing practice may make do with small meals.

If an interruption occurs:

Solar yoga practice has a cumulative effect and it can always be resumed with the exact time where we left off after months of pausing. For example, if we reached 20 minutes of gazing, and then took a break, we pick up the practice by starting with a minute, and extending a minute more each day, until we come to the 20 minutes we had already had. We will achieve this after 20 days. Afterwards, we can go on with the old practice of daily prolonging by ten seconds. Therefore, 20 minutes and 10 seconds, the next day 20 minutes and 20 seconds, then 20 minutes and 30 seconds, etc.

If we have made a minor interruption, lasting from several days to several weeks, we can resume simply by continuing from the number of minutes previously achieved and then continue by adding the regular ten seconds.

After nine months

After nine months or when you come to 45 minutes, you should stop sungazing because solar science forbids further it for the sake of the eyes. The body will empty out as you stop sungazing, and it will be some time before it recharges. You will be able to do this by looking at the sun for 15 minutes at any time of the year, when you are in need of renewal. At that point, you should start walking barefoot on the ground for 45 minutes a day during the period of one year. Only a relaxed walk will do. There is no need for speed walking or running. Grounding is crucial, and the body receives this in direct contact with the earth. Any available time of the day is fine, however, you should do it when the earth is warm and you can comfortably walk in the sunshine. During winter days, this grounding is something you can do at home if you have electricity. All you need to do is to connect the copper wire from the grounding in an electrical socket to your feet, with maybe a copper plate to stand on.

Walking barefoot is as important as sungazing because it closes the full circle of energy between the sky and the earth, through us, as a conscious subject of the sky and the earth. When we are aware of that, who we are and what is happening, it becomes many times stronger.

There are two factors we need to understand: the energy of the sun in the form of light, and our consciousness. They should be united in us. The energy of the sun is the source of existence, and consciousness is the outcome. In between is the earth, with nature and life. The sun gives life on earth, but when we consciously enter this process, when sunlight connects to the earth through us, then two new factors begin. One is that we, with conscious participation in creating life, begin to realize ourselves; and the other is that nature itself and sunlight achieve their ultimate goal, which is for them to be brought to awareness through us. Before this, without our participation, this process was happening spontaneously. In the conscious subject it becomes conscious, and as such returns to the divine absolute. This process between the sky and the earth created our being. When we consciously take part in it, it is as though a child opened his eyes and smiled at his parent for the first time. While we are looking at the sun, the divine accepts us like this, like a parent whose child is looking him in the eye for the first time. Only in man do the light of the stars and nature discover themselves as the same divine existence. Only in a conscious man do they achieve their final purpose and the reason for their existence.

In their outer expression, these factors appear separate, but fundamentally they are the same, but manifested in a variety of ways, some subtle, and others gross. What happens on the outside on the gross material plane in the form of the sun, planets, life energy, and the cosmos, contracts in its outcome in the most subtle of ways: into a conscious subject, into self-consciousness. In the consciousness of our soul, everything that exists intersects.

To receive the energy of the sun, awareness of the energy and its recipience is needed – awareness of consciousness is required. That constitutes self-consciousness. The potential for consciousness is all around us in the form of life energy, which governs the lives of average people. It is completely conditioned and led by outer influences. Self-consciousness is the higher factor: it is the awareness of consciousness itself, of oneself, of the one who is conscious. Only a consciousness like this can have a will of its own. It is a completely new factor in nature that did not come about naturally; it is a result of work and effort of the conscious subject to strengthen and maintain pure awareness of himself independently of outer conditioning.

Self-consciousness is a higher and more subtle factor, and as such attracts energy which manifests itself through lower, grosser forms. Self-consciousness is the most powerful energy receiver, its finest user, and router.

When we are conscious of ourselves during sungazing, of our whole being, as in meditation, such self-consciousness impacts the energy collected in the following way. Energy travels from the sun to the earth, and the earth absorbs it and breeds life. This happens spontaneously everywhere. Plants act as mediators through which photons from the sun initiate life processes on earth. Man is also a mediator; his life efficiency is far greater than that of plants. When man becomes aware of this process, of the transformation of solar energy into life through nature and his body, and that he is nothing but a tube that conducts the energy of the sun to the earth, when he becomes a conscious subject of the whole process, the process does not continue spontaneously as it did before; instead it finalizes in him as the conscious subject. The conscious subject acts as the plug on one side of that tube, a conductor so that the energy no longer goes through, but accumulates; and increases, it becomes one with the consciousness and the conscious subject.

The consciousness that creates the whole life started from the sun and got to its final destination, to the conscious subject. In him, it became aware of itself in the highest way possible, in a divine way. A man who is self-conscious and gazes at the sun barefoot returns the divine consciousness to God in the most subtle way, the most proper way, through himself, with full awareness of the whole process, creating a unity of consciousness and existence. Such existence becomes divine.

With consciousness such as this, we absorb divine energy directly, and with it the divine will, correctness and everything it brings with it.

All other ways of addressing God, all prayers, are like ranting in your sleep compared to sungazing with understanding such as this. This is the only way to look at God directly, the only way to experience him directly. Everything else is an act of avoiding direct confrontation with the divine.[32]

The key factor in solar yoga is consciousness; the conscious soaking up of sunlight, its understanding and the understanding of this whole process, and not the sunlight itself.

Sunlight and energy have always been around us, as well as in ourselves. However, people who unconsciously reside in the sun do not achieve the effects of solar yoga because they do not take part in the process consciously. When we are aware of this energy process, it multiplies tenfold and yields all its fruit.

Consciousness is the factor that actualizes everything, that turns potentiality into reality and leads it toward its outcome.

The secret of man's realization is in taking part consciously in what already is, and not in achieving anything new. In that way, we have always been one with the divine, with the Absolute, but the enlightened is only the one who participates consciously in the overall unity. Always and at every moment this unity actualizes through awareness in its presence. Initiate your conscious participation with solar yoga. It will help you to expand conscious participation in the divine to all other activities and spheres of life.

Consciousness plays a key role in solar yoga, and generally, those who find this feasible to master are advanced meditation practitioners. Truth be told, it is solar yoga, and yoga without meditation is not yoga. The fastest and the best results can be achieved if we consider sungazing as a form of meditation.

I will present a form of meditation that is appropriate for solar yoga in my experience.

What is the attitude we should adopt when we start with meditative sungazing? We should always have in mind that with sungazing we finalize the whole process of creation, or emanation of the divine. If there has ever been any place in the physical universe where the absolute consciousness or God manifests, it is bound to manifest in the form of the light of a star. Are you looking for God? There he is in the sky. There would be neither you nor the world if he were not there.

However, the sun itself is not God; but the divine finds it easier to manifest most powerfully through sunlight.

The sun is the 'Father who art in heaven' who sent his only son (an individual human soul) to save man from the darkness of unconsciousness he experienced after his fall into matter. The son was born on 25th December, when the sun starts to rise in the sky, following a new cycle of life. The son returns to his father only through death and resurrection, through the death of bodily and individual limitations and awakening in pure consciousness, which always exists because it is existence itself.

With sungazing, a conscious subject dies, his bodily aspect is terminated, and he resurrects in the divine consciousness which enables everything, because he is gazing at its primordial source, at what his soul was as absolute consciousness before oblivion in the physical body. He uses the same method to awaken himself. That explains why he no longer lives off bodily food. The sun is the source of our soul. The soul has via the sun consciously created the earth we tread on, the plants and animals, and all living forms, to be able to return to itself through the conscious and complete personality of man, well-designed and brought to a state of awareness in the most intimate and experienced way. Love and goodness are the only indicators of the maturity of this experience.

Almost all of the ancient forms of religion, all across the globe, celebrate the sun as the only God. The first Christian monks (and Buddhist monks and yogis) used sungazing as a source of food and sublime spiritual life.

In Rig Veda it is stated that the sun is the visible eye of the universe in which man resides, Purusha; it is the same Man in the physical universe, his innermost essence, the divine consciousness which enables his awareness of his own being and the whole of nature as a witness (*sakshi*).

With such awareness we should start sungazing.

The sun knows itself through our eyes. We know ourselves through the light of the sun. The cosmos and the earth unite in us as we stand barefoot gazing at the sun. In our awareness of ourselves, in the experience without thoughts, in the pure, timeless existence of 'I AM' here and now, sunlight/divine light/consciousness find its ultimate goal and fulfillment.

We should not visualize sunlight getting inside of us through the eyes and with every breath because it is already in us. We have always lived off it. All of the life energy in the world comes from the sun and is present here already. Sungazing is the practice needed to activate the energy from within us, with full alertness. All we need to have full use of this energy is to be aware of ourselves, and not attract and absorb it in another way.

To accelerate this self-knowledge through the sun, the whole body should be included; this means we need to deal with energy consciously. This exercise alerts dormant kundalini energy, but in a spontaneous and moderate way. Kundalini needs to be activated consciously, with our participation. Then, we know what is happening to us and the power it entails is ours, easily controllable. If kundalini rises all by itself, spontaneously (or using some other methods), we become its victim, because we will not know what to do or what is happening to us. It is extremely harmful and dangerous. Activating kundalini is uniting consciousness and existence (energy) in us. We know how deranged we are in this Omega point world, in our ignorance and wrong way of life that keeps us identified with the physical mind, which separates consciousness from existence. Activating kundalini smashes all the malfunctions that originate as a result of the separation between consciousness and existence. For that reason, the consciousness of our physical mind may also shatter if we are identified with malfunctions and ignorance. We must liberate ourselves gradually of this identification and ignorance, to be able to face the divine consciousness and existence.

To be able to activate kundalini properly, consciously, and moderately, we should, while gazing at the sun barefoot, with an extended breath (through the nose) lift the energy from the base of the spine upward, all along the spine to our eyes, to the third eye or pituitary gland in the centre of the head. The tongue should touch the palate softly. We should feel that in the pituitary gland, all of the energy of the body we have uplifted is collected, and is tied to sunlight through our eyes. While it is still there, we hold our breath, while simultaneously gazing at the sun directly. We should remain steady, holding our breath, and all the power in the third eye, with the only sensation of the presence of here and now as 'I AM', while experiencing the sun as the outer projection of our third eye and Selfhood – for as long as we can endure. When we can no longer hold our breath, we slowly exhale through the mouth.

It is enough to do this several times during one solar yoga session.

This also means our energy, sexual most of all, should be preserved so that it can transform itself into the higher centres, chakras, or levels of consciousness. If we absorb it through the eyes and then lose it, we will get nowhere.

Cessation of food intake and overcoming sexuality are common consequences of rising kundalini to the heart chakra, and exceeding the function of the first three chakras, characterized by sexuality, food, and sleep. Those three characteristics of our being disappear with uplifting kundalini during sungazing practice.

This concludes the description of direct prayer, addressing the divine from the outside by implementing some physical activity.

Prayer as Contemplation and Devotion

The most supreme form of prayer is contemplation, in which we give ourselves away to the divine and disappear as a separate individual. Any separation between us and the divine is erased.

Contemplation is a direct commitment to our divine source within us.

On the outside, there is only God, and the activity of the mind is the only reason why the illusion of us being separated from God exists. That is why contemplation is performed via utter stillness of the being and mind. That is a way for us to be united with the divine whole.

Divine consciousness is the foundation of the being, and we get in contact with it when our whole being is still, on all levels, both physically and mentally.

It is like clearing muddy water; it becomes clear once it becomes still. Then you can see the bottom. The same works for the bottom of your being; we see the eternal divine existence when we calm down the movement of our body and mind.

Our physical, emotional, and mental movement is mechanical and happens following our habits, but we accept it as destiny that we never get to question. It blurs our vision and our whole life is disturbed. When we calm down and consciously testify to our body and all of its movements, we rise consciously above the body, we gain superiority over it, and in doing so we get considerably more energy. When, in the same way, we testify to our feelings, we rise above their mechanical functioning that ties us and makes us lose our energy and consciousness. We do not deny our feelings, but we rise above blinding attachment to be able to understand them better. Here, in spiritual practice, overcoming means better understanding, greater sensitivity. We are only bound by the things we do not understand. The same applies to thoughts. When we testify to our mind and all our thoughts, we rise above the patterns that keep mechanically repeating and we become more conscious of the cause of all our thoughts, we see directly the true nature of what we were thinking about.

The words of a prayer that can be used while practicing this have the sole purpose of giving form to the mind, a thought's contents, to prevent the mind from moving out of control. Once the mind is given some form, some content, then the independence of the essence of man's mind becomes evident; we realize it is something more than the mind itself; it is the consciousness behind the mind and every thought.

When man becomes aware within himself of the fact that he is consciousness, independent of body and mind, he then automatically knows the absolute divine consciousness which is the foundation of everything. This happens because we are the microcosm, and because a multitude of consciousnesses do not exist; it is all one divine consciousness that branches itself out into all of the individual forms.

On this simple rule the science of meditation is fully based - the one that has been conveyed to us in Patanjali's Yoga Sutras. Buddhism has its roots in this practice; Buddha became enlightened through the practice of meditation. All of Buddhism is, in fact, an extended form of meditative practice. Buddhists made the first coenobitic monasteries. Buddhist missionaries were in

Alexandria in the first centuries A.D. They spread their teaching there. The first Christians accepted the coenobitic monasticism and adjusted it to their teaching.

Stillness of being must be followed by an appropriate lifestyle that induces stillness and dedication. This is contained in the ethics and instructions that are identical in both early Buddhism and Christianity.

Without a completely proper life, complete stillness is not possible, either of the body or the mind.

Man knows divine reality with the essence of prayer and true spirituality, in conquest over the body and mind.

Man knows the divine to the level he is able to defeat his body and the bodily mind, by attaching himself to the higher mind and strengthening the presence of consciousness of the soul. This is the process in its entirety.

The fight over the body starts by controlling the physical conditions of living, by avoiding worldly behaviour that fires up and traps the mind; then control over diet which should be light, but the next best option is vegan or vegetarian. Fasting has always been a necessary precondition for good prayer.

Once the affinities of the body have been put in order, the believer has achieved his goal of prayer and contemplation, total submission to the divine.

Only then is the believer fully aware of the true nature of the divine; he sees that the divine has always been present in everything that exists, it is no different from existence itself, or from himself, from his body and his every thought. He sees he has nothing to fight for but maturity and restfulness of this kind.

Whoever has not disciplined and overcome himself is capable of imagining many things. The mind is capable of everything, it can mimic God, not just the devil.

The road to this goal appears hard only because of illusory attachment of consciousness of the soul to the body. It is as hard as we make it.

That is why man in prayer and contemplation does not know God, nor does he approach God, he only liberates himself from his illusions.

RELIGIOUSNESS AND MIRACLES

It is hard to distinguish religiousness from the desire for the miraculous, from the belief in saints who have 'supernatural powers', and from holy places where people find remedies for ailments, and focus instead on the power of some higher force with healing properties in this gross material reality we live in.

These religious aspirations are not only a reflection of the need for solace, a compensation for helplessness, but they also have a scientific explanation. Not in mainstream science, of course, but in esoteric science that is as old as mankind. This science reveals that there are dimensions other than the one we function in - the material plane we are able to perceive with our senses - that have a deciding and overpowering role over the dimension we currently reside in.

Higher dimensions affect the lower ones. Whenever this occurs it is perceived in the lower dimensions as a wondrous manifestation of a 'higher force'. The reason for this is that beings on the physical plane can sense physical phenomena only; they cannot perceive the higher planes, so anything from there seems unknown and miraculous to them.

However, the problem with perception does not end here; it extends to further interpretations of the higher planes. We are on the lower plane, limited by physical senses and the physical world we live in; anything that comes from higher dimensions we tend to interpret as 'otherworldly', as though it were 'supernatural', and therefore 'miraculous'. Additionally, we ascribe this functioning to either God or the devil. In reality, all of this functioning belongs to the same nature that we live in, but that we are currently unable to see because we do not see all dimensions. We do not see the process of causality that extends across all dimensions. The part of nature we cannot perceive we interpret to ourselves as 'higher worlds', which we usually call 'heaven' and the 'kingdom of God', since from our perspective all of these phenomena appear to be somewhere higher up.

The 'otherworldly' plane is actually the astral, while the 'kingdom of heaven' or paradise is the higher astral where negative vibrations and entities no longer exist (as they do in the lower astral), but there are still recognizable shapes from our world (perfectly beautiful nature, colours, and so on). Individual souls of the deceased go there and make their way back to this world.

The higher dimensions are not 'up', nor are we 'down'; the issue here is one of different frequencies of electromagnetic fields, which all of reality consists of. Our senses are tuned so that we are able to perceive a relatively narrow frequency range and act within it; hence, we cannot detect any other frequencies (this explains why we do not remember our stays in the higher dimensions). They are simply more subtle or gross, not 'higher' or 'lower'" in any way. That is all. There are no miracles, nothing is 'supernatural', everything is a part of nature, we just do not perceive it all.

Although we do not perceive the higher dimensions of nature,we nonetheless reside in them when we sleep or are otherwise out of our body. We use them all the time: when we feel and fantasize, this is a function of the astral; when we think we are in the element of air, when we are filled with energy and exaltation because of some vision that inspires us to act with our whole being, this is the element of fire, which is between the air and the astral. It is all in us, but our unconsciousness and oblivion make us project it outwards.

All of this was depicted in the science of Sânkhya, which details all of the categories of nature: Prakrti, the physical world and all of the higher dimensions, as the same field of nature, and the spirit, Purusha, the divine consciousness which is transcendental to all phenomena of nature. This Purusha is man's true essence.

Man is composed of all the dimensions of nature. This makes him able to perceive them all and work with them. The man who has developed all of his capabilities is one who has opened himself to all the dimensions and who can function in them. He has erased the boundaries, and stopped projecting outwards that which is in him, which is himself. He has created nothing new, he has merely opened himself to what is; he has ceased to be locked in the senses and the physical body. The power of his functioning has extended beyond his physical body, and he is able to use energy - that is to say, frequencies of the higher dimensions - and, acting via them, induce consequences on the physical plane. This happens all the time, but now he can see it and affect this phenomenon because his consciousness is harmonized with the consciousness of the higher realms and he is able to take an active part in the ongoing processes.

He sees the phenomena of higher dimensions, where space and time are contracted into a single phenomenon, where all causes are in their unmanifested state, and he sees how all will be manifested on Earth. This is called clairvoyance. If he joins his energy with this, if he manages to master his body's energy, then he is able to impact his environment using energy only. To use energy in this way and affect the environment means recognizing the unity of energy within and outside of us.

An onlooker who has no awareness of the higher dimensions can only see this man performing miracles, and calls him a saint.

This works well if he is a respectable member of the ruling religion. If the same were performed by someone who is not a member of the local church, he is made to seem as an evil wizard to the church followers, a Satanist assisted by the devil himself, someone who tricks people with wonders, a warlock who should be burnt at the stake. These are all problems associated with miracles and failing to comprehend the functioning of the higher dimensions. Many people have lost their lives because of this.

Opening up to the higher dimensions and being able to work with them is possible so that man can harmonize with the divine consciousness which enables everything, which is everything. To use the language of the Bible, he goes back to paradise and becomes like God. A saint is a person who can prove his unity with God, in practical terms. Above all, this is something he needs to do himself. He can manifest this to others only to inspire them, to help them recognize and realize it within themselves. People need inspiration, a practical demonstration of what they read in books and debate. Demonstration of power is justified only if it goes hand in hand with self-knowledge, as a part of practical training.

If somebody demonstrates the power to manipulate people and direct their attention to a God other than the one within themselves, this is abuse.

There are places, temples, and objects that are connected with saints who had powers. They had a positive and inspiring effect on people during their life, and they continued to do so after the death of their physical body. To them, death made their job easier.

Their goodwill should not be abused. For example, when we go on poisoning our body for years and as a logical consequence we fall ill, and medicine fails us, we turn to a saint for the cure. This would be as if you took a big shit and said to the saint: 'Clean this up, will you, you are a good and hard-working fellow, you can do it.' Saints are not the cleaners of our junk. Their job is to teach us by giving us a personal example of how not to make mistakes, and how to become better human beings.

Esoteric science explains in detail how man can perfect himself so he can perceive the higher dimensions and learn to function in them. In the work of Patanjali's Yoga Sutras, a whole chapter is dedicated to acquiring powers, *siddhi*. In the beginning, it is said that when (through meditation) complete concentration of consciousness is attained (unity of the state of consciousness called *dharana*, *dhyana*, and *samadhi*) then supreme unity called *samyama* is achieved.

This remains vague to many commentators because samadhi denotes the highest state of consciousness one can attain in meditation. *Samadhi* brings insight into the complete unity of existence and consciousness; it is the disappearance of time that divides consciousness and existence, that divides our inner dimensions from the outer world. The point is that *samadhi* is initially attained only occasionally. The states that precede samadhi are *dharana* and *dhyana*, and they refer to the power of keeping your focus permanently on the object of meditation (breathing, *yantra*, *mantra*) until *samadhi* is finally attained. Patanjali tells us that when *samadhi* becomes a permanent state, like *dharana* and *dyhana*, it is then called *samyama*. At this point, all powers or *siddhi* come into full effect.

Samyama, or the permanent unity of consciousness and existence, is a complete unity of our body with consciousness, energy, and the entire outer world, the cosmos. When this is achieved, we have the power to act completely. **Previously, at least a tiny difference existed between our consciousness, our body, and the outer world. To the degree such a difference was present, we felt helpless, separated from God. To the degree this difference is diminished by us, we receive the power to act, and we are in unity with God.** At first, it manifests through bigger insights. Wisdom and insights precede the power to act. Many advanced meditators have the capacity of insight, psychic abilities, and powers of perception, although they have not been endowed with the power to impact physical reality, *siddhi*.

We would be in serious trouble if all those who do not have a grain of wisdom or insight have the power. The higher consciousness of our souls, which rules this world, will not permit this.

It should be said that there are such individuals, who are without any insight or wisdom, but who through perseverance and practice manage to attain certain powers - mostly those that enable them to have influence over other people and take their energy. They are called magicians. They base their power on receiving or becoming acquainted with the principles of the lower levels of the higher dimensions, or by being in cahoots with beings of the lower astral, inorganic beings or demons. Beings of the lower astral do not produce energy, only people can produce energy, and that is why these beings need to take it from people. It is always a case of exploitation of life energy. Although magicians can enrich themselves with energy by stealing from other people, in the end they will pay the price. In the holographic universe, theft is not an option.

Complete unity between our deepest awareness of ourselves, our body, our energy, and the outside world has always existed; it is a reality that we have not paid much attention to. By proper contemplation we remove the obstacles that prevent us from seeing reality, and we realize there is nothing that is apart, everything is One, everything is divine consciousness itself. Nothing but the divine consciousness and presence exist. To see divine consciousness means seeing that there is nothing else. This is the void or sunyata that Buddha spoke of.

This is all we need to know about religiousness and miraculous powers. There is nothing extraordinary or supernatural.

SEXUALITY AND RELIGIOUSNESS, TOGETHER FOREVER

All religions have very strong opinions on sexuality, which border on obsession. This is perfectly justified as sexuality is necessary for the survival of the species, for the survival of all life.

Let us first analyze what happens in the process we call sexuality.

Special 'sexual energy' does not exist, nor should anything be done with it. There is only one energy, and it causes different consequences depending on the level of the being it is manifested by - specifically, through which chakra it emanates. If it manifests through the second chakra, the consequence is sexual activity. If the same energy manifests through the third chakra, the consequence is work that is beneficial for the community. Through the fourth chakra, there is an experience of unity with existence, in harmony and love. Unlike the second chakra where love is experienced only through physical contact with the opposite sex, in the fourth chakra we experience unity with existence, in numerous activities of human endeavour, in joint experiences where we find beauty and meaning, with humour. In the second chakra, we have sex, in the fourth we make love with all life. In the second chakra, we merely attempt to experience what we experience in the fourth as a permanent state. If this energy manifests itself through the fifth chakra, the obvious consequence is creative expression through words and deeds, we write poetry and philosophy, religious debates. True understanding is the most important expression of love that we share. If it is manifested through the sixth chakra we see and experience what words cannot begin to describe; for the first time we see the unity of everything, we see everything as energy. In the seventh chakra we participate with our whole being in the unity of everything, divine consciousness is our consciousness, God's will is our will, divine energy is our energy. There are no longer any differences.

Therefore, the only real issue is the focus of energy and consciousness.

This focus decides what man will do in the world and how he perceives the world.

This issue is the cause of all battles for man, and has concerned man since his early days.

The next thing to understand is that, for energy to move throughout man's body, the rule of free will applies. Energy can move freely, but it can also get stuck. It can be manipulated in a number of ways - not just by mental convictions, but with certain interventions and practices as well. It can be manipulated consciously, and even more so unconsciously. Man can perform this manipulation on himself and other people, without them being aware of it.

A good rule of thumb is that when man is glued to his convictions, religious or otherwise, this means that all of his energy is stuck in one chakra, and deformed. Such a man is obsessed with one type of behaviour, and he cannot change it without some outer intervention. The truth is that energy cannot be stuck in one chakra without it becoming deformed in some way. When it is conscious and proper, it flows, it circulates and brings forth all possible experiences. When it is jammed it is deformed, as is the consciousness of man. Energy cannot stagnate and be deformed without a similar effect on the consciousness, because they are connected, like two sides of the same coin.

Energy can be blocked on one level of consciousness, in a certain chakra, only if it is disturbed, which means that the functioning of the centres of consciousness, the chakras, may be upset in some way. One centre can take on the role of another centre and start making decisions on behalf of the true centre. This means that consciousness is on a lower level than energy and overall function, that consciousness and energy are not well-balanced and on the same level of functioning; we think one thing and speak openly about it, but do something completely different in private. For example, if the consciousness of the third chakra works by identifying itself with the energy of the second chakra. What happens then? A textbook case of adultery: an impeccable husband, a respectable member of the community and a politician (a characteristic of the third chakra), is found cheating on his wife, because of his excessive sexual drive (caused by the second chakra). In such cases, we can say that his brain is between his legs.

There are much harder cases than this, when consciousness is inspired by the higher centres and connects and identifies with the energy from the lower centres; this is a recipe for religious fanatics. If consciousness inspired by the higher centres becomes attached to the energy of the first chakra, then this is the most dangerous position of all, because it affects life itself; such a fanatic takes human lives out of the most supreme ideals, and finds meaning in sacrifice - first others, then himself. He physically manipulates people and their lives. He believes he has to act on his faith at all costs, doing something drastic. If he hangs on to the second chakra then his deranged faith will be in a somewhat milder form - such as a priest who rapes little boys, or a cult leader who abuses a large number of women and children with a Bible in his hands. If he is a rich and respectable Arabian sheik, he will go to a luxurious European hotel and organize a gay orgy with prostitutes trashing the hotel facilities with his feces, and all of the damage will be paid for in full.

Therefore, the trouble with the motion of energy rests on its freedom to take a turn at any point and in any available way (it must be free for it to be effective and creative). This means that all people have diverted off the right path toward God. Everybody is in need of correction. This is why sexuality gets condemned as sinfulness in man.

Energy diverts from the right path and becomes blocked most easily in the second chakra because, while exiting the first chakra, it becomes polarized for the first time into sexes - but is still pretty far from the higher centres. There is very little consciousness, but a lot of energy. The great number of stupid and negative things man does with the energy of the first chakra is because it is the most distant from consciousness of the other centres. The function of the first chakra we see in aggressiveness while fighting, physical conflicts of any kind, rows. Why is this so? Energy from the first chakra is expressed through physical action and has no awareness or understanding to make this action right, and therefore is too often used in the wrong way. Violence in any form is a wrong action. If the energy of the first chakra is aimed at the higher centres, at least to a minimum degree, it gets manifested in adrenaline or extreme sports, in healthy and positive aggressiveness, in the fight for a noble cause.

The deranged energy of the first chakra teams up with the sexuality of the second. This is the worst combination ever: the joining of the first two chakras, without sufficient consciousness, is when one decides on behalf of another when they do not know their boundaries and their roles, when they become mixed up and cannot be distinguished any more. Excessive attachment to the first and the second chakra leads to sadomasochism; sexuality is connected with the energy of the body in all possible ways. Due to this connection, the worst misdeeds and crimes are committed, crimes that are always connected with deranged sexuality. In fact, most crimes are based on deranged sexuality.

The next thing to know about energy is that the body of man is designed so that energy can circulate throughout all the centres. If energy moved without obstacles, in the way it is meant to, it would automatically move to the highest centre and man would instantly attain God-knowledge, the highest consciousness possible. The body is designed for this. However, this does not happen because consciousness interferes with energy's movement, and since it is not mature it tends to be seduced by impressions and experiences. Such consciousness is followed by energy. It does not go anywhere without consciousness.

If a certain activity is repeated several times, the energy gets attached to this function, and habits result. If the consciousness is weak, it will become a slave to such energy functions, to such habits.

The next regularity should also be remembered: it is enough to have a minimum presence of consciousness to release great energy; a bad habit gets repeated incessantly while consciousness is passive, and the reverse effect occurs when we wish to set in motion and preserve the higher consciousness; to do this all of our energy is required. If we start to lose energy in the lower centres, even a little, consciousness falls under their influence, at least temporarily. Energy can function with minimum consciousness, but to keep consciousness in a higher state takes all of the energy we have at our disposal. It is like having a barrel full of water; to keep the water level high, all of the holes that water could flow out of must be plugged. If there were even the tiniest hole, the level of water would drop and the whole barrel would be empty.

To keep ourselves in the higher energy centres we must not lose energy through the lower centres; we should not do what is typical for the lower centres if we wish to remain in the higher ones. We must be whole to be conscious. We cannot serve two masters, we cannot be split if we wish to be fully conscious and dedicated to the purpose of our life.

The problem is that consciousness is neutral and functions everywhere - so much so that it justifies its functioning through every chakra. When we impact any chakra with our consciousness, even the lowest, it seems like the best idea in the moment, completely justified and necessary. In reality, the more we affect the lower centres with our consciousness, the more justified it seems to us, and the more attached we are to such functioning. In the lower centres, energy is stronger, and it binds consciousness more powerfully. This is why it is so hard for us to get rid of inferior drives and obsessions.

A strong attachment to consciousness in the lowest centres has justification of its own. It causes the consciousness of our soul to attach to the physical body and this world. Sexuality (the second chakra), next to life energy (the first chakra), has the strongest attachment of the soul to the body. If it were not for this attraction, the consciousness of our soul would be a lot more free, independent, and life as we know it could not happen in its present form; we would be neutral observers of life and not active participants in life's drama. We need to be heavily involved in our lives to develop further. For this reason, identification of the consciousness of the soul with the body and all of its activities is of crucial importance; what we truly need is a passion for life. Chakras represent varying degrees of identification of consciousness of the soul with the physical body and this world, degrees of passion, illusion, and clarity; the lowest centres are the most passionate and illusory, while the higher ones are the least.

Amongst everything else, religiousness deals with sexuality because it has the most allure for the deception of consciousness of the soul, its bondage to suffering and separation from the divine state. If the ideal of religiousness is to return consciousness of the soul to its original state, to 'save our soul', then it must focus on sexuality, which has the strongest pull of the soul to the body.

We can give some practical advice here on how to resist our lower drives. Whipping ourselves will do no good. This will only fire up the passions of the lowest chakra. A negative attitude or condemnation will not do much good either. All we need is understanding. Obsession with sexuality is best overcome by becoming aware of its essence. This is the way of tantra. When something is completely clear to us, when we have become aware of it fully, it can no longer trap or deceive us. We are through with it. Awareness, in itself, uplifts us. It is necessary to become aware of the process of the origin of obsession and desire. It appears in thoughts first, as an idea that justifies itself in a myriad of ways, then it focuses energy toward its gratification, sets the imagination in motion and drives the body to do what it wants. A process such as this is present in all of the passions that consume us, whether it be sexuality, aggressiveness, or any other activity. To stop the process, we need to deal with it at the very beginning, to be aware of its first thoughts and plans. This is achieved by recapitulation. Once our urges are satisfied, we should quieten ourselves and by recapitulation, in imagination and memory, we should go back to the beginning, to when the first thought appeared. After several experiences of this sort, we will be able to observe the moment of origin as it happens, and we will be able to stay fully aware of the whole process of its realization. When we become conscious of the whole process it will no longer have a stranglehold on us; instead, we will be the masters of it. The more aware we are of the idea itself and the thoughts that incite passion, the less influence those passions will have over our life.

A change in breathing is also welcomed. Each state of consciousness is followed by a certain rhythm of breathing. By changing the rhythm of breathing we can change the state of consciousness. It is enough to strongly exhale all the air from our lungs, bend forward at the waist, and then with empty lungs straighten up, trying to keep the lungs empty for a few moments, or for as long as we can. When we can no longer endure, we should let the air fill our lungs, until normal breathing resumes. It is enough to do this several times and the rush of heated passions and obsessions will be neutralized. Our mood will change completely. This is a way in which we use breathing to pull the energy from the lowest chakras to the higher centres. This works for all passions, aggression, and hatred, and our attachment to illusions. All of this will change with a change in breathing.

It is also necessary to change where we are, to change the circumstances in which passions (anger, illusion) take hold of us, to distance ourselves from the individuals we normally socialize with who invoke lower passions in us (hatred, illusions). We can do this when we become aware of the origin of our passions, and we will do so if we put this to practice.

These instructions help to overcome all of the obsessions which enslave us, temporarily or permanently, and which relate to the lowest chakras. This can be sexuality or uncontrollable outbursts of anger and hatred, or an affinity for illusions through substance abuse.

What is also important to know is that everything happens in cycles, that rise and fall like a wave. Recapitulation will bring us an awareness that our strongest passions, obsessions, hatred and anger are transient; it will bring greater alertness when a wave of stirred passions and obsessions starts to move, the way it rises and then finally disappears. The key moment for us is to resist the wave, to stay unscathed by it in the moment of its peak, knowing that this too shall pass.

An awakened man who is whole is one who has learned to surf the waves of natural cycles and all phenomena, in his body before all else. He always maintains his awareness of himself, independent of the states the body and mind may find themselves in. People who live in illusions are like small children who identify with every wave that moves them, drowning before long.

Abstinence is not necessary for everyone. If there is a true relationship based on love, there is no sexuality; they make love and it always uplifts them, their energy permeates one another in a healing way and activates the higher chakras. In true love, they may attain the highest spirituality. If true love is absent then abstinence is the best solution, so energy can accumulate and be redirected to the higher centres. Therefore, we uplift energy in one of two ways: via a love relationship with someone else, or by ourselves.

Whenever we have sex without love, we lose energy. It stays trapped between the first and the second chakra. Only the experience of love can uplift this energy to the fourth chakra.

That is why abstinence has always been the best solution for those who are on the path of spirituality, and due to circumstances are without a love partner they can share their growth in awareness with. Some need to go down this path alone for karmic reasons, and others need help and support.

When we say 'uplifting energy to higher centres' what we mean is this: ***realizing that we can have an orgasm with every chakra***, not just the second one where we experience it through physical contact and energy exchange. When we work and receive recognition in professional and social settings, we experience an orgasm in the third chakra. Through cognition that we are one with the cosmos and nature, we experience orgasm in the fourth, heart chakra; we are then in love with all beings and the overall existence, as well. Orgasm can be experienced in the fifth chakra when our experience of unity with the Wholeness is expressed in a way that people can understand us when we convey understanding. Orgasms of the fifth chakra are manifested in a smile of the deepest understanding, during long talks, writing, painting, and composing. An even higher orgasm can be experienced when we discover the direct impact of divine consciousness, always and everywhere, in everything, as the living conscious force. This is the orgasm of the sixth chakra. In the seventh chakra, we finally reach the climax and do away with all of the illusions that drove us to believe we are apart from divine love, and understand that we have been trying to find it in indirect, even wrong ways.

This all happens to us when we 'uplift energy' into higher chakras, when we stop losing it in the lower centres.

This is of great help to those who, for some reason, cannot find their orgasmic fulfillment through the second chakra, and who do not have an ideal sex life. This does not signify loss, at all. Naturally, it is beneficial that the second chakra functions properly, for energy to travel to the higher centres, but as we have already concluded, this development does not always happen correctly and many deviations can take place in the second chakra. It is a more frequent occurrence for consciousness to get stuck here, rather than go up. This makes it easier for people without a fulfilling sex life to uplift their energy and realize it in the higher aspects of existence, rather than during sexual intercourse, because they are not trapped in the second chakra. Instead of suffering because of it, they should use this situation as a blessing in disguise. It is more likely for us to find the right partner in a person who we work with, while attaining higher, creative goals, one we share ideals with that belong to the nature of our higher energy centres. If we can share with somebody the passions of the third, fourth, fifth, or sixth chakra, only then can we share passions of the second chakra without problem. If we find the ideal partner for the needs of the second chakra, chances are slim that he/she will be suitable for mutual growth to the higher centres. We can love someone much more deeply if we share the principles of the third, fourth, and other higher centres, than the first and second only. Love of the higher centres is much deeper and more lasting because it gives more awareness of the meaning of life. Love of the first two centres is only energetically strong, which makes it more attractive, but it is relatively short-lived if it does not get uplifted to the higher centres.

Therefore, those who have a 'good sex life' should not fool themselves that they are truly realized; maybe they do not have love, maybe they are burning in the fire of passion and are glued to the second chakra, to the point they are unable to rise to the higher centres of consciousness, energy, and pleasure. Apart from all the passions the second chakra has to offer, a person is lonely unless he/she is realized in the higher centres, together with their partner. One does not have to be physically alone to be lonely. A much harder form of loneliness is when you are with your partner and you do not share the passions of your heart and soul, but live side by side your whole life. The higher the centres we can share our consciousness and energy, the happier and the more fulfilled we are.

The movement of energy throughout the body is manifested in physiological and biochemical processes. In the pituitary gland, a substance is secreted: dimethyltryptamine (DMT), which is the molecular link of the physical body with the higher consciousness, with the consciousness of the soul. DMT is set to accept the consciousness of the higher mind in the body, to conduct divine consciousness in our being. DMT circulates throughout the whole body, from the sixth chakra to the first, and connects them all to consciousness of the soul, and from that point goes back to the sixth. This happens in the space of one calendar year - it makes a full circle in the space of 365 days. The circling both begins and ends on December 22nd, during the time of winter solstice. This circling was initially calculated to be the ideal state; people rarely manage to realize this because they lose the energy of their consciousness through the lower centres, since they are identified with the functioning of those lower centres. If man manages to finalize this circling without interruption, he then attains the highest consciousness and God-knowledge, resurrection.[33] If we manage to become aware of all energy manifestations in all the centres, then DMT is not wasted in the lower centres, but finalizes its circling in the pituitary gland with its fullest potential.[34] Then DMT does not need to go again through the lower centres, to connect them with the consciousness of the soul, because it is already present in all the centres – all the centres are equally connected with the consciousness of the soul – and a path toward the seventh chakra is wide open, and our being merges permanently with divine consciousness. All our energy and all our centres, all the states of our consciousness, become permanently joined with divine consciousness, with existence itself.

This is all well-presented in the esoteric meaning of the New Testament. Events, words, and deeds of Jesus throughout the whole of the New Testament have been aligned in such a way as to reflect the esoteric meaning of the Zodiac. In the end, Jesus attains resurrection on Golgotha. This is the name of a hill that in reality does not exist anywhere in Palestine (Israel). In translation this name means skull. Therefore, Jesus attains resurrection on the skull. This was a symbolic way to say that resurrection happens when our life energy unites with consciousness and arrives at the seventh chakra, at the top of our skull. Simply visualize a cross on the top of your head where Jesus was crucified. This is the true meaning of Golgotha.[35]

Because of all this, sexuality in religions has been maximally controlled, to make sure no one gets enlightened or resurrected. Institutionalized religions do not serve the purpose of leading us to enlightenment, but to maximally stretch out the Omega point in you, to the ultimate limit of madness and illusion. These manipulations are generally orchestrated by tying the consciousness to the lower centres. The lower the consciousness is, the stronger faith is, because in the lower centres energy is stronger and consciousness is weaker, and more deranged. The characteristic of the lower centres is greater polarization; consequently, consciousness is more polarized by opposition and conflicts of various kinds. Man who is in conflict with people, the world, and life, who is overly identified with something, always has disturbed sexual energy, mixed with religious fanaticism. The property of the higher centres is greater balance and understanding.

This is the only way that you can be forced to reach insight yourself and raise your consciousness to the higher centres in order to achieve the purpose of your existence - through the experience of conflict and opposition.

The fact is that you are the only person who can do this, there is no outside help, *there is no collective salvation*. The essence of consciousness is that it is always personal, unique, and it springs from you alone, from your soul. Consciousness cannot be given to man from the outside, and no religion can play a part in it. Not even God is of help. Any attempt to find God and divine consciousness in the outside world, to somehow get all results through our faith, is the negation of true religiousness, blocking the true bond with the divine – negation of the truth that we already are the divine we aspire to merge with.

The situation here is like sex: nobody can do the merging but you.

Sexual merging gives us for a brief moment the experience of blissful consciousness of unity; the ego disappears together with individuality and we dissolve in eternity, through this experience of the greatest unity with another being. When we get to know somebody deeply and intimately enough, we find God in them. That is why orgasm is the most desirable experience. It lasts for a short time and is given to common folk as a prelude for the real and eternal bliss and wealth that awaits us in the highest chakra. All we need to do is to become aware of the process.

All spiritual practice can be reduced to learning to do consciously what we would do instinctively, unconsciously. *What we do with full awareness does not repeat itself, it does not stay on the same level.* Consciousness itself releases us from everything that is low and uplifts our energy toward the higher centres. Consciousness has the natural propensity for ascension, like a balloon filled with helium. Therefore, make every move conscious; vipassana in bed is the real vipassana; a slow walk with focus on every step we make is for old people. Spiritual practice is not found in abstract teachings and dogmas. It is in life itself, here and now. It is life itself, here and now.

Sex is inviting to us because it gives us the feeling of unity with another being, the feeling of unity we lost when we were born and became egocentric individuals alienated from the whole and other beings, when we started to learn religious commandments and theology, or science for that matter. However, we are always in this unity, but we fail to observe it; our body is in physical unity with planet Earth and is in no way separated from it; like the cells in our body that belong to us, we people are as cells to our mother Earth. Our essence, soul, is in no way different or separate from the divine Absolute. We should simply become aware of who we truly are. The sons of God. Brahman. Purusha. Adam Kadmon.

Everyone on a spiritual path sooner or later is confronted with the issue of sexuality and what to do with it, because they see it as an obstacle to religiousness. The answer lies in the cognition of the true nature of reality, knowing that existence itself is here and now, in every possible form, the highest divine consciousness and presence. In the holographic universe, everything is One. In the divine reality, there is nobody else, there is no duality. The more we approach it, the more we become liberated and lose our need to find sanctuary in somebody else. This is what we were naturally and passionately searching for in the first two chakras, through sexuality, through a bodily relationship. As we continue to grow in self-knowledge and God-knowledge, in awareness of the higher chakras, we see our unity with others and we feel less inclined to realize it in a rough way. The nature of our energy bond with existence grows more subtle; in the fourth chakra we discover love for all, we learn that love can be experienced and exchanged in all possible ways. In the fifth chakra, an understanding word is usually enough. In the sixth, a mere look is sufficient to convey love and understanding. This is a way to surpass 'sexual needs' through a rough exchange of energy with 'others'. A look full of love and understanding equals physical orgasm, only it is in higher dimensions, much closer to the divine reality. That is why it is nearer and dearer to us, it lasts forevermore in us.

The closer we are to the divine, the less we need a rough exchange of unity and love. With the cognition of the divine we share love, we do not look for it, because we have plenty.

It is a big mistake to think we can attain the higher centres of both consciousness and love by denying ourselves the lower centres. We must not deny ourselves anything, because it is all divine. All the opposites within and without should be experienced with maximum awareness, and only then will we be able to rise above. It is consciousness that uplifts us, no denial ever does the trick. If we deny ourselves a certain aspect of life, it only means that we have not adequately known and accepted it as the divine.

In conclusion, we can say that the relationship between sexuality and religiousness is the same as the Alpha and the Omega, yin and yang, where both are right when the former is right, the latter is right, too. And vice versa. Sexuality is problematic only when we are not religious in the proper way, and likewise, our religiousness is wrong when our sexuality is wrong.

RESURRECTION IS THE GROUNDING OF THE SOUL

Depictions of God-knowledge as a method of ascension are widely present in all forms of religiousness. Ascension is also connected with the idea of heaven or a heavenly kingdom. Whenever believers address God with an idea or a prayer, they look up. This upward orientation has its reasons and should be properly understood.

The idea of heaven and ascension to God should primarily be understood in the context of the dimensions which existence consists of. Our position is here, on the lowest material plane. Therefore when we look up, we turn to the higher dimensions.

It is common knowledge that in esoteric science, all of the higher dimensions are placed within man. Man has been instructed to turn inward, to himself, to know himself, because the 'heavenly kingdom is in us'.

Ascension is closely associated with the idea of resurrection. What we mean by that is exceeding the limitations of the physical body and uplifting oneself to the higher dimensions, closer to God. The religiousness of people who are tied to the function of the first two chakras assumes that resurrection is to do with life after death, overcoming death in some form. Since their notions cannot exceed physical limitations, their identification with the body, they view this phenomenon from the perspective of the physical body. More developed religious people of the third, fourth and higher chakras naturally assume some form of rebirth during their physical life and with resurrection open themselves up to the perception of higher dimensions.

In any case, the ascension to God or resurrection means opening oneself up to the higher dimensions, knowledge of higher dimensions by means of opening perception - not only understanding theoretically, but concretely, through spiritual discipline and mastering one's body and the energies of the body, and together with that mastering the mind. *Mastering the body always means overcoming the limiting influences the body has on our perception.* The more we master the body, the greater our ability to perceive the higher dimensions.

We will take a closer look at the nature of higher dimensions. They are by no means as abstract as the mind trapped in the body imagines. Higher dimensions are our feelings and imagination (astral, the element of water); our energy and will with which we decide from day to day what to do with our energy (the element of fire); our intellect (the mental world above astral, the element of air).

Since we are not aware of the true nature of the higher dimensions that are in us while we are here in our physical body, we are also unaware of the deeper motivations of our being, our actions, and our mind. This means we are unaware of the higher causes of our life, and with this we are unaware of the consequences of our actions. This means that we are unaware of divine presence and intervention.

When, through spiritual discipline, we open up to influences of the higher dimensions, or better yet when we learn to exit the physical body and enter the higher worlds directly, and experience their existence and the nature of their functioning, in person, we become aware of our whole being and start doing what's in our best interest. When in astral projections, we go to astral many times, we open ourselves up to the influences and vibrations of the higher dimensions, we increase our creative potential to a far higher degree than we ever could through reliance on the physical body alone. By recurring visits to the astral we, in a way, dig out a tunnel for better communication between the lower and higher dimensions.

The astral is also a world of feelings and emotions. When we are awake and conscious in this dimension we are aware of all our feelings, and everybody else's too. Practically this means that we cannot hurt anybody else emotionally through an unconscious and irresponsible act, because we feel the effect it has on the other party. Our feelings become objective, they are no longer subjective, we have more than one angle to view them from. This is called empathy. A direct consequence of a conscious stay in higher dimensions is maturity of emotional intelligence, the greatest compassion for all beings, for all of existence. There is no better way of acquiring emotional maturity than through out-of-body experiences to become acquainted with the astral world.

When we master the energy of our body, we master the dimension above the astral, and we have our will. Practically this means there is no longer anything we can do unconsciously and spontaneously, merely acting on an outer impulse, a challenge or incentive, but we always act out of our free will, independent from outer influences. Then we can hurt nobody with our willful conduct, because we experience it as though we hurt ourselves.

By mastering our body's energy, we master the omnipresent energy, and then when we act it looks as though we perform miracles, we move things, we heal. All of this energy is the same, joined into one; there are no divisions in the energy that is the foundation of existence, it unites all forms of existence. When we master it in ourselves with our consciousness, then we are masters of it everywhere.

Additionally, if in meditation we manage to master our mind, then we can go on to an even higher dimension and begin to understand the causes of all mental states. Then we can see the reasons for certain thoughts in us, and as a consequence we can see the same in everybody else. It becomes possible for us to communicate not only with people but with plants and animals. With such mental maturity, it becomes impossible for us to hurt someone in our thoughts, or even to think something bad.

We become incapable of wrongdoing and hurting people; once we have mastered the higher dimensions of our being we are in full capacity of impeccable perception - mental, energetic, and emotional. We then become infallible, we see the true nature of all things, nothing eludes us, we have perfect cognition.

This all happens in man once he resurrects. He is closer to God by becoming more aware of the true nature of his body, energy, feelings, will, and thoughts themselves, his mind. This is a way in which man knows higher worlds, the 'kingdom of heaven'.

In doing so one overcomes everything that is bodily and wrong (sinful). Man errs only if he is closed off into subjectivity, if he fails to see himself from the outside, objectively, from a higher perspective, if he does not feel and understand how the recipient of his actions experiences his actions. Man is sinful if he closes himself off into the lower dimensions, into the illusion of bodily separation, into mortality or the laws of rebirthing, until he matures and stops acting subjectively.

Every sinner has converted himself once he becomes aware of himself from a higher perspective, from the point of view of other people, his environment, or his victim; when he stops watching the world from his own viewpoint only, when he becomes aware of what he does to his victim, how he/she feels and how the victim sees him. Then he, at least a little, opens himself up to the influences of the higher dimensions and feels the general unity of existence, of all living beings.

When man feels the general unity and connectedness of all life energy and consciousness, he then feels responsible for his actions. It is not possible to be responsible for one's actions without awareness of the unity of existence, which in religious terms means without the unity of divine consciousness in everything.

This all has another name: conscience. Conscience is consciousness of the higher dimensions, consciousness of the higher mind and consciousness of the soul. When consciousness from the higher dimensions, for an instant, manages to reach the low physical mind, this mind experiences this contact in the form of conscience.

Finally, when we speak of ascending toward God and resurrection, it all boils down to ascension of the physical mind toward the higher mind and consciousness of the soul.

To put it even more plainly, the mind projects everything into the exact opposite of what is real, like a mirror image. The mind is, in fact, a kind of a mirror. It would even be more accurate to say that there is no ascension, nothing is up or down, the universe is a hologram and everything is contained within everything already. *The true nature of the ascension of man's mind toward the higher dimensions and higher reality is in effect an insight into what is here and now, which is possible only through appeasement of the physical mind and ego, their stillness.* Due to the function of illusions, which are essential to the mind, this appeasement seems like ascension.

Stillness is not a religion, it is a science, the science of meditation presented in detail by Patanjali in his work 'Yoga Sutras'.

Stillness of the mind exists in religions also, in the form of the monastic practice of asceticism. Its purpose is for an individual to learn to master his energy and will, the body and mind. The original definition of overcoming sin is metanoia, which means overcoming the mind, transcendence, or appeasement of the mind.

Stillness of the mind is the only way to get closer to God. Any other attempt to get closer to God is yet another illusion of the mind.

In all of the previous explanation, we can find the true meaning in the words: 'know yourself and you will know God'.

Transcendence of the mind is the true meaning of resurrection.

However, on this opposition point of the divine, everything is reversed - even the understanding of resurrection. From the perspective of the mind, we imagine it to be some kind of ascension, going up somewhere. However, it is quite the contrary. *Resurrection is the act of descending consciousness of the soul into the body.*

The whole process of manifestation of divine consciousness through nature and existence is a process in which all of the possibilities of divine consciousness are manifested concretely. The outcome of this process is the physical world we live in. Our life exists as consciousness of our soul descends into matter, becoming more and more materialized - which has no negative context, only positive. *Materialization of consciousness of the soul is a complete and concrete manifestation of divine consciousness.* Anyone who considers materialization as a negative process has a very naive preconception of the matter. Materialization is the most positive occurrence in divine existence; the divine manifests the most in physical form, as form itself, as all possible forms, all possible processes, as life itself and the meaning of life. Nowhere before has this been an option. God receives the most substantial form there could ever be in his physical form. God is the closest to us here, although it appears as though he were the most distant. He manifests his likeness through man's body. Our souls have created this world and embodied themselves in the physical body. This whole process is the process of embodiment, of descending consciousness of the soul into the body, into physical reality.

However, this descent has not been finalized yet, it has been going on throughout the whole process of the existence of the human race. It is a continuous process. *When a soul completely lands on the ground, in physical reality, when it consciously masters physical reality, then consciousness has manifested itself completely on the physical plane, it has finalized its emanation entirely, it has realized itself. Man who has undergone this process has resurrected.*

Man who has fully manifested his soul in this world, who has landed completely, can now begin to fly; he is in possession of all powers. He has mastered the physical world. Man who has not landed consciousness of his soul fully still levitates and wanders in the imagination of the astral and the mental world, where all illusions are very much possible. Such people wander in their illusions, fascinated by various contents of their unconscious, while being here in this world. That is why the work of people in the real world is still under the influence of various unconscious contents and influences. Such a man is still helpless. He must, therefore, use tools and learn through work. The whole affair is the reverse, but it introduces a paradox. People who have not yet landed on the ground of reality of this world must work and learn how to master this world. Human souls have still not fully manifested themselves in this world.

Grounding the soul and its actualization in this world is, in reality, man's return to himself, to his authenticity. It happens first in meditation during the *samadhi* state. When we think we are a little outside ourselves, experiencing oblivion of ourselves and identifying with the contents of our thoughts, this is a split. This schizophrenic split away from oneself is even greater when we speak, and greater still when we act. If we recorded ourselves in the heat of the moment, when we speak and act, and later went over the recording, we would appear to ourselves like somebody else, like we were in a dream, like schizophrenics. We would not recognize our voice even. This return to ourselves is what the essence of Christianity is trying to convey through resurrection. It is not going somewhere else, but a return to one's true essence, otherwise known as the soul. An old man dies on the cross so that a new one can be born. The ego and the physical mind die so that we can open ourselves up to the higher mind and consciousness of the soul.

The process of materialization of consciousness of the soul manifests as cultural and civilizational development. It is a negative process, it is the testing of the Omega point, its stretching in all possible ways, experiencing all the wrong ways of functioning in order to become aware of the right ones. Until it hits rock bottom, until it gets crucified on the cross of physical existence, consciousness of the soul cannot be fully itself in this world, it cannot resurrect and exceed this world.

Therefore, the process of resurrection is the opposite of what our twisted mind sees. *The process of resur-*

252

rection is complete awareness of the soul in the body. The body then disappears. God is revealed in us as the eternal present. Then we discover the 'kingdom of heaven' here. We truly transcend the body (resurrect) when we become aware of it, for what it is. Then it disappears as a special phenomenon. What remains is divine consciousness as the only reality. In consciousness of the soul, it has always been the only reality, any other kind is not an option. In other words, *man resurrects when he finally masters the physical world completely, when he learns to do what is right, to put everything in its proper place, when he arranges life to be comfortable for living, when he shows true understanding for everything and everyone.*

If you wish to enter the kingdom of heaven, then very carefully and with the greatest respect, like you would show to God, watch everything (even the tiniest) in this world, and everything around you. Only then will you be able to see that the kingdom of heaven is in you and all around you (the Gospel of Thomas).

All in all, resurrection is overcoming death. The only death is our ignorance and unconsciousness.

MAN IN TEMPLE OR TEMPLE IN MAN

Temples have always been special holy places that are completely different from this world, places which enable man to be nearer divine consciousness, where he can connect with God more easily.

Man connects with God in contemplation in a temple. Contemplation is an individual and inner process of direct cognition, whereas a temple is an outer place that inspires contemplation. They are connected in the following way.

The word 'contemplation' comes from the Latin word contemplatio, which etymologically denotes attaining the highest place (templum), from which seeing is objective and accurate. It is made up of the prefix con, which signifies connectedness, synchronization, and templum, a temple or holy place in which a bond with the divine is made possible, to receive messages from the divine. Since the issue is not some outer temple, but an inner experience, the word 'contemplation' practically means attaining an inner sanctuary, a sublime state in one's being that enables connection with the higher, divine consciousness of the soul, to harmonize with it. It is a change of consciousness to a higher level, transforming one's being into a temple of divine presence.

Several things indicate the following.

Firstly, not all places are alike. Some are more favourable than others, they have a different vibration. Some vibrations uplift our consciousness and some lower it. A temple, by definition, is a place where our consciousness is uplifted.

The very existence of temples as holy places and their apparent difference from their surroundings marks the difference between the holy and the profane, heavenly and earthly, positive and negative. For mankind in the early stages of development, such distinction between the holy and the profane was a simple introduction into the culture of differentiation, everything right from everything wrong.[36] That was an elementary form and the initial stage in differentiation between the conscious and the unconscious. Such differentiation was the foundation of culture. Temples have always been the centres of culture, objects which stood out from all other architecture, the greatest investments of knowledge and skill were put into them, from pyramids to cathedrals, and we owe the most impressive buildings in existence today to the knowledge acquired during the building of temples in the past. Over time, man's knowledge and skills multiplied and perfected, and were used to build famous cathedrals,[37] whereas in modern times this knowledge is installed in smartphones, microchips, and nanotechnology. This is the same process of awareness that keeps getting perfected.

An additional point to be understood about temples and holy places, which also relates to the functioning of the mind, is that the state of consciousness is directly dependent on actions, and not just some place, and actions are directly dependent on the circumstances man is in. We all behave differently in different places and different circumstances. This is due to the fact that we have many Is, not only one. Our I is our current state of consciousness and mind. Since these states tend to change, we have many Is.

Division of our personality into multiple I is conditioned by space and time, because our I shift in space and time. There is a certain space and time when our I manifests. We have one I at work, a different one with our family, a third with our company, we have a different I for every person we socialize with, and yet a completely different one again when we are by ourselves. One special 'I' we have for religious celebrations, and another when we are having fun with somebody or with ourselves. It is enough for us to find ourselves in a certain setting, and the I that corresponds with this setting is activated.

Naturally, our Is are by no means separate, but joined together, giving us the illusion of continuity. We can see them changing only when we change mood, or forget something. Some go on for longer, some are stronger and some are weaker, some seem to have a positive effect because they originate under positive circumstances, and some are negative because they originate under negative circumstances. Man's unconsciousness is a complex fragmentation into a multitude of Is.

What is relevant here is that there is always some 'I' which is closer to man's true being, which is open to consciousness of the higher mind and consciousness of the soul, and through it to divine consciousness. This 'I' should prevail over all the other Is. A conscious and awakened man is the one who has only one 'I', only one personality under all circumstances.

In the same way that our true I (one that brings us closer to ourselves, to our soul) exists, there are places that are closer to divine consciousness. 'Holy places' have an atmosphere in which it is easier for man to open himself up to consciousness of the higher mind and soul, to divine consciousness.

When one kind of energy is constantly added to a certain place, it becomes packed with this energy, and any new person feels and receives this powerful vibration. It helps. It seems to be no coincidence that such places were carefully chosen to be locations where earth's magnetism is the strongest, where lines of magnetic fields intersect. When a ritual is performed in such places and certain emotional energy is input, it begins to affect the wider environment along the lines of earth's magnetism. For the energy and vibration of the ritual to be stronger and to have the maximum effect on its surroundings, it must be performed in places where the meridians of earth's magnetism intersect.

On the surface of the earth, there are energy meridians that resemble those of the human body in the system of acupuncture. Earth's meridians make a grid that forms a pattern. Energy is greatly enhanced in locations where the energy flow intersects. There are places with fewer energy lines and ones with a considerably larger number. Where the greatest number of lines intersect, energy is at its maximum. It has been discovered that these places house ancient temples and megalithic structures. For example, one of the places where a number of earth's lines intersect is Rosslyn Chapel, Stonehenge; another is the Gizeh plateau in Egypt with the pyramids as the energy focus, etc. This can be seen in the image that shows lines of the earth's energy fields.

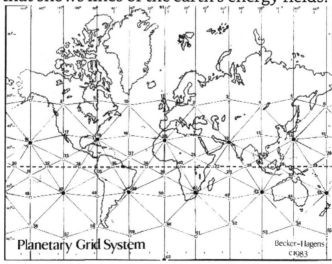

Planetary Grid System

Becker-Hagens
c 1983

The Greatest number of intersections of energy meridians are in places well-known for their magnetic whirlpools and other strange deformations of space and time. The picture shows one such whirlpool in the Bermuda triangle; another in West Africa, in Mauritania, where the Richat Structure is located, a gigantic circular construction; in south Africa one such intersection is on the exact location of a megalithic structure by the name of Adam's calendar (the Blaauboschkraal stone ruins, Mpumalanga); followed by one in south Pakistan in Mohenjo Daro valley, where one of the oldest known civilizations once lived; and the place called Devil's sea located south-east of Japan, known for its similarity to the Bermuda triangle.[38]

There are smaller lines whose intersection gives places of increased energy power, where the temples of Europe are located, and the most visible are in France.

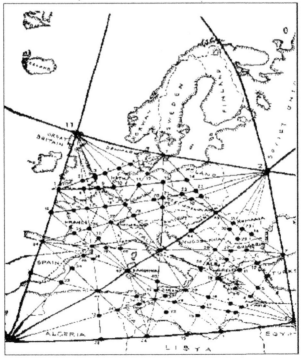

Temples exist to inspire people to be more conscious, more themselves, to have some place where their consciousness can rise above banal mundane issues, and open themselves up to something that is eternal and divine. In temples, man connects with the energy of the Earth, and via this with the sky and the whole of the cosmos.

Temples are necessary for man number one and two, young souls that still need objects, those that find their sanctuary in outer objects. Mature souls find their only true sanctuary within, by connecting to the divine, through meditation.

A multitude of I is not wrong or harmful, quite the contrary; this multitude is necessary for the individual consciousness to be able to express itself in a myriad of ways, or all possible ways. If we had one I only, we would not develop and we would not have a wealth of versatile experiences. The multitude enriches the experience of divine consciousness through individual souls of people. Only those who are unaware of the true nature of the divine, of the fact it manifests itself through a multitude and differences, start conflicts when they face differences. A multitude of religions also provides for a wealth of religious experiences, it is not a mistake in itself. Only unconscious people can create conflict out of difference in religion. One who sees God in every religion knows God truly. He also sees God in everything, in the plethora of all possibilities, in all oppositions as well as above all oppositions.

If believers were as attentive as they are in the temple, if they had only one I in the temple and the street and their home, this world would be paradise. Unfortunately, what they keep doing is projecting the ideal of one I into one God, and behaving in a schizophrenic manner amidst the multitude of their Is.

In temples, prayer is conducted, a spiritual practice of uplifting the consciousness of a split mind toward one, higher mind, and consciousness of the soul. Religious objects help with this.

This practice is performed in meditation with souls that are mature, completely independent of religions and temples. For a mature soul, the body is the only temple.

The first Christian communities in the early centuries of Christianity did not build temples. They called themselves ekklesia, a 'unity of people who think alike', they gathered together as like-minded people and exchanged experiences. That was all. Later, when the Christian movement became political, the first churches were built. At that point, the church was proclaimed to be the 'body of Christ'.

The human body was considered to be the true temple of God because man can only know God within, and God expresses himself the most creatively through man in this world. The oldest temples, such as those in Egypt, were built according to the measures and principles of man.[39] The oblivion that man experiences in the consciousness of his soul, in this Omega point of ours, is reflected in the fact that he became completely unaware of the true nature of his being. That is why he projected his divine essence outward, into outer temples, and he replaced awareness of his divine origin with religions.

Therefore, we can safely say that man started building temples the moment he forgot himself, forgot his true divine nature. It could also be said that he built temples to be a reminder of his true nature he had forgotten about. Maybe it is the most accurate to say that temples exist for those people whose consciousness functions in the first three chakras only.

It's required to extend the consciousness we have in favourable circumstances, such as in a temple, in prayer or meditation, to all other circumstances and activities. This is the function of the fourth, heart chakra. Such a man experiences divine consciousness everywhere, not in temples alone; he sees it as the energy of divine love that is life-giving.

We must never do the opposite, introduce the frustrations of everyday life into a temple and mix them with faith. People whose consciousness resides in the lower chakras usually do this. Such believers reach the conclusion that their faith is the best and the only true one, that all the other infidels should either be conquered and brought to reason, or if that does not prove to be adequate, then killed. In this case, religiousness becomes political and stops being religiousness.

We should always export the consciousness we attain in prayers and temples into the world and everyday living. Never the other way round.

The principles and regulations of ordinary life should never be brought into a temple and used to form our religiousness with.

Religiousness should influence our life, and our life should not influence religiousness.

When we enter the temple we leave our mundane life behind. Entering a temple is a form of drill. When we exit the temple we should give to the world the divine consciousness we attained in the temple. That is what temples are for.

HOW TO EXPERIENCE GOD
AS THE UNCONDITIONAL LOVE

We live at the point that is the exact opposite of the divine Absolute. We have ascertained the reasons why this is so. We often experience the opposite of love here - it could be said that opposites dominate this realm. Life is invariably cruel and tough. However, it is important to understand the nature of the freedom that is present in this world. The fundamental nature of the point opposite of the divine is the complete freedom of everything to manifest itself and to be the way it sees fit. This means that the nature of our world is not particularly evil or good, but is simply free to manifest as everything it can be. *If something is bad, it is so because a conscious effort has not been made to make it better.* Bad things raise our awareness of how we can go about making them better for everyone. The only thing that is of value here is work and the results of work. Such is the principle of consciousness in this dimension. Divine consciousness gets expressed here through action and reaction, through karma, through work and the results of work. Everything bad or imperfect can be corrected and upgraded. The whole of human civilization, throughout all of the past centuries, is an illustration of this. Work makes civilization. In fact, civilization is consciousness applied through the working process; it is a concrete, material reflection of consciousness. A perfect and orderly civilized life is a reflection of divine love.

Divine love does not fall from the sky. It always aspires to manifest itself through man. It is all very simple: if man needs love, then it should be manifested through man, so that it is human love and not 'heavenly'. Heaven acts as a mirror. If we want love, we should be love. If we want our image in the mirror to be happy, we should smile. We have explained that the universe is a hologram, everything is interconnected with everything else. This comes close to saying that the universe is a mirror of consciousness. This means we should always be what we want to be. If we would like to find true love, we should give love first. Because, if we do not know how to give love, how will we know how to receive it? Giving and receiving are two sides of the same coin.

Let us go back in time and remind ourselves of the single 'divine particle' whose vibration creates everything that exists, including ourselves; it is of divine nature, it is everything we do, and everything that happens to us.

The experience of this unity is the experience of divine love. Divine love is not something abstract that happens rarely, on special occasions. Divine love is every kind of love that happens everywhere, in any conscious being capable of love, in every act of kindness, love, and understanding. Sometimes all it takes is a look full of understanding to convey it. These are all fragments and different expressions of one universal divine love.

In the same way as a multitude of consciousnesses does not exist, and each individual consciousness is just an expression of the universal divine consciousness that manifests as outwardly as existence - there is no multitude of different kinds of love; any expression of love is either a minor or major reflection of the one divine love that enables everything. Therefore, if you have ever loved anyone or anything, you have already experienced divine love.

Consequently, we only learn of divine presence through love. Reality can never be truly known without love. Love is the condition without which it is impossible to know reality.

We live in a dimension which is characterized by the dialectics of opposites. This is simply a way in which consciousness manifests here; we mature and learn by experiencing oppositions. Such is the natural order of the world we live in. We experience ultimate opposition here, such as the absence of love. Due to this game of oppositions, we need to experience the lack of love to become more aware of our need and the importance of love. This is the only reason why there is a lack of love, not because it is objectively absent from this world, but to make us aware of its nature, need, and importance. Everything we do in our lives, we do because we need love. Every act of violence we perpetrate as an angry reaction to the lack of love. Love is the only cure for violence and evil.

If we experience a lack of love, it is not because there is none, or because we are not worthy of love; it simply means we should manifest it firstly ourselves. *Divine love has two aspects in this world: one is when we get it from the outside, and the other one is when we manifest it ourselves from within.* We can best understand the two aspects of love by studying the example of children and parents. Children expect and receive unconditional love from their parents, and parents give it. Expecting to receive love from the outside is a childish, immature phase. Our ability to give love to others is a mature phase in human development.

However, the second phase depends on proper understanding of the essence of love, which is its unconditionality. The ability to give love grows to the degree that the love we give is unconditional. This means that we enable existence with our love, instead of pursuing personal interests. Love is immature when it is a form of trade, or if it imposes anything on the loved one. Love is unconditional only if it loves the being as it is, if it helps it to be what it is, its own and free. We want this because the true nature of love is such.

The closest expression of divine love in this world is parental love. A hug of a parent is like the hug of the divine. The same is true for the hug of a child.

Divine consciousness of the soul is best seen in this world in the face of a child. The body of a child is small, the individual mind and personality have not developed yet, therefore the big consciousness of the soul manages to manifest itself more easily - there is nothing to overshadow it. The aura of a child shines with energy of the soul. This is what attracts us to children - not only because they are small - we are attracted by the seriousness and dignity many small children manifest in certain moments, which exceeds the consciousness of an adult. We are attracted to their creativity, which always comes from consciousness of the soul. Grown-ups have alienated themselves from the consciousness they had as children, because they have toughened up in their physical mind and personality. Adults have a more radiant personality. Therefore, when we become like small children, we will go back to the divine consciousness of the soul.

Children teach us the lesson of unconditional love. They ask it of us and in doing so they teach us to manifest it. Children teach us more than we teach them. When a child gives you their little hand, full of trust, to lead them through life, a truckload of responsibility is suddenly on your shoulders, you cannot swerve, you cannot do what your little mind and ego would like, but you have to act properly and be responsible. The most righteous and the most responsible you can be. Divine consciousness teaches us through a child's being, through the exchange of giving and receiving love. And both parties grow and mature by giving and receiving love. Besides, we owe our lives to lovemaking. Therefore, it is not unusual that our whole lives revolve around the issue of love.

If you have no one to give you love, then you should change that by being the one who gives love. Unconditionally. This is the other way for us to find true love in our lives. The first way, to receive love only, is the way of a young and immature ego. Giving unconditional love is the mature and creative way, unselfish; it is the overcoming of ego. If we observe it from the perspective of the limited mind and ego, we think we must get love first, in order to give it. The higher mind and consciousness of the soul already know that we have love, that existence rests on divine love; all we have to do is to manifest it. Some force activates our heartbeat continuously. Are we grateful for that? We breathe continuously. Do we show gratitude for the fact that air exists? The Sun shines. Are we grateful for that? It is all a reflection of the divine love that enables existence and most of the time we are not even aware of it. Religious people in ancient times were aware of this. They showed their appreciation to the Sun for shining. But not today. In modern times religion is theology only.

By giving love we actually get it, we discover that we have always had it. We enjoy when we have love to give. In fact, our maturation, overcoming our mind and ego, is in realizing that unconditional love is here and now, readily available as the source of everything. Mature people always manifest it, even in the most difficult of circumstances. Difficult circumstances exist in our life to teach us to manifest love always, not only when we receive it or when it suits us. For this reason, true love is always unconditional.

We must understand what the term 'unconditional' regarding love truly means. It is the kind of love that asks for nothing, but gives itself unconditionally, which is identical with existence and life. While living and doing all sorts of things, absorbed in our thoughts and illusions, we fail to notice the amazing intricacies of life in us and all around us, the enormous effort put into everything which maintains life. We deal with our petty issues of everyday life while at the same time existing in the divine and complex universe. Each cell of our body is more complex than the Mercedes automobile industry, divine consciousness was necessary for each cell to be created, divine consciousness is necessary to keep it running, divine consciousness connects the functioning of all cells in the symbiosis of our body. This very complexity of life is the true face of divine love; the more effort and creativity was put into it, the more love is present in it. What do we usually think about when we are suffering? The only cure for any, even the greatest suffering is an awareness of the nature of our being and divine power, and all the creativity that life holds in every single moment. In other words, insight into reality removes all suffering.

When you are in deep sorrow, do not pray to God to save you, but find a textbook on biology and read about the functioning of a cell. It will help you.[40]

To understand the presence of divine love we must always be aware of the 'divine particle' everything is made up of; or to simplify matters, everything that exists is the vibration of the divine being itself, its conscious intent. Although it is quite useful to be well-informed, to be aware at all times, direct experience of permanent awakening is necessary. I can go back to the moment when I experienced it: I went to fetch a glass of water. At that moment I saw water as a conscious form of the divine, as the element which chose that form to enable life for me, to quench my thirst. I saw all things around me, all the elements, the floor I stood on, the building I lived in, the walls, all the things useful and necessary for life as a conscious, living form that exists with conscious intention in the shape it does, to make my life possible, and for me to become aware of them. All of them were becoming aware of themselves through me.

I can recall a detail from a documentary into water research, where one incident based on a true story involving castaways seemed very vivid. They floated aboard a boat for days; there was no more drinking water left. One of them, out of desperation, took a handful of seawater and prayed over it; he asked the water to turn itself into drinking water to save their lives. Afterward, he tasted it. It was no longer salty, it had become normal drinking water. It answered their prayers because it was conscious creation. Of all the elements, water is the closest to consciousness, it can respond the fastest to a conscious request, it reacts to our feelings and words because it is mobile, fluid. Other elements feel the same as water, but due to their grosser nature they are unable to respond quickly enough in a way that we can see. This incident also shows the impact our consciousness has on our environment, similar to telekinesis, but more than anything it shows that we exist in a conscious environment which enables our lives, owing to conscious intention. Although we live in a big world and move freely, we are as taken care of as a child in its mother's womb, like fish in water. Divine love is all around.

Some say that this same nature kills us, water drowns us, not every castaway will have seawater turn into drinking water. Maybe this is so because we have not asked for it with our whole being, or we have done something wrong, because we do not experience the outside world as something conscious whose purpose is to serve us, but rather we view it as an alienated enemy environment. Therefore, that is how it responds to us. Nature reflects our consciousness like a mirror; such is the characteristic of the holographic universe. I remember one more event that happened a long time ago. A child managed to crawl in between the grids of a lion's cage in a zoo. It went, overjoyed, to stroke the lion's mane. It came out unscathed and equally happy.

The divine whole sees us in a much wider context than we see ourselves. We are attached to the body we have and we judge from its perspective, and it sees our soul, to which this body is only a dream. Death is not a negative occurrence, at all, no matter how important life was. From the highest perspective, life and death are like batting an eye. That is why we die so easily if we do not act with our whole being, if we do not use all of our potential.

Dr. Murdo MacDonald-Bayne, a doctor with the experience of spiritual enlightenment, in his childhood and with complete connectedness of his mind with consciousness of the soul, managed to slow a fall from a high place using his conscious intention, which helped him to survive. All wonders are possible when we have consciousness of the soul, with which we see existence as conscious and living, as our extended being.

Divine love is all around, it is everything that exists. We are always in it, and it enables us in all possible ways. If we suffer at the hands of something, it is only because we failed to use the full potential of consciousness, we did not act properly because we were in conflict with nature.

Maybe we as people, in our alienation of the Omega point, are the only place where divine love is scarce, where it still needs to be discovered and manifested through us.

The omnipresence of the divine was hinted at in religions using words of admiration and veneration toward God. A relationship with God is always accompanied by veneration. Once you become aware of the true nature of the divine, you will feel veneration toward the glass of water you are holding in your hand, toward everything for that matter, to the same degree you admire God.

The 'unconditional' in love means the absolute, what exists always, irrelevant of everything else, something that cannot be threatened by anything. Unconditional means it is always available, without any conditions. It means it does not impose itself, it exists like the freedom of choice. We can only attain unconditional love in this dimension of ours through the freedom of choice of our individual consciousness, through our will to express it – as well as to receive and accept it.

If we do not have love, as individuals and as a nation, it does not mean there is no love, but rather that we have not chosen that option yet.

Unconditional means that divine love is something we can accept and express with our will and consciousness. Acceptance and expression must not depend on anything, or on one another. Therefore, the unconditionality of divine love here means that it is connected with consciousness and will, with actions. Although divine love exists as existence itself, like the air that gives us life, it depends on conscious acceptance, which is possible only by understanding its nature, or by conscious expression, which is also possible only by understanding its nature. In both cases, divine love is connected with consciousness and with actions.

The final understanding of the term 'unconditional' in divine love shows that it exists independently of all conditions and circumstances. This means that if conditions are unfavourable and hard, if our life situation can be described as living in hell, if we are surrounded by hatred and alienation, if love is to be found nowhere, our job is to create it independently of all these circumstances that constitute our current reality. In fact, then it is needed the most. Moreover, it was not there, because nobody had manifested it. Unconditional love is independent of all conditions. When negative circumstances and difficulties surround us, divine love seeks to manifest itself through man. When conditions are fortunate and pleasing, divine love descends on us like sunlight. The beauty of life and bliss are the manifestation of divine love; we are blessed when we recognize the fact that divine love is all that exists.

Therefore, this 'unconditional' is two sides of the same coin: when love comes from the outside, and when it manifests through man and his deeds. It descends by itself when there are no obstacles in its path, when the weather is bright and shiny, when there are no dark clouds in sight. However, when the weather is gloomy and bad, when there is a shortage of love, nonetheless love must manifest itself, there is no other way. Man must manifest it regardless of conditions and circumstances, despite everything – unconditionally. There was no love because man did not manifest it. He created hell for himself, as he was in the business of doing deeds contrary to love, contrary to life.

If our experience is that there is no divine love, this is because we have not become aware of it as the nature of existence itself and for this reason we are unable to manifest it through us, through our acts of love. Divine love never imposes because it is omnipresent, like the ground we walk on, like the air we breathe. It is waiting for us to become aware of it and manifest it through ourselves. Outwardly it is manifested and developed in the form of nature so it can receive its most concrete embodiment, a human shape, and achieve understanding as the final result. Nowhere does divine love manifest itself so effectively, beautifully and clearly as through man, in human deeds of love and understanding.

The most beautiful phenomena in this world are created by people who love. People who are merely on the lookout for love invariably cause situations which display immaturity and lead to destructiveness.

If you manage to manifest love despite circumstances, despite even the most adverse circumstances, your love will be unconditional and as such it will have divine properties. If you manage to create a love like this while you are in hell, divine love will flood you automatically, like a reflection in a mirror.

If a person has never experienced unconditional love, if he grew up in hard and cruel conditions, it does not mean love is intended for the lucky few, and never for him. Quite the contrary, it is unconditional, and is not intended for anyone in particular - it is always available. If you have never experienced it, it only means it is your task to create it even though you never had it, and to do so unconditionally. Be love, spread love although you did not have it, unconditionally – for the very reason that you never had it. A love like that, which comes from our goodwill only, is truly unconditional and is the closest to divine love. The love we receive is always weaker in strength because it may be overshadowed by interfering circumstances and insufficient understanding. But the love we manifest from ourselves is much nearer and clearer to us, it is much closer to the original divine love. Therefore, if you wish to experience real divine love, manifest it from yourselves, do not sit around waiting, because what you will end up getting will always be second best, it will depend on the presence of the one who gives you love. The other party who is giving you love had to create it themselves.

This is very important as an example of love we give to those who do not have it. A little reassurance is all it takes for them to receive encouragement to express true love themselves. If they never feel it, it will be hard for them to believe that it exists at all. That is why you should always give the example of love: somebody is bound to notice it, and who knows when to pass it on. Expressing love is very important, like food and water. In fact, food and water are the necessities of life, while love itself is the purpose of our life, whether we are aware of it or not. Without food, we die, and without love, we kill ourselves, in all possible ways.

Love is also important for learning and cognition. Love is another name for cognition. Nothing can be known without love. Love is the energy of cognition, what attracts us to know it all the way through. Love is cognition that surpasses the mind. The mind is logical and sees only what the senses perceive. Love is consciousness that exceeds space and time, that exceeds the senses and broadens perception into infinity. Our emotions are the intelligence that surpasses the physical body; with it we see what the physical eyes do not see, and we understand what the mind cannot.

Love connects everything the limited mind divides. There is no conflict that love cannot solve. All conflicts originate as a consequence of a lack of love and understanding, that only love can produce.

The consciousness of our love broadens our horizons and merges what appears as incompatible – and in doing so it uplifts us to divine unity. That is where it originally comes from.

The only way for man to have divine love in his life is to give it himself. Often people who did not grow up in a warm, loving environment are not aware of its importance, and do not know how to give it sincerely. They remain narcissistic till the day they die. Those who never had it but were able to materialize it from nothing, to manifest it from themself, have truly known the greatness of love and always have it round themself. Since he has it within, he can never lose it. There is no other way to be surrounded by love except to create it ourselves. It is what is expected of us.

This transition from immature and passive expectations of love, to receive it always, to the mature phase, when we learn to give it despite difficult circumstances, unconditionally, is the most important and the most critical transition for every man, but for all of mankind as well.

In fact, the development of human civilization depends on this alone: how to arrange the world to meet the needs of man, and to make it a world with love in abundance.

RELIGIOUSNESS
AND THE DEVELOPMENT OF CIVILIZATION

The development of mankind should be viewed in the same light as the development of a child. Children cannot make judgments and decisions for themselves because they do not have sufficient life experience, hence, they need guidance, help to encourage them to grow, a proper upbringing. Any parent knows how difficult it is to make a child switch from playful imagination into physical reality, to make them think in practical terms, to connect the concrete with the abstract, to stop spontaneously doodling on paper and start learning to write proper letters; to put belongings in their place and not throw them about.

The same principle applies to mankind. It develops in pretty much the same way: it learns to create everything it needs, to recognize phenomena and the laws of nature. Religions have always provided much-needed help in rearing nations, and the whole of mankind. They had an educational purpose. They represented a father figure, which mankind needed desperately.

The oldest forms of religiousness had taboos and tribal laws. All religions have a very strong ethical component, but the educational function of religions is best seen in the so-called ethical religions, Judaism and Islam. The most important aspect of these religions involve coaching their followers on what to do, from the moment they wake up till the time they go to bed, even how to relate to their dreams (there are situations where they are forbidden to interpret their dreams). Likewise, they are advised what to wear and how to behave in their everyday lives, down to the last detail. Everything is prescribed for them, from menu and fashion to the highest cosmogonic issues. They have a reply to every question, written in some 'holy book' that must never be questioned. Punishments for disobedience are severe, tolerance barely existent; if conversion does not succeed, a death sentence will follow. For young and immature souls, ethical instructions of this kind were necessary.

There are religious practices that organize life for more advanced and mature souls, such as Christianity in all its forms. Apart from rules on how to live, which have been reduced to only 'ten commandments', there is a little more freedom in the choice of clothing and behaviour, while the psyche is still trained by means of dogma.

All of this was a big help for people learning over time how to live in an orderly and harmonious way, as much as possible, and to learn to lead disciplined, hardworking lives. Such organization had a mirror effect on the environment and cities became orderly and well-planned.

There have always been so-called clashes of civilizations, which are in fact conflicts between the varying degrees of states of consciousness, work ethic, order, and discipline, the ability to organize life in a civilized and meticulous manner, to make settlements and cities suitable for a cultured life – as opposed to immature state of consciousness and culture that permit lack of order, work, and discipline, that can be seen in the way they organize their towns and cities, void of any development over long periods of time.

Such clashes of civilizations are still very much present today.

Maybe you have not been informed of it, but this planet is destined for development. Civilizations and nations that do not take part in the development of material and spiritual culture, whose basic intention is to remain in their vegetative state, unchanged for thousands of years, who make do with comfortable living, or worse yet, make do at the expense of others, will not have their way. They will be prevented in their game.

The reason for this tendency in man is not only the immaturity of young souls but the nature of soulfulness too. Spiritual people see divine consciousness all round. They do not see a need to change or perfect anything. They see that God is perfect, and they choose to surrender themselves to him. They sit in the cool shade all day long, drinking tea in between prayers (while women do all the work). Therefore, some form of coercion is necessary to make them work and organize their material environment. The problem is that coercion often uses wars and guns as a last resort, and sloths also tend to defend themselves with guns, claiming their God told them not to do anything. God decides everything, all they need to do is submit to him. We have mentioned this previously. The right measure must be found to balance this out; too much coercion will make people lose their soulfulness, consciousness of the soul, and without this, everything is lost. All endeavour present in this world is for making sure that the divine consciousness of our souls finds a way to express its creativity better.

The truth is, the majority of problems in this world exist because the right balance has still not been found between various forms of coercion and manifesting spirituality.

Systems that force people to grow are institutionalized, and some of the greatest are religions.

In the first place, there is the Roman church or Catholicism, then all the Protestant churches.

The influence of religion on material development and work I am able to describe quite vividly from my own experiences, which will make sense to everybody.

I spent one summer holiday in Paris, in the early eighties of the past century. I was wandering through the city streets and, at one point, found myself on the Eiffel Tower. On the second platform, I was waiting for my lift, and a group of tourists confused me for a moment, jostling and bustling around me, so much so that I stopped at the entrance to let them walk through. An elderly gentleman in uniform, who was in charge of the movement of the elevator, grabbed hold of me and forcefully pulled me inside the elevator at the exact moment when the iron door was closing. He saved me from being caught in the heavy door. I do not know what would have become of me if that had happened, I believe there was no sensor to block the door at that time, but my prospects would not have been so good. I thanked the gentleman for helping me while the other tourists laughed.

Now when I describe the awareness of work ethic, I cannot but remember this gentleman who was only doing his job, completely invisibly, but at the right moment he did the right thing without hesitation. Up until this incident, my life was relatively carefree, relaxed, in a favourable setting; I was reading poetry and philosophy, I had never had a job before and never gave it much thought. Work and responsibility were not my focus at the time. This event was very eye-opening. I saw the city in a different light from then on. In the Holy Heart basilica (Sacre Coeur) on Montmartre, I felt the chill of its dark walls (at least it was dark back then), and ascetic wooden benches as I listened to the priest speaking. Next to the basilica, I enjoyed watching the flower beds and feeding sparrows from my hand. The contrast between the inside of the church and the outside setting of the whole city was huge. Every detail in the city was artistically well-executed, every bench, lamp post, and bridge were an ode to creativity and beauty, nothing was only utilitarian in its expression; intelligent design seeped through every building. The Eiffel Tower itself serves no purpose, functionally it is unnecessary and pointless, it is the single most needless object in the world, but it is the most attractive tourist destination in the world, because it was created to glorify an invisible sense, aesthetics, and aspiration toward higher realms. Its structure is perfectly positioned to overcome Earth's gravity. This tower is a sculpture which with its vertical composition expresses an aspiration of overcoming the conditionality of this world, which is what we generally call culture. It is the greatest artistic object in the world.

Notre Dame is also impersonal and cold inside, only its walls reveal invisible architectural ingeniousness. But on the outside, it invokes admiration as an integrated part of the city's structure. This city appears to depict the unity of consciousness at its best - or, at least, it aspires toward this goal. Cities are places where roads, people, experience, and information intersect, where awareness of existence is collectively developed and perfected. It is the definition of civic political culture.

Eastern Europe paints quite a different picture. Orthodox churches are majestically decorated, priests are ornate beyond belief, contents from the Bible are painted on all walls in breathtaking frescoes, church rituals are magnificent – yet the environment surrounding churches is untidy and often dilapidated. Often there is nothing but mud around the churches. City planning and buildings and roads maintenance never became part of the living culture in these countries; law and order are not high on their list of priorities. Père-Lachaise cemetery is orderly and beautiful, like a small town; Orthodox cemeteries are untidy and muddy. Most cities are like this because the work ethic of the people living in them is like this. Naturally, there are many wonderful cities and squares, but if you leave the centre of Moscow for example, you will find ugly places to live in. What has been built to be of use is regularly maintained. In fact, everything that has been engineered across Russia and Eastern Europe that has a positive effect (from architecture to government policy, and in accordance with modern standards) has been done under the influence of Western Europe. Unfortunately, this is not enough. For example, in Russia, the rule of law is missing. Unlike the Anglo-Saxon and continental legal system, Russia today knows 'intuitive law'. This means that there are written laws, but everybody knows they do not have to go by the book; additionally, there are unwritten laws everybody abides by because they know there is real power behind them.[41]

In China they do not have even this. The communist party uses feudal mentality to impose digital slavery on the masses. In India, almost every desk clerk sees himself as the master of karma of all his clients. He decides what working hours to choose for himself daily.

In the East, too much emphasis is put on the symbolic expression of faith, and too little on culture and all other aspects of life.

Muslims have this blown out of proportion. Mosques have been built splendidly, stone rosettes seem to have landed there directly from the imagination of sculptors, but the streets of the biggest Muslim cities do not even have a sewage system. They have some advancements only because of the influence of the West. You can get Coxsackie bacteria from water even in the best hotels (I was a witness on one such occasion).

Further in the East, this discrepancy between religious ideals and quality of everyday life is even more evident. India is probably the best example of a negative relationship between religiousness and living culture. Religiousness and living culture are pointing in opposite directions there, as if one exists at the expense of the other. They not only have no sewage system, but they also do not have toilets. (Only recently have they started building them.)

City planning is a far cry in many other religions and cultures also; in some of them it does not even exist in the form of an idea, let alone in fact. This is due to the fact that religiousness is not properly understood and applied. Only when man becomes aware of their unity, will he live like in heaven, like on Elysian Fields in Paris.[42]

Any employer knows what we are talking about here, how hard it is to find a good worker, and even harder to make him work well always.

To avoid any confusion, it is not primitivism that is the issue here, but the immaturity of young souls. They can often be positive; those people are joyous and playful, spontaneous, and cordial, but they are like small children and it is hard to force them to be orderly, hard-working, and self-disciplined.

There are two reasons for lack of order, work, and discipline in people. The first is karmic immaturity and there is no cure for this. They are simply primitive and cannot learn. However, some mature souls find it hard to adapt themselves to order, work, and discipline, which is necessary for the building of this world, but since they are more soulful, they are closer to consciousness of the soul, and therefore more laid back and careless; they would rather play and have fun than work all day. Even when they work, it is hard to discipline them, to make them respect a certain business code; in the workplace they cannot distinguish between what is private and what is professional. This often has a soothing and positive effect on a tense working atmosphere, but often enough it also impedes work. Such soulful people, who are like children, should be distinguished from the first type of karmically immature, who simply do not have the intelligence for work and creation. People who have consciousness of the soul, but not the discipline to support it are often ingenious and creative. However, they are that way only individually, not collectively. They are very attracted to discipline and creative endeavours, but they are the minority.

All discipline related to work is so individual consciousness of advanced souls can spread into the whole community, for spontaneity (which is the characteristic of young and immature beings) to be regulated.

It is very important to find a balance between manifesting soulfulness and the need for discipline. In the early stages of capitalism, people (children included) had to work in hellish conditions. Over time, working conditions have gradually improved, but they have still not come to an ideal balance – the need for work discipline to be maintained, and to make it beneficial for all people. It is hard to achieve such a discipline, but it must be made into an ideal.

Living culture and arranging the living environment through work, order, and discipline is the primary characteristic of Catholicism. We know what Catholic schools are like.

There is a problem in Western Europe too, amidst the cultures that deal with the development of civilizations. They go to the other extreme. The immaturity of young souls is suppressed by an overly disciplined approach. This is visible in Anglo-Saxon culture, and that of Protestants, Nordics, and Germanic people. Material culture is the most developed there, but soulfulness and heartiness suffer as a result. These people are cold and pragmatic, alienated amongst themselves, and more lonely than ever. Soulfulness is best expressed in literature and films,[43] and in family relationships to a certain degree.

Utilitarianism and pragmatism are of use for work to be well-organized, for everyone to accept their role and weight of responsibility in the division of labour. However, if suppression of spontaneity and soulfulness goes to an extreme, the work itself becomes futile because it does not serve man; man is a slave to work and to owners of big capital, corporations that do not distinguish man from a common tool; they walk over everything human to achieve their goal, which is not even in the interest of people.

Civilization without soul kills people and nature.

Still, such pressure in the West crystallized the question of consciousness of the soul, more accurately the secret of life. Consciousness of the soul is the biggest issue today, as never before in history, quantum physics merged with spirituality. Some of the most renowned advocates for the synthesis of ancient knowledge and spirituality with new science are: Michael Talbot, Lynne McTaggart, Dr. sc. Amit Goswami, Bruce H. Lipton, Gregg Braden, Rupert Sheldrake, Fritjof Capra, Neale Donald Walsch, Eckhart Tolle. In their words, the essence of religiousness is expressed in terms of modern science, in a way which completely eliminates alienation of people from one another and consciousness of the soul.

The heart of the problem is to find a balance between order and chaos.

Soulful people are representatives of the transcendental consciousness of the soul which is based on freedom and creativity. That is why it is so hard for them to adjust to order, work, and discipline. Creativity never comes from order but from freedom, from mess and chaos. Order and chaos have always existed intermittently, like yin and yang, because life is full of both the unpredictable and predictable, the known and the unknown. Chaos is not destruction and evil, but the freedom that breeds creativity and new ideas. *Order needs occasional chaos to allow creation. Chaos needs order so it does not end up as destruction and the negation of life.* Order and chaos are the Alpha and the Omega of life. *This happens on this planet and in this society, in space and time.* There are people, cultures, and civilizations that bring order and development, and others who bring chaos. There are times when order rules, and times when chaos rules, and they change all the time. There are territories on planet Earth where chaos dominates, and territories where order dominates. *The former needs the latter.*

It is not hard to see that truly soulful people find it easy to adapt themselves to work and they enrich any type of work with the utmost creativity. They can see that order helps them express their soulfulness through work more creatively.

Therefore, the main task of development of the world is to help soulful people act in a more orderly and disciplined way, to learn to work diligently, and not for the dictatorship of discipline to be imposed at all costs, like the elite in the West are trying to do now.

The upbringing of people cannot be performed by churches and religion only, the normal worldly life of ordinary people should also be included. The worldly domain of the aristocracy and secret societies took upon themselves the raising of mankind, using coercion and duress. Aristocracy exists with the idea to set a good example for people to look up to, with their behaviour and looks. Kings, princes, and princesses have always been idealized. They were, at least in the beginning, the role models people should look up to. However, some of them have forgotten their original purpose and become self-willed degenerates who go on parading in adorned costumes as though they were in the middle ages. Their educational purpose is long gone now, everything is reduced to rituals and parades; in modern times, they are idols for mediocrities.

Still, they managed to do something. For example, we in part owe the layout and development of modern cities to them. Victorian England saw the first multistory buildings, the first built-in toilets (which sadly exploded at first due to accumulated gases that stank horribly, until some Lord came up with how to solve the problem with pipe curvature), steps were not always of the same size and people tripped over and broke their necks; this has at long last been perfected. They initiated industrialization and the development of the modern world. The economy is entirely under the control of aristocracy, which owns all the corporations and banks, which also form coercion and duress and are still a long way away from humaneness and fairness, but without the free market and competition of goods, services, and large capital, there would be no development in the modern world.

The role of ethical religions has also been modified over time; they have not kept up with the development of civilization, they have not managed to change, and gradually they became out of tune with modern times. Ethics in religion had its purpose: to teach people normal behaviour and life. When people collectively rose above the situation found in previous centuries and started having quality lives, it was because they became aware of what to do themselves and what not; but now those same religions prove to be an obstacle more than guidelines for future growth.

The chief characteristic of modern times is the destruction of old religious concepts while embracing new customs of living. Globalism was introduced by the informational connection of mankind via the Internet. The Internet destroyed the old forms of religiousness. It rendered them obsolete. More than anything, it brought to the surface all of the lies and deceptions most religious institutions use. Information does not have physical obstacles like it used to.

Religions that have suffered the most are conservative religions like Islam, Judaism, and Orthodoxy. In the previous centuries, they offered true sanctuary and safety to immature people, they gave them valuable lessons, but nowadays the quantity of knowledge and the availability of information have brought forth the advantage that people are now capable of learning and raising their level of awareness by themselves; they develop an inner compass and they know what to do and what not to. They do not need some Semitic God to boss them around.

A clash between western civilization that advocates complete freedom in everything, and Islam, Orthodoxy, even Orthodox Judaism that offer safety in tradition is taking place before our eyes. However, their safety is mechanical and prevents the development of human awareness that enjoys challenges and the freedom to experience everything it can experience. Young souls fear freedom like this, for good reason; they feel this is a diversion that could lead them down the wrong path. That is why they crave the safety of traditional religions where everything is written out for them what to do so that they do not have to start thinking for themselves. Nonetheless, such safety cannot last forever because eventually it will hinder the future development of mankind.

A form of coercion is required to make young souls leave their comfort zone of traditional religions and the dictatorship of ethics they provide. Let us hope the element of pressure will not have to be a third world war.[44]

Man's development begins as a passive accumulation of rules of what is right and what is not, and ends with man's full awareness of the facts, ascertained using his own mind and without any outside assistance. He can do this only if he connects with consciousness of the higher mind and consciousness of the soul. At that point, he has complete freedom to act in accordance with his will because this is the only way for him to perfect his will and knowledge, by facing the consequences of his actions. When he manages to perfect himself, only then does he connect himself with the divine consciousness.

Man can never connect with divine consciousness by following authority blindly, because he is not in possession of his will.

Only when, through connection with the higher mind, man has his will, a completely sound will, only then will he be truly free, and then divine consciousness can act without obstruction because the will of man is completely harmonized with the will of the divine. God acts freely only via a completely free man whose will has been harmonized with the divine.

The key factor for manifesting consciousness of the soul in this world is the freedom to act, freedom for man to be completely aware of what he is doing, and, accordingly, to start making decisions on his own. That is a way for consciousness of the soul to be manifested, and via the consciousness of the soul, divine consciousness itself to manifest. There is no other way. That is why New Age and globalization insist on all the rights and freedoms of man to be implemented.

And so we come to the point that the end goal of all religions cannot be accomplished in the religions themselves; they must disappear to make way for a worldly life, while the worldly life should refrain from savagery and rampage and continue to be a worthy successor of religious ideals and aspirations. Worldly life should offer the freedom every individual soul needs to be able to express itself properly.

The first phase of worldly life is rampage, freedom for the sake of freedom, especially the lowest drives; a rebellious demolition of all the limitations religion has imposed on people. This is the current phase of our development. A higher form of worldly life will be when freedom and consciousness are properly understood, and when they get the right direction, aimed at achieving the purpose of existence, the same goal religions aspired to long ago when they were at their best.

Therefore, worldly life must be an upgrade to religious life, to enable the realization of the goal of religions, and religious life should be free from all the boundaries of faith and dogma and identical to the ideal worldly life.

When they become perfect, religions and worldly life will in no way be different.

Until such perfection happens, there will be conflicts because this process is neither small nor simple; additionally, it is quite slow because the levels of consciousness between people vary. Some are pulling forward and others pull back; there is always someone with a better solution, but if the solution is based on a 'better' interpretation of the 'holy scriptures', instead of encouraging better consciousness of an individual, it will deepen the conflict.

Maybe this manual will help facilitate better understanding and harmonization in the ongoing change.

DEMONISM
AND THE DOCTRINE OF AWAKENING

We must draw a clear line between authoritative but educational demonism – which permeates all the lower forms of Judeo-Christian tradition and all of its sects, together with all of the polytheistic pagan religions – and the doctrine of awakening to which systems like early Buddhism and Sânkhya belong, (Patanjali's) Yoga, (philosophic) Taoism, and the esoteric traditions of Sufism.

Educational demonism entails all the religious traditions based on rituals, on institutionalized and dogmatic interpretations of revelations received from the outside, from higher, 'divine' forces or by prophecy, which are all authoritative and dogmatic and contain either some mention of sacrifice, or offering sacrifices, real or symbolic, or impose a victim mentality on man. All of this demonism is used by rulers when they work on stretching the Omega point to its maximum.

The doctrine of awakening contains all of the practices that drive man to awaken from unconscious naturalness, and liberate himself from ignorance and being a slave to the forces of nature, even the highest, a practice which is conveyed directly and personally because they enable him to experience the presence of the divine consciousness himself. The doctrine of awakening is, therefore, based on spirituality, which is a result of man's maturity alone and can be regarded rightfully as the authentic and the only one that is appropriate for man - the human one. Demonism, on the other hand, is based on influences which come from the outside, which are imposed by some 'higher force' and which must be accepted through collective imitation, drill, or force. Such 'spirituality' is pseudo-spirituality and all the religions based on it are pseudoreligions. History, which is packed full of wars between such religions, is the best indicator of the inhumane character of such 'spirituality'.

The doctrine of awakening represents those truths that are revealed by personal maturity and working on oneself, always in a unique way. Demonism represents those 'truths' which came from the outside, ready-made and unchangeable, which the law imposes on everybody collectively (such 'truths' often get dictated by some Draconian God).

The doctrine of awakening (Buddhism) invites man to become aware of the highest reality himself, because Buddhism considers man to be capable of such an undertaking. It makes man an active participant in realizing the divine purpose. Demonism always makes man passive and negative by making him feel guilty or sinful, it teaches that man suffers from 'original sin' and is therefore incapable of being aware of the highest reality, he can only be a servant or a slave. Reality is only what some higher entities or authorities present as reality, what always comes as ready-made from the outside, and what is written and learned by heart as tradition, dogma, or law.

That is the basic difference between demonism and man's authentic spirituality. Demonism is always *received* passively, outwards, and passed down through tradition and institution (church), while authentic spirituality is manifested individually, it is *created* in the process of individuation, as personal maturity (that is to say, as a mature person), it is attained through direct experience and complete participation in the highest reality of existence and sense. Demonic faith is always determined by nation (tribe) and territory, its tradition no different from nationalism. That is why demonic 'spirituality' is always violent and exclusive, while the spirituality of an awakened person is universal and cosmic, it is gentle and accepts everybody with love, regardless of religious (and other psychomental) convictions, it sees and loves only man himself, and not his metaphysical illusions. Reality is manifested through an enlightened man; he radiates spirituality like a star radiates light, he expresses it with humour and freedom, while the demonic believer always looks like a servant or a slave, or an advocate of 'divine truth,' or a politician at best. He accepts 'reality' with his mind only, he learns by heart what he thinks is reality, while an awakened man has become a reality which is the result of the being itself, of every man and all life (Luke, 17:20-21).

The teaching of Jesus is the doctrine of awakening, but later, after the founding of the church, it was turned into demonism. It is important to know the first three levels of all the great religions (Judaism, Christianity, Islam, and Mahayana Buddhism) belong to demonism, while their higher, esoteric levels point to enlightenment (a mystical overcoming of everything).

Both parts are necessary. Everything has its reason.

We all in ourselves constantly confuse these two forms of existence, learning and performing actions. Sometimes we are obsessed, sometimes awake and sensible. Essentially, demonism and awakening are two states of consciousness, passive and active. One tempts and stimulates the other, like Alpha and Omega. Therefore, demonism and awakening can be viewed in this light, as the Alpha and the Omega of our consciousness and religiousness.

RELIGIOUSNESS, FOLKLORE AND CHURCHES

The difficulty in telling demonism and the doctrine of awakening apart is partly due to the influence of tradition and folklore.

Turning religious experience into (national) tradition is the lowest form of living. It is then folklore, not spirituality. Many 'religious' people today identify national mythology, magical ritualism, and folklore with the religion they have belonged to since birth. Tradition is always an imitation, and as such represents the lowest form of the experience of existence. It is a natural way to regulate the behaviour of an unconscious man, it informs him that certain conduct, belief, and even style of clothing have stood the test of time and are therefore error proof. Constant repetition of such a model creates a habit, through which man acquires his identity in society and the world.

All traditions (religious and social) exist to the degree that man lacks identity in himself, in his Self, in the consciousness of the soul that reveals existence the way it truly is.

Man does not know himself as a unique personality in the universe, as long as his mind is spontaneously turned to the outside, fascinated by objects. He attains vague awareness of his existence using outer molds constructed by traditional ways, language, and belief systems above all else, also territory, tribe, nation, and even traditional costumes.

The less integrated people are as individuals, as whole persons in themselves, the more they identify with a nation, tribe, or tradition.

The less they have of themselves, the more they are in need of some outer form of identification, according to some traditional pattern.

The less they see themselves as human beings, suitable for divine consciousness, the more they fight each other over differences in faith and tradition.

It is wonderful to see people from different traditions that love and respect each other. They, in the best way, manifest their human nature, their soul. Then their religion achieves its purpose.

Spiritual evolution moves toward man's direct self-knowledge, toward liberation from the mold of traditional conditioning.

However, traditions have always been turned too easily into institutions.

Apart from physiological needs, people have an equally strong need for a spiritual sense in life. This need on the collective plane is fulfilled by institutional religions, churches. The key elements of life, such as birth, weddings, death, dates of historical significance (religious holidays), must be connected to a higher, cosmic aspect to receive their spiritual purpose. This job is done by religious institutions in the form of symbolic rites and rituals because *symbolic and ritual imitation is the only way to satisfy the illusion of spiritual fulfillment on the collective plane.*

In the pyramidal structure of society, its lower part, the wide foundation with the greatest percentage of people, those who cannot directly and personally know spiritual truths, have their spiritual needs met in a symbolic way, by ritual and collective imitation. Churches satisfy these needs, they are completely made up of symbols and rituals. Therefore, churches are institutions of socio-political character, but not spiritual. The church is a service for mass consumption and the manipulation of people, not a spiritual institution, and as such it is important and necessary; the vast majority of people have use of it, if for nothing else then for inspiration on the path to spirituality, keeping faith and a reminder for ethics and morality.

True spiritual realization is possible only as a personal experience, never as a collective. All misconceptions about the interpretations of spiritual truths stem from this illusion, because they were associated with a church that has nothing to do with them. A church only uses terms that refer to spirituality; it uses them in a strictly symbolic way, never fundamentally, hence the misconception that it deals with spirituality at all.

An additional proof to support that claim are all the religious wars that had institutionalized churches behind them, if not in words then in deeds. Strong individuals that had attained personal spiritual experience were always in conflict with the church. Churches always persecuted those who managed to connect themselves with true spirituality (Gnostics, Meister Eckhart, Jakob Bohme, Giordano Bruno[45]...). On the other hand, they were always connected with rulers and collective interests. Although there is an exoteric and esoteric aspect of expressing spirituality (monasticism) within the church itself, it is controlled and permitted as an illusion and imitation only. The independence of spiritual cognition and its free expression is not allowed.

Institutionalized religions (churches) exist to the degree that people are unconscious, and to that degree they are useful for cultivating people by preserving tradition; but not to make them more conscious, to keep them restrained and controlled. That is why religions consist of laws and prohibitions. Tradition does not change people but keeps them within the confines of a mold. However, that, too, is good for them.

Institutionalized church, like tradition, is a counter-measure to the unconscious rampage of man, and this is the only thing it is good for. It always becomes evil when it is portrayed as 'spirituality' – because collective and national interests, which constitute the church, are given spiritual significance, which is absurd and always leads to violence and genocide.

All religions (except for early Buddhism), and especially the Judeo-Christian ones, serve as control and manipulation over people. The greater evil would be to allow an unconscious man to do whatever he wants. In such a way, indirectly, rulers help the unconscious man – not so much to become conscious, but not to cause greater harm.

RELIGIOUSNESS AND TIME

In its original form, religiousness saw the world as it is, as the eternal present. For that reason, it measured time in cycles, according to the seasons, and rejoiced in the renewal of life. The foundation for religiousness was the Sun, and the change of seasons was the centre of religious activities and festivals. The basic symbol was the equilateral cross with bent arms, which depicted the change of seasons.

The primary goal of Judeo-Christianity was to supersede the renewal of time in cycles and place it into historic linearity toward a certain goal, which means to make it conscious. We have the Christian west to thank for a singular time measured all across the globe.

Time is the primary mode of existence in this world, and awareness of time represents awareness of being. If the time process periodically mechanically renews itself, it remains unconscious, and no finalization of the maturing of existence through consciousness can ever be attained. Besides, nothing can be produced if a segment of the production process is perpetually repeated, nor does any process make sense if it does not yield a certain result. Although recurring time predisposes cosmological wholeness of existence and participation in its perfection, it must be realized across all dimensions and the whole being must take part in it.

Unlike the eastern concept of cycles of time (existence), the western man has been exposed to the influence of Judeo-Christian linear, historical time. He, too, moves in circles of the timeless wholeness of being, in much the same manner as any man of the east, but with the difference that he does it concretely and objectively, following a straight line, step by step. He experiences every step along the line of natural manifestation of the divine, and that is why he was able to express these experiences objectively in detail through arts and sciences. This walk, following a set linear pattern, has become the chief characteristic of the western world that dates back to ancient Egypt, which produced what is the most valuable in Judeo-Christianity.

Therefore, the East sees the entire circle, wholeness, and does not want to walk the line of this circle; whereas in the Judeo-Christian West this same circle is not viewed as a whole, but as a line meant to be covered step by step. It is the same circle line the East sees as a whole, but refuses to acknowledge as a task to be accomplished. The East deals with the whole as the timeless present and the West linearly observes time, to be able to view the whole down to the last detail.

Only in linear time can we manifest all the possibilities of the divine consciousness of our soul in all ways, with all details.

This circling of the maturing of existence set in time is applied in practice by a westerner in the most concrete way, through the alchemy of personal experience that inevitably leads to death and resurrection. By experiencing his walk in the form of a linear realization over a period of time, he loses sight of the original wholeness of existence, which the man of the east has well-preserved in his vision, but has become one-sided as a result. Linear set up of time has, however, enabled the West to become productive on the physical plane by developing technology. Advancements in technology of the West should be understood in accordance with the alchemical concept of the maturing of being on its path to consciousness. It is, after all, in accordance with the original meaning of the ancient Greek word tehnos, which denotes the way something is permitted to manifest and become, to crossover from the covert to the overt phase.

The event that initiated this linear walk along the timeline was the occurrence of Jesus Christ. It marked the starting point of history and the time of human maturation in divine consciousness. Jesus initiated historical development of mankind toward spiritual awakening, because Buddha showed it could be done, it could be an individual human achievement. Additionally, a message was implanted that spiritual authenticity is achieved through work and history, through death of the 'old' and birth of a 'new' man, through resurrection, i.e. transcendence. Hence, the measuring of time starts with his birth.

That is why, from the equilateral cross with arms bent at right angles, swastika, the symbol of the cycles of time, the only thing that remained was only the cross,[46] and in the central position, a man was placed. The idea that man should resurrect, overcome natural causality and conditionality, and not passively serve natural cycles that go on repeating themselves, was here introduced. The character of Jesus is based on solar symbolism to show that nature serves to liberate man, and not to enslave him.

The purpose of Christianity is to set time in a linear order toward a certain goal, unlike the renewal that happens in cycles, so typical of old cultures. A cyclical view of time refers to natural phenomena, and dependence on them, while linearity is a way to come to the end of time, for it to be transcended. That is why the teaching of Jesus had death and resurrection as the key elements of transcendence.

The linearity of time induces technological development, which is nothing but the alchemical perfecting of nature to be suitable for the presence of divine consciousness, its fundamental aspiration to overcome itself. (The father of modern science, Isaac Newton, was an alchemist). In the same manner in which an individual must learn to harness its being and perfect its way of existence to be suitable for divine consciousness, man must also perfect his way of living to harness nature and to be suitable for divine consciousness. Ecological crises and technological abuse show the degree of our immaturity in harnessing these potentials.

The essence of the appearance of Christ is in the following: God, which is the Absolute and beyond which nothing is possible, is in itself the pure consciousness that enables everything. Through everything that is manifested God projects itself in the form of individual souls that raise the level of their awareness by gathering impressions through all of the manifested aspects of God itself, in the form of the cosmos and life. In this way God personally and concretely experiences and affirms all of its aspects, that is to say, it affirms itself from the perspective of an independent and self-sufficient individual. This is how God affirms himself from the aspect of an individual being. To put it differently, all human souls are God himself who has projected himself to know himself through individual experience (this is why it is said that we are made in 'his image and likeness') – because he, without this projection, cannot objectively know himself, in much the same way he cannot see himself. For objective insight, the experience of separation is needed. We are Gods on a self-knowledge training course. Why would God need self-knowledge in the first place? The Absolute is timeless in himself, complete and therefore abstract.

That is why he needs affirmation of himself from the other side, from the (seemingly) separate and independent individual which will through the absolute divine essence know himself, through the illusion of time and the very process of cognition, of his own will, as its will and its essence. Only at the point, when an individual soul, divided from the divine whole with its will and personal consciousness, knows and accepts the divine whole, its manifestation through life and existence becomes complete, perfect, and finalized.

This is the true background behind the archetype of the son of God who leads people to salvation, and God almighty that proclaims himself through his son. The scene of crucifixion and resurrection is the archetypal pattern of the crystallization of an individual and his transformation in the form of the 'victim' with an initiatic death on the cross. The cross represents the outcome of the differentiation of consciousness across all of the elements and dimensions, as well as the process of individuation – after which a new man is born: God-man, an individual personification of God. That is how an individual, which has of its own will personally recognized its divine nature, comes into being.

Before Christ, the divine was only a faceless Absolute unaware of himself. Christ is the principle of individuation with which the Divine becomes objective and personally aware of himself - in man.

You could say that in a way God created this little game with himself by firstly projecting himself into oblivion, like in a dream, so that he could as an individual soul, the most intimately and the most concretely, personally experience all aspects of himself; (has he done a good job of all that he has created/manifested?). That is why in vedanta, all of the projected cosmos is considered to be a dream, an illusion, and man's awakening is God-knowledge.

Since the phase of individuation has such a strong centripetal force, so that he could never liberate himself of his own accord – which is the ego phase – God installed a kind of an alarm clock in the form of Lucifer, the angel light-bearer, whom he put in the role of one who wakes individuals from their egoic phase and illuminates the entire process. Since the only right way to awaken is to understand this phase, awakening is possible only by means of pressure and coercion. That is why the suffering of man happens, the outcome of which is depicted in Jesus on the cross.

Lucifer performs his job of the awareness of the process of individuation by means of coercion and duress in all of the dimensions, on the higher astral planes through his demonic forces, and on the physical plane through his human hybrids, Illuminati (and their servants, the Freemasons), who love Lucifer as their God.

As a result, man awakens through the ordeal of resurrection in self-knowledge, and by knowing himself he knows God in himself and knows that God is all. By this act, God at the same time finalizes his emanation in the self-knowledge of an awakened man.

History finalizes in the conscious, in a resurrected subject.

***

To understand the concept of time in religiousness, it is necessary to understand eons. Eons are periods of time that last for 2,160 years. They are based on precession. Precession is the movement of the point of spring (or autumn) equinox due to slow rotation in the direction of the earth's axis. The rotation of the earth's axis makes a full circle in the space of 25,920 years. This means that it occupies one astrological sign for 2,160 years.

Around 4,000 B.C., it entered the constellation of Taurus, when the symbolism of the bull was in the centre of religious worship (the Cretan civilization); around 2,000 BC it entered the constellation of Aries, and then symbolism of the ram was the centrepiece (Roman civilization). It entered the constellation of Pisces about 2,000 years ago and the astrological symbol of Pisces (fish) became the main symbol of Christianity. The age of the universal man, Aquarius, is soon to follow.

Everything has always moved in cycles, but they do not go spinning in circles, in eternal repetition of the same thing. Only to a mind that is completely conditioned by nature does it appear as though nature keeps going in circles. A truly religious man, one who has transcended the mind, clearly sees that it is divine providence for the cycles of nature to serve the development of a conscious subject, man.

THE VARIETIES OF RELIGIOUS EXPERIENCE

Religion is (ideally) in its essence an outer reaction to inner reality. This projection has a development that mirrors man's development. The oldest religions saw God in everything, as the spiritual source of nature; man was in unity with nature and the divine Spirit, but an unconscious unity; he did not have objective knowledge of nature or the divine consciousness that enables nature, much like he did not have awareness of himself and his position in the whole affair. Man needed to acquire individual consciousness of himself, and early immature consciousness of oneself always manifests in the form of an ego, a detached individual, seemingly alienated from the divine whole and nature. The phase of forming such an ego in people was expressed in a corresponding projection of God, Jehovah from the Old Testament. He represents a complete projection of the alienation of man from nature and the divine whole, a projection of the ego, hence the fury and violence of his actions - a fight against enemies he sees everywhere and in everything. Only an unconscious individual alienated from the whole can be violent; awareness of unity does not allow for conflicts with anyone or anything because it would be a conflict with oneself.

The idea of God developed in all sorts of ways in Judeo-Christianity. They are known to everyone who knows the history of religions, so we will give only a brief reminder of them here.

The oldest idea of God in Judaism was elementary, it belonged to the realm of big elements. It was the idea of

God as tetragrammaton, a four-letter word made up of the Hebrew letters Yod, He, Vav, He. This formula (JHVH) represents the four-pole principle of the universal creation of the world through four elements: earth, water, fire, and air. At the same time, it represents all the dimensions of existence and it could be said that such an idea of God corresponded with the principle of creation which exists in the universe. It is expressed in Kabbalah and the 'Genesis' book of Moses, but only at the beginning, in the first chapter. From the second chapter onwards the true principle of creation disappears, the dynamics of which are expressed through the number seven, and God is depicted as an inorganic being - therefore, he transfers to the realm of the astral. He (in an anthropomorphic shape) strolls about in the cool shade of heaven and asks questions he does not know the answers to (Genesis 3. 8-9). This is a typical description of inorganic beingness and is not a description of the Creator, but of someone who has arms and legs.

Jehovah of the Old Testament is the personification of the forming of the human ego. Judaism is therefore completely restricted to the body and ego; all of its teachings are reduced to a collection of regulations of what to do and what not to do with the body, and how to discipline one's behaviour. In those days, there was no other way to cultivate the primitive consciousness of people, so the role of Judaism had positive connotations. This was an important phase of man's transition from unconscious unity with nature to objective awareness, to divine consciousness. The same role was attributed to the Christian church during the early centuries and the middle ages; with all its negative characteristics, it was the only way for the human ego to be cultivated and for a unique civic (European) culture to be created – which is the foundation for the actualization of divine consciousness on this planet.

The phase of forming the ego is important in both the development of a child and the whole of mankind; the ego is the shield that enables the soul to function in the body and the outer world; the ego concretizes awareness of experiences. Without an ego, man has disrupted behaviour and finds it hard to constructively express consciousness. Only a proper ego can be overcome; the more correct an ego is, the easier it is to overcome; an immature ego out of balance is the greatest obstacle.

The next, higher phase of the idea of God arises with the occurrence of Jesus Christ. He embodied divine consciousness into living reality with his own being and by doing so he validated it on the level of personality. With Jesus Christ, God obtains his most human face - he becomes man. This is the Christian standpoint which even the modern church advocates, but the early Christian and Gnostic standpoint indicated more clearly that in Jesus Christ, God was saved from his demonic nature (astral creation) and elevated to a higher ontological level. In Jesus Christ, God becomes a personality from an impersonal and inhuman force, and his creative power is determined as love – which is recognized only when the energy of creation becomes conscious, which can happen only in a personality. For that reason, Jesus Christ divides The Old from The New Testament.[47]

The purpose of the occurrence and actions of Jesus is in overcoming ego, *in connecting man's outer actions with his inner essence, with his divine soul, in merging the heavenly with the earthly*. In all of his teachings and actions, he manifested the relationship between the inner divine soul and the outer embodied individual. He used the notions of the Father and Son only because these notions were comprehensible and commonly used in the environment where he lived and worked.[48] By giving the ideal vision of a perfect, authentic Man he initiated the fundamental differentiation between natural-demonic (*Prakriti*) and spiritual in man (*Purusha*). Therefore, he persistently banished demons from people who were possessed and proclaimed himself to be the Son of Man, to stress that he was different from the creation (sons) of demons, i.e. inorganic, astral (or is it this 'Of Man' his allusion to *Purusha* in the teaching of *Sânkhya*). Many sermons of Jesus can be found in Gnostic gospels (*The Gospel of Thomas*) and point to the perfect union of man's personality with the general principle of salvation. He testified of God through personal example, he spoke of Him as of Spirit and truth that cannot be found in temples. That is why conflict between him and priests and hybrid rulers occurred; God was and is a national fetish, they have for the past three thousand years successfully established monopoly and trade over human souls.

The character and the teaching of Jesus represent the biggest preservation of the interests of the soul on this planet, while the soul lives in this world and plays its role, and that is to go through the process of materialization and contribute to the transformation of nature.

The teaching of Jesus, and later the Judeo-Christian culture of coercion and pressure, is intended for young souls who have only started their process of incarnations.

The Eastern church has tried to be more consistent in its differentiation between the divine consciousness and protection of the interests of the soul than the Western church. That is why the split between Rome and the Byzantine followed suit (1054 A.D.). The Eastern, Orthodox church, has preserved stories of the true disciples of Jesus and the experience of the soul in this world; the importance of inner prayer leads a monk to see the uncreated light of the soul, and in mystical theology, it preserved the understanding of the words of Jesus that God is the freedom that enables existence and he is, therefore, love, that with its energy saves all creations, every single man as well as all of nature. Orthodoxy condemns sin, but not the sinner. This is the meaning of the Jewish word *tzedakah*. The translation into Greek was correct in the notion of *dikeosini*, which denotes the division of goods into equal parts, without any differences (Matthew 20:1-16, Sermon on the Mount). With its falsified translation into the Latin term *justicia divina*, God's will is attributed to the narrow juridic sense for mundane legislation that generates conflict between good and evil. Owing to a view such as this, the righteousness of God is reduced to violence that stems from the political and schizoid notion of good and evil that does not exist in nature.

That, too, has its reason for existence because, with juridic condemnation of sinners instead of sin, coercion of man grows stronger, hence the Catholic and the Protestant social system have become far more progressive than that of the Orthodox, which forgives man for everything in the light of 'goodness of God', which condemns sin and not the sinner, and with this disables disciplinary measures necessary for the material cultivation of life.

However, although it is backward in the material sense, Orthodox culture maintained development of the soul. The essence of Orthodoxy is in submission and preserving man's soul in the expression of unconditional love and goodness by which God enables everything, which is the expression that brings man one step closer to God. The essence of the Western, Roman church, is to impose coercion and duress through Judeo-Christianity on people to fulfill the process of materialization of the soul, thus finalizing the transformation of nature toward divine consciousness; or, in short, to implement consciousness of the Divine in this world.

Both methods, the Orthodox and the Catholic, are necessary because man must not forget about his soul while dealing with affairs of this world. The challenge is that neither of these methods should become one-sided and self-sufficient, or oppose one another. This is exactly what has happened throughout history though. It will continue to happen until man becomes aware of his true nature and his true role in this world.

The process of materialization is a negative path for the soul, but such is the plan for this world. It is hard, which makes it all the more worthy. I am not familiar with any other planet in the universe that has this type of role, so valuable and indispensable as the Earth: to conduct through man consciousness of the Divine Absolute across all aspects of existence and all dimensions.

The fundamental problem of Orthodoxy and Islam is that they stick to one aspect of the interests of the soul, its aspiration toward transcendence, toward the divine as its source, and very often overlook why the soul came here in the first place. It is here to conduct consciousness of the Divine through man and onto the whole of existence, 'Thy Kingdom come. Thy will be done: on earth as it is in heaven'. This implementation of divine presence on earth, man must do through himself, with his actions, when he learns all of the processes of creation and working with matter and all of the physical laws. No prayers or ritual magic will make the 'Kingdom of God' fall from the sky.

***

We have seen how the idea of God in Judeo-Christian tradition developed from the elementary principle of creation, onto demonism, to its ultimate overcoming in the personality of Jesus Christ.

At least four mystics have appeared in Christianity and spoke of it differently, trying to elevate it to a higher level, to the level of the higher mind and consciousness of the soul. The dual concept of God was thus created: the covert and overt. An attempt has been made in Gnosticism and in the work of Meister Eckhart to differentiate between God (which corresponds with consciousness of the soul) and the Divine (which corresponds with the Absolute). This is followed by the works of Saint Dionysius the Areopagite, Jakob Böhme, and Nicholas of Cusa, in whose work we can observe suspicions that God is like the unconditionality of the Absolute. However, these are not the only forays into a higher understanding of the purpose of existence. Their apophatic theology is an example of the highest cognition one can utter, but cannot be included in the doctrine of awakening since it was still theology, the teaching of God, while simultaneously presenting unconditionality from everything. They all end up as a discrepancy of 'learned ignorance' (*docta ignorantia*) and 'union of opposites' (*coincidentia oppositorum*).

It is very well-known in the East, particularly in Buddhism, to never refer to God as a person. Not because they do not know of him or negate him, but because they have perfect knowledge of this, hence, overcome it, in what is more than anything the unconditionality which enables God and personality to be, and at the same time liberates them from everything – in nirvana. Unlike Christianity, Buddhism is aware of what is above the principle of creation and aspires toward it. **Buddhism is the only one that directly affirms the highest consciousness of the soul.** This makes it the closest to divine consciousness. Its practice of spiritual awakening is identical to the goal of Sânkhya and Patanjali's yoga.

The original teaching of Buddha represents the most direct path of liberation of the soul and the purest testimony of its essence, but independently of the soul in this world, independently of the role souls have in this world, which is to go through the process of work and materialization and to contribute to the transformation of nature.

Buddhism is teaching intended for the most mature souls, in terms of karma, that strive toward complete liberation from the cycle of incarnations. The process of incarnations for fully self-conscious souls is nothing but suffering. Buddhism is the science of complete maturation of the soul in this world, to set oneself free from all the illusions this world imposes on us. That is why the necessary precondition for Buddhism is abandonment of worldly life, and starting a new life as a homeless person.

Once the soul becomes fully aware of itself while still residing in a physical body, man becomes enlightened or awakened, he walks and talks like Buddha, he knows who he was before physical birth, not only what he did in his previous life - which is as irrelevant to him as his current life has become - but who he was in the absolute sense. Such a man is as liberated from this world as any true Buddhist, who has implemented Buddha's teaching on the path of purification in practice (through meditation and discipline). He, then, sees the world from the perspective of the soul, exactly the way Gautama Siddharta described when he became Buddha after awakening in Bodh Gaya. Buddhism is the only completely non-violent religion toward all sentient beings because it represents the only testimony of a completely conscious soul. Everything that was written in the original Pali canon of Buddha's speeches and teachings is the testimony of an awakened and liberated soul, including the way it perceives life in this body and world, and what it does to set itself free from everything that is not authentic and causes immense suffering. The core of this teaching from the perspective of the soul is that everything that exists 'is not mine, it is not me', starting with the body, feelings, and mind, together with all the contents of the mind; to be always aware of what makes a body, feelings, and the mind; to always reside at the very entrance of one's senses.

However, Buddha does not state anywhere what the soul itself is, since his testimony comes from the enlightened soul itself. Consequently, it cannot state anything about itself, because it is the source of everything. The soul is an expression of divine consciousness that is unconditioned and without attributes, it cannot be identified with anything, the mind can only testify that it is pure voidness because that sounds the closest to the truth from the perspective of the mind, although it is not the truth, it is just the least wrong of all descriptions. The voidness or *sunyata* Buddha speaks of is, therefore, the description of the soul, and not actual emptiness. When in this world the subject of the soul is debated, *sunyata*, voidness, or *nirvana*[49] is the best compromise the mind can make in its ability to comprehend. In the same way an eye cannot see itself, the testimony of the soul cannot describe itself, it can only describe what it is not and how it is able to release itself from everything it is not. More picturesquely, the mind can only understand and ascertain what it sees before itself, whereas the soul is always behind the mind. Therefore, what is required is a meditative turning point from the mind to Itself, numbness of the mind, its emptiness, and this emptiness of the mind is the only emptiness in Buddhism, this emptiness of the mind is in effect purity, and the crack through which an unconditioned soul may manifest itself in this world through the mind. That is why the essence of Buddha's teaching is nothing but the path of purification (*visudhi-maggo*), without a description of the endpoint of the path. Subsequently, Buddha never spoke of the goal but only of the path, the middle way between two extremes, which means between materialism and idealism, beyond the scope of proving God and soul, as well as their negation. If Buddhism spoke about the soul and the divine, whether to affirm or to negate it, it would be the proof that it is not the testimony of the soul itself, and it would not be the middle way. It would merely please the requirements of the mind for descriptions and getting attached to those descriptions. All the other teachings strive toward that goal.

Since he was truly awakened, Buddha spoke from the highest standpoint, the way enlightened ones are able to see. Speaking of sunyata or voidness and the non-existence of the individual self, he wished to express in words that in the whole universe nothing happens, absolutely nothing – except what the Absolute does to himself. However, he did not speak of the Absolute because it cannot be perceived in any way, as it is not an object or anything outwardly. The Absolute is ourselves, in our essence or soul. Since there is no time in the Absolute, it cannot be said that it does anything, not even to itself. And yet, it cannot be said that it does not do anything, since life exists. Therefore there is nothing to be said about reality. One should only awaken in it.

Since original Buddhism is the greatest testimony on the essence of the soul while it still resides in the body, and represents a direct path toward its liberation and awakening during life in the body, it posed the biggest threat to the plans of rulers, hoping to implement the process of materialization of the soul through Judeo-Christianity. For this reason, they took on the task of translating Buddhist teaching from its original language, Pali, into western languages, and placed it in the hands of Freemasons and Jesuits. This was orchestrated in such a way that while translating they made subtle modifications to the Pali term *atta*, which corresponds to the Sanskrit *atman* but does not mean the same. *Atta* in Pali is a personal reflexive pronoun and simply means I, self or own, while the meaning of the Sanskrit *atman* covers Selfhood or Being, which corresponds with the term 'soul' in the West. The core of Buddha's teaching, which constantly repeats *anatta*, and means simply 'it is not me' or 'it is not mine' - referring to everything that is of the body and mind, which he later names as factors of being - Jesuits and Freemasons translated as 'this is not my soul or my Selfhood', with the conclusion that nothing has permanent properties, the soul included, therefore the soul does not even exist. By doing so, they turned Buddhism into a religion without a soul, that negates the soul, which is as far away from the truth as possible.

Buddhism does not negate anything, it simply leads to awakening. Awakening is not possible through negation, but only through a supreme understanding of the true nature of existence. In effect, everything Buddha said regarding anatta is the same that quantum physics discovered of matter; he spoke of the illusion of substantiality, materialistic individuality and ego, and against metaphysical establishing of Selfhood as a mental projection, which would also be an illusion.

The same was done with the other key notion of Buddha's teaching, cittam, by translating it as consciousness. The accurate translation of the Pali term cittam is detecting, thinking, activities of the mind. They translated it as consciousness itself, which enables the mind and detection, even alertness itself. At that point, Buddha's teaching became absurd; in translations he states that one should 'abolish the consciousness itself' to be able to attain the state of nirvana. In the original it reads that one should overcome the mind and opinion, not abolish the consciousness itself, which is the basis for wakefulness and enlightenment Buddha taught. What else is awakening if not awareness? How could consciousness possibly abolish itself, apart from becoming unconscious? Hence, 'abolishing or numbing of the consciousness itself' became the foundation of modern interpretation of the goal of Buddhism, nirvana, depicting it as numbness in nothingness. The numerous criticisms of Buddhism, naming it the 'religion without soul' stem from here. This absurdity comes from the falsified translations of the essential terms of Buddhism and has remained, unfortunately, unrecognized by all modern academic interpreters of Buddhism. Today, Freemason authors are trying to prove that Buddha never existed, that he is a mythical figure, based on myths that originated centuries after Buddha's life.

All of this makes ignorant people think Buddhism negates the personality and soul, although Buddha's speeches are abundant in detailed instruction on how to become a fully conscious and integrated individuality, descriptions of what a human soul experiences after death, not owing to the self-will of some God, but as a consequence of actions (karma). The whole of Buddhism rests on strict meditative practice, conducted with constant focus of attention or awareness, and anyone who knows this can confirm that man cannot sit still for five minutes, relaxed and mindful, if he is not an integrated personality with soulful maturity. If man is whole and mature as a person, he is focussed during Buddhist meditation. An integrated personality is directly linked with meditative mindfulness.

Buddhism fully entails an integrated personality and does not speak against it, but insists on the experience of its overcoming because personality, as the centre of the circle, has a very strong attraction, and if that were to become the subject it would automatically, become the end of freedom, instead of its beginning, as is the case in Vedanta and Christianity.[50] Buddha never spoke against the soul or God, only said that any concept of soul or God is wrong until we grow to be a whole person, that anything we are able to envisage is not itself, that it becomes impossible to envisage anything other than what it truly is – our essence especially – because we are that already. We should simply be what we are.

With any form of imagining, we project, separate, and lose what we are – by imagining something we are not. This is because of time. The mind projects time while our essence is the timeless present. With our mind and the process of thinking we derail from the timeless present and our authenticity, into some imaginary time and existence. The only thing Buddha was pointing toward was stillness and numbness, appeasement of the mind (tranquility and contemplation), transcendence of all the functions of the mind. Any notion is an obstacle to transcendence. *We cannot speak of anything that is beyond the mind because that is the way to achieve a counter effect.* Everything that is beyond is the fruit of the experience of transcendence. Besides, the very idea of personality points to this: it can only be reached personally. Also the concept of awakeness: one who is not awake cannot be taught how to be so, one can only be awake, here and now.

Everything Buddha spoke of regarding selfhood (pali: *atta*, sskt: *atman*) refers to the ego and egoism.[51] As an enlightened man (and he was only too aware that all of the answers man receives from the outside have a counter effect), he must give his answers based on his cognition; nothing can so easily cross over to its exact opposite as a personality, especially when it judges based on insufficient experience; most people do not have enough information about it, thus placing it on a lower level, accessible to them, to the world of senses, turning it into ego. Buddha knew that only a whole person can directly become, and even that for a short while; the stage of an integrated personality is brief, followed by suprapersonal wakefulness, into submission which enables (personality included) everything, into the higher mind and consciousness of the soul.

Buddha's goal was the highest, therefore he rejected everything lower. His apophasis is the most consistent because he does not mention God, sometimes in the negative context only,[52] although Brahma, the supreme God, is known to him not from tradition only, but from personal experience: it was Brahma who asked Buddha to announce the truth to the world when he chose to become silent after awakening. Here we have a humourous twist: while the western mystic prays for God to show itself to him, as the truth, Buddha was asked by a God to reveal the truth.

The realm of the astral absorbs all concepts and mental projections and gives them living form. Like a gigantic mirror, the astral world reflects all expectations and states. That is why, to a devotee of each religion, only their deities can show up – never somebody else's. The importance of apophatic theology and Buddhism is that they have this fact in sight, and all of the focus is put on the removal of all attempts of that kind. Only then, in the silence of a calm mind, is it revealed for what it truly is.

Zoroaster affirms knowledge of the higher mind because the very name of God, Ahura Mazda, can be translated not only as Supreme Wisdom but as the Highest Wakefulness. Mazdaism is a model of religion that strives toward true spirituality. The idea of one supreme God Creator stems from Mazdaism, the idea of resurrection, eschatology which promises universal salvation, the myth of the Savior, and the proclamation of the Holy Spirit. The influences of angels are also well explained here, which Judeo-Christian tradition later took over, especially the church (together with all the elements), not bothering to change some of the names even - but it degenerated man's freedom of choice, which existed in Mazdaism, to slavish servitude to authority. Mazdaism is one of the sources of Judeo-Christianity, which has nothing original in itself.

Apart from Judeo-Christianity, India in the east is an even better example of demonic overturns and influences. All the people who refused to align with the ruling elites, were, at one stage, accused of being demons (*asuras*). An attempt to overcome demonism is Shankara's advaita vedanta and it reaches as far as the principles of Selfhood. Nowhere have philosophical and religious orientations expressed the experience of consciousness so successfully as they have done in India, from extreme materialism to the highest idealism.

Opposed to all of this stands Buddhism, fully committed to the awakening of the soul from all conditionality of nature. It is the complete accomplishment of the doctrine of awakening and is therefore named after it.

318

While all other religions can be rightfully considered mind control, Buddhism, due to its differences from all the other religions, is a religious practice of deprogramming, or mental hygiene. Consequently, Buddhism is not a religion but a science of awakening.

***

The original teaching of Jesus and Gnosticism is the most perfect teaching on the nature of the soul ***while it resides in this world*** and is heavily conditioned by the body and karma, but with emphasis on liberation. By establishing the Christian church and imposing Judeo-Christianity on people, with the added corrections in Gnostic teachings that relate to direct liberation and placing the church as the inevitable mediator in that path, Christianity has become a way souls are led through the process of materialization with necessary coercion and duress. It was not a straightforward decision to use the Catholic church for this task, it was indirectly engineered by Reformation, and especially Calvinism, making it the leading figure in the development of the material culture of the Western world, later followed by a global process, and always in cahoots with Freemasonry.[53]

The original teaching of Buddha represents the most perfect testimony of the soul itself, ***irrelevant of reincarnation and functioning in this world***, as well as its direct liberation from any karma and incarnation. As such, it is necessary for this world to be its heritage, a light and a way out, and the final absolution from karma and all of life's drama.

In this world, Jesus and Buddha complement one another and become a whole that is needed for the souls of this world.

Judaism and Islam have the purpose of causing chaos in this world, polarizing opposites between heavenly and earthly options, which will stimulate the soul to grow faster.

The role of the East is to safeguard the heritage of the soul and direct liberation of the soul.

The role of the West is to lead the soul, by means of Judeo-Masonic dictatorship, through a negative process of work and materialization, to transform this world in divine consciousness, to make the soul experience all of the aspects of nature with the presence of divine consciousness. One of the initial stages of this process is the development of technology. For that reason, the West has developed material technologies, whereas the East has kept the truth about the soul and techniques of transcendence, i.e. the liberation of the soul. The greatest civilizations in this world have been India and China, who were even made aware of some of the most advanced technological achievements, but failed to use them and saw the beginning of the twentieth century from mud and bullock carts, because they did not have the Judeo-Masonic conspiracy to help them develop a material culture for themselves.

The merging between the East and the West is well under way, brought about by the development of technology and material culture in the East. Additionally, the West has been introduced to the spiritual heritage of the East.

The true future of man in this world will begin when the traditions of the East and West recognize one another as being complementary, and unite into an integrated development of life. Only then will the presence of man in this world be authentic and whole. Only then will man become a truly cultured being. Man will know who he is in his transcendental essence, and what his job is while here in this world; he will know how to express the consciousness of his transcendental soul in this world with scientific precision.

Our mind craves scientific knowledge the most, the highest knowledge of nature, to be able to accept the all-mighty consciousness of the soul and express it properly, in accordance with this world.

Only then will he be able to balance out the development of the power of science with the omnipotence of our soul. Science will be a physical expression of the soul in this world. It is not possible to separate the action of the mind and science from the question of the soul and its functioning in this world.

Maybe to some, their uniting and harmonizing appears as overly idealistic and mission impossible, but all the chaos in this world exists because it is being divided now.

TRUE RELIGIOUSNESS
IS TRUE UNDERSTANDING AMONG PEOPLE

All divine consciousness is one in the entire manifested world, in every form. The individual forms by which it keeps manifesting are the only difference between them, which include all of the forms there are, all beings and the whole of our cosmos.

One divine consciousness is in every man, its manifestation through character and temperament is the only thing that sets them apart - as well as individual life experience, the shape of the body, and personality. These differences exist for the sake of versatility of expression, not for separation.

People communicate with each other all the time, not just in words, but in deeds. Whenever things 'click' between them, when they reach a level of perfect understanding, divine consciousness has recognized itself. Hence, the corresponding feeling of bliss and love between people that follows true understanding. True love is nothing but true understanding. The bliss of love is due to proximity of consciousness of the soul. The act of love is always a mutual division of consciousness of the soul.

When people fail to understand each other, it breeds suffering and plight due to alienation, due to distancing oneself from consciousness of the soul. Then we have an individual mind and a feeling of being closed off in the body.

This is the law: every negative and wrong action and all alienation is an act of the physical mind when it prevails; every right and positive action and all understanding is induced by the presence of consciousness of the soul and its predominance.

When two people understand each other, divine consciousness connects with itself, God reunites with this world; God manifests in this fashion in this world. Understanding is merging the one same consciousness that was in different forms in two men. It seems as though this division into a myriad of forms has caused the divine consciousness to suffer, and once reconnection in understanding happens, it experiences the exaltation of love. Love is when two separate forms unite. Hence, the pleasure and the feeling of fulfillment in people who experience it. There is love in them. When there is love, all the differences in manifested forms disappear.

To be able to become properly religious you should try to understand thy neighbour. Nothing else is needed. Especially those who lack understanding; they need your attention the most. Do not accept his logic, do not increase misunderstanding, but decrease it. Lack of understanding in others should always be interpreted as a symptom of their need for understanding.

With an increased level of understanding among people, consciousness of the soul is also increased, and with it the presence of divine consciousness in this world. This is easier than it seems because at every single moment we perceive and communicate, divine consciousness everywhere acts as life itself. We learn to understand, always and at every moment. Our whole lives comprise learning to communicate and understand ourselves and other people, that is to say, ourselves through other people, and to perfect others by perfecting ourselves. As a consequence of failure, we are born again to be able to learn better. Therefore, stop killing yourself and others by employing misunderstanding. Only you suffer as a result of a misunderstanding, and understanding is staring you in the face all the time. It is this whole life and cosmos of ours.

Every moment of life, every act and deed are here for us to be able to understand them, our whole life as well as our body and every action has the chief goal of perception and understanding.

Our whole body was designed with the purpose to perceive and act. Perception and action are mutual. Perception exists only because of our need to understand, and actions are there only for our tendency to express understanding.

Your actions are illustrative of your understanding. Show your understanding with your actions, no matter how small or insignificant they may seem.

There is nothing as important as understanding. Every single instance of it counts and is needed for this world, for its improvement and corrections. Do not hide your understanding. Always show it, but do not impose it! The only reason for suffering and negativity in this world is a lack of understanding among people and its improper implementation.

The biggest misunderstanding is that understanding is somewhere, far, far away, out of our reach, that should be gained; you should get it to be able to manifest it. However, everything is quite the contrary. Understanding is at the foundation of existence. Like a spring that starts pouring water once the prophet strikes a rock with his staff, understanding, too, springs from wherever there is goodwill and awareness that says **one consciousness is in all of us, in life itself**. Always have that in mind when you are arguing with someone.

It is not hard to recognize the one divine consciousness that is in us and in every other being. There is only one universal way of overcoming a lack of understanding and conflicts between people: recognizing that one divine consciousness is in all of us.

How could divine consciousness be any different when we are all conscious beings and aware of the same life; when our whole lives we seek understanding and love in other people; when we all live together in the same divine world!

THE NEW INFORMATION AGE AND RELIGIOUSNESS

The global information society demands a new form of religiousness.

Three key events shaped the development of modern civilization.

The first was the appearance of Christianity and the linear measuring of time.

The second was the appearance of modern science with the founding of the Royal Society in London in 1660, and the publishing of Newton's Principles (Isaac Newton: Philosophiae Naturalis Principia Mathematica). This marked the beginning of science from its foundations and doing away with mythical and magical views of the world.

The third was the manifesting of Serbian genius Nikola Tesla.

Although Tesla appeared before the discovery of quantum physics, in his practical work he bypassed all the inaccurate speculations of physicists and based his findings on the physics of aether, previously officially rejected by physicists – although his patents based on the physics of aether revolutionized the modern world.

Information technologies and telecommunication are based on three patents by Nikola Tesla from the 19th century: one was the wireless transfer of signal and energy (mobile phones), the second was four oscillatory circuits in resonance (a remote control, something satellites and navigation cannot do without), and the third was AND-gate logic circuit (I gate), the logic circuit in all computers for the selection of frequencies by which screening of the correct and incorrect information is put in operation. Additionally, the modern world is set in motion by Tesla's electromotors, lasers, and radio signals, and the whole world is lit by his bulbs.

It made the world a global community for the first time in history.

Global information connection changes everything, including religiousness. It is not and cannot be the same religiousness as before Google and the smartphone.

Living culture in earlier times was to a great extent based on the slow and laborious transfer of information, and its concealment. Those who had information were in positions of power. Information in previous centuries was scattered, brought forth symbolically; today it is presented in complete form, that much has been facilitated, although there are various ways of hiding information even today.

However, in the modern world, there is a different problem regarding information. Previously, information transfer was slow, done mostly by people, but the depth of information was considerably greater. People were much deeper in their thinking in centuries past, they explored the divine depths of the being to a considerably higher degree. Everything we know about God and the most profound secrets of life we have from those ancient people, who did not even have the Internet. Knowledge depended on personal experience. It depended on the authority of the person who presented and shared it. People communicated by looking each other in the eye. Today communication is without any kind of contact, but instantly traverses the globe. This makes information false and shallow despite its speed. Speed and availability in modern times eliminate direct communication. The quality does not lie in the speed but the depth. Speed can easily create an illusion of depth and quality. The world of media exploits this to the fullest, they compete in bringing information and disinformation to us because they know the first news hits the hardest, nobody reads denials of damaged parties any more.

However, everything matures and people are gradually becoming more aware of this problem. In the future, awareness of the correctness of information will surely mature regardless of the speed information is transferred at.

Religiousness reveals the greatest depth of human existence. In the modern information era, religiousness must change in order to keep pace, it cannot be like before. External forms of religious expression must be altered, simply because they have become redundant. Previously they were needed to show the spirit of the time, they were in accordance with the age they belonged to, now they no longer are, and ultimately they have become an obstacle to the very purpose of their existence. Religiousness goes against itself if it does not go with the flow, if it does not change in accordance with time, if it stays the way it used to be.

What we have in mind here is a way of modernizing religions to the point of broadcasting them on the radio and TV, placing church in campers, and 'distributing Jesus' to people by the side of the road, making all religious activities virtual and accessible to all. The issue, however, is greater availability for the depth of religiousness. Without understanding the deeper sense of religiousness, danger occurs: like providing immature and unconscious people with free energy. That would further fuel their immature thoughts and chaos and destruction would follow. If religiousness in the old form, in its outer forms, can be imposed on everyone through global information connection, its depth and meaning would be further lost.

Due to the instant transfer of information a proper understanding of religiousness is necessary. Religiousness of earlier times had the form it did because the transfer of information was slow, hindered by many obstacles. Such were the physical conditions of its transfer and maintenance, and it was adjusted to that. Nowadays, things are different, physical conditions for the transfer and maintenance of information have changed, the obstacles have gone, and it is high time for the essence of religiousness to come to the fore and become the only contents of religiousness; it is time for outer forms to disappear.

The outer forms of religiousness, rituals, symbols and dogmas, were used to separate people because they were based on either territorial or national restrictions – and based on a lack of information of other and different people that inhabit this world. Because of information separation in space and time, people had no awareness of others, and conflicts were always imminent. The biggest development in cultures originated at the point of their mixing.

There is an additional tendency to continue with deception, for one world religion to be made, which would be a concoction of the outer forms of all the big religions (perhaps resembling Baha'i).

True religiousness of the future is one based on the universal, divine consciousness of the human soul.

All the previous forms of religiousness served the purpose of gradually bringing people to this consciousness. Their outer forms are obstacles in the modern world.

Before the work of Nikola Tesla, bringing people closer to this goal could not take place.

His works were based on the physics of aether, and aether is the physics of our soul, of divine consciousness. The physics of aether is based on the timeless present, there is no separation for it in either space or time. Information connection brings us closer to the divine consciousness in which everything is connected and recognized as One being.[54]

This is an ongoing change happening before our eyes. Because of this change, all the modern conflicts happen; they are, in fact, conflicts between civilizations, and civilizational conflicts are nothing but conflicts of time, our resistance to a new age. It is a resistance to making man become a true man, to rid himself of old illusions. All modern conflicts reflect one truth: man today cannot be a false man, he cannot, and must not live in the illusions of the past, he must manifest the consciousness of his soul because the speed and transparency of information and deeds will automatically make him feel the consequences, he will come in conflict with the timeless present, which is divine consciousness, and the outside world. This is what we witness as time speeds up. The gap between cause and consequence is getting increasingly small.

The higher speed of information, the stronger power to act, and having to face consequences sooner rather than later, is indicative of our ascension and integration with the higher dimensions (air, aether, akasha). Space and time are more united there than in the lower dimensions, where phenomena and objects are divided across space and time, the way they are on the physical plane. Since these dimensions are in us and we are made up of them, this means that we now discover and know about higher consciousness far more, we learn of divine nature, in us as well as around us. Such wholeness does not put up with falsehood and actions, which are not authentic and harmonized with reality. Consequences manifest directly.

It calls for a new social system which will not be based on assets and territory, like in Roman Law, but on the original generic community, which does not mean going back to the stone age but complete freedom to access assets as well as information, freedom based on the factual state, on human values.

A long time ago, people could not survive in any other way but to share everything they had, to be humane with one another because in their experience and their religiousness they knew and felt that they were living in a world which is connected to one whole. It was a generic community, in which people were valued for their human qualities and deeds. Naturally, immature people always existed, who were incapable of being human, so they grabbed goods by force from those who were producing.

Today, when we are connected in space and time, there will be no other way for us to survive and overcome this chaos, which is a result of development, but to stop stealing from others because the gap between cause and effect is getting smaller by the minute, space and time are shrinking; we should become the people that we are in our essence, the way religiousness taught us to be: sons of God, manifestations of divine consciousness.

The heart of the matter is that we cannot be anything else because nothing exists outside of the divine consciousness.

All destructiveness and all trouble, both individual and collective, happen only because we are trying to be something we cannot be, and are given the liberty to keep trying, nonetheless. The logic of all our problems is so simple.

By understanding all of this, we may stop all of these illogical and unnatural tendencies, and become well-harmonized with divine consciousness which is the only reality.

This manual should contribute to such understanding.

WHEN WILL THE END OF THE WORLD COME?

This is a question that is of most interest to religious fanatics. They eagerly await God in the form of a terrorist that would destroy the world and all sinners, but conveniently take on a limited number of his obedient flock. When a date with round numbers starts to approach, they prepare for Armageddon.

The answer is simple: unless they bring it on themselves, the end of the world will never come.

In the same way that the world did not originate in time, it will not disappear in time. We spoke about this at the beginning of this book, albeit in abstract terms. Now we may be pragmatic and round off this whole story.

This world did not come into being 'at the beginning of time' but each moment of it, which is always present, consists of the vibration of the divine that moves from nothing into something, from the space of akasha or the quantum field into a form or mass. Every moment this keeps happening, here, and now. In its entirety.

As Tesla put it, this initial manifestation is light. All mass, and all the physical world and life are made up of its photons.

Photons expand constantly, but not in a chaotic way, without reason or aim. They constantly travel at the highest speed because they are returning to their source, to the divine Absolute.

Where does the light find its source?

Definitely not somewhere outside the universe, but somewhere within it.

In Zarathustra Nietzsche said: 'Oh great star! What would your happiness be if you did not have us to shine for!'. His words are confirmed by the latest cosmological theory of the Strong Anthropic Principle,[55] which claims that the universe exists the way it does for the very purpose of forming a conscious subject, man. If the fundamental cosmic constants were any different, life would not exist. Therefore, light created the cosmos and man to be able to return to its divine source through man, through his self-knowledge; for as long as man gazes at the stars, their light reaches its destination, it achieves its goal. When the light of the stars enters the eyes of an observer and becomes his consciousness of himself, the purpose of the manifestation of the universe has been achieved. Therefore, stare at the stars as much as possible.

The end-goal of the cosmos is in man's self-knowledge, in understanding the cosmos. His self-knowledge does not happen all at once. The whole of human history and development helped to build it. That is why culture exists, as well as civilization and technology, so that the light of the stars gets recognized for what it is. Once it enters the eye of the observer it has achieved its purpose, but it is required that it enters the eye of a civilized and aware observer who will be able to understand the nature of light, to recognize the nature of existence as divine consciousness; as man's self-awareness.

The ultimate purpose of the manifestation of divine light is for it to be consciously recognized in everything, even in the darkest corner of the universe: a man's mind that thinks it is separate and different from the Divine consciousness.

Man was simply made as a suitable place in which this event of recognition may be accomplished.

Once this happens in man, god-knowledge begins to manifest as beauty and compassion. This is the ultimate purpose of the manifestation of the universe. It is the purpose of existence in general. Time then stops. We feel this when we are blessed in self-knowledge.

The ultimate purpose and the 'end of the world' happen whenever we manifest understanding, of any sort, either small or big. When we become aware of something completely.

When we share this consciousness, it is experienced as joy and love. The ultimate purpose and the 'end of the world' begin when we, as a result of understanding, forgive and give love and understanding. Then the Omega point turns to Alpha. Then the kingdom of heaven descends on earth. Then the end of the world as we know it ceases to exist, this world of unrest and suffering.

When we say that the end of the world is achieved once we manifest understanding, we mean that the whole of the universe has existed with that goal alone: for man to come to understanding, to goodness, and self-knowledge. The whole cosmos is a theatrical scene in which man plays the final act.

The world originates as a form of manifestation of divine love. Only when divine love manifests through man does the world fulfill its intention.

The world exists as unrest and disharmony. When in man harmony and peace are created, restlessness is finally over.

This world comes into being through the oblivion of consciousness of the soul. We experience this as our birth in the physical body. When we know the consciousness of our soul, while we are in our body, then the world disappears as the world of estranged objects, and reveals itself as divine consciousness and presence, as our being.

The world disappears with transcendence of the mind. In man who attains a calm mind in meditation, the whole world becomes calm, the universe achieves its final purpose in him.

Therefore, the only way for the end of the world to happen is for us to awaken to our essence, to the divine soul.

Man is a microcosm. The creation of a child and the cosmos is the same thing. If you wish to find out the secret of the origin of the cosmos, get to know a child. If you would like the world you live in to develop properly, learn to treat the child properly.

Then you will also use religiosity correctly, as a master, you will not even need to think about it.

Then you will be a role model for religious people.

ENDNOTES

[1] This also means that matter is nothing but a light whirlpool of photons, the energy particles. This has already been proven experimentally. Electrons, protons and neutrons can be created from light. By their combination, all the other elements are made.

[2] This omnipresent energy is something Tesla spoke of as the "energy of aether". It is the energy of the quantum field. Other names for it are "zero point energy", "vacuum energy" and "dark matter".

[3] We all know that the Bible speaks of the creation of the world. It appears that somebody in the past altered this text. Advanced research into the Bible's original language clearly indicates that there is not even a mention of the world being created from nothing, but only a division of what was already available, already existing, through intelligent design.

Mauro Biglino in his book 'Bible Is Not A Holy Book' (Mauro Biglino: La Bibbia non è un libro sacro, Orbassano, Italy, 2013) reveals results of the accurate translation of the Old Testament from ancient Hebrew, from the Masoretic text Codex Leningradensis. He proved that a thorough linguistic analysis of the original text shows that terms like "God", "eternity" and "creation" do not exist in the Old Testament; The works of prophets originated after the events they allegedly prophesied. The first six days of creation in the Bible comes from the Sumerian text Enuma Elish, as does the story of Noah and the flood; Adam is not one man but humankind; God's ten commandments did not relate to all people, but only to the organization of community life within one tribe, while they killed, robbed and lied to all the others at will. The name of God was Elohim, which in translation means 'the ones that from the sky came' or the "most holy", and is always plural.

From these texts, mere chronological accounts of one tribe's rise to power in the Middle East, priests of the Roman church created theology - but not before the middle ages, and with completely different meaning (the one we know today). There is a fundamental difference between the original texts of the Bible and their theological interpretation. When an average believer in modern times speaks of the Bible, he does not refer to the original text, but the theological interpretations and dogmas that were imposed in the middle ages. He does not know the real text of the Bible.

[4] An alternative to such a God is either the belief in God as a big ghost we summon during our magic rituals in churches, or the belief that God is in fact a super powerful extraterrestrial who came to this part of the universe a long time ago, did what he had to do, and then left, leaving us to our own devices to cope as best we can. Proof for this is abundant in the Bible, as Mauro Biglino proved. This idea fits with ease into the pattern we present here, if we know that aliens are part of the same divine whole, like we are. Besides, creating such a complex world is labour intensive, a technologically demanding undertaking, especially since it required the creation of the whole solar system, and not just the Earth. It does not happen in an instant, using a magic wand. For such a task God needed some great architect, an architect with advanced

technology. Esoteric knowledge reveals to us that they existed in reality, and they came from the star system of Sirius. My personal experience with them confirms this.

[5] Meister Eckhart: Deutsche predigten und traktate.

[6] On the Moon, see more in my book: "Moon - Magnet for the Soul".

[7] Isha Schwaller de Lubicz, *Her-Bak: Egyptian Initiate* (New York: Inner Traditions International, 1978).

[8] Among the many games human souls brought into this world, theatrical performance is a reminder of the principles of functioning in this world. Performing a drama on stage, in literature, is the greatest reminder for human souls while they are in bodies of why they are here and what they should do. Famous writers are old, big souls that remind us of who we are. William Shakespeare (that is to say, Francis Bacon) knew all of this too well when he wrote: 'All the world's a stage, and all the men and women merely players'.

[9] *The Good, the Bad and the Ugly*. A brilliant film by Sergio Leone from 1966. Three men meet in a round cemetery, shaped like a mandala, the symbol of Selfhood or divine consciousness. It is also an amphitheatre, a playhouse of our lives. The buried treasure they all seek is in an unnamed grave, which symbolizes every man. The Good man (nameless, or potentially any man) defeats the Ugly or evil man, whereas the Bad is hanged on a cross, the symbol of religious morality, as the only support to keep him alive. In the end he is liberated out of mercy.

[10] Many criminals testify to this (the ones who do not belong to the organized crime) in their confessions during psychiatric examinations: they were not in control of themselves, many of them even heard voices that drove them to commit a crime.

[11] At the end of the nineteenth century, the founder of psychology as a science, Wilhelm Wundt, established that there is no soul, but only psyche. The functioning of the psyche he attributed to material causes only. This is exactly what science has been doing to this day.

[12] The complete alienation of people in this world was best depicted by a director Gaspar Noé in his films "*Seul contre tous*", 1998, and "*Irréversible*", 2002.

[13] In the first editions of Encyclopedia Britannica there was abundant information on Grand Tartaria, the native country of ancient Slavs which stretched across Western Europe to China. The more recent editions have the data erased. Rulers who use deception in their rule were not comfortable with true history.

[14] Religiousness cannot be divided from the history of humankind. Religiosity and history together reveal the meaning of human existence. To understand religiousness properly, we must first be acquainted with the story of man's origins. It is, by all means, as 'unscientific' as religiousness itself, equally fantastic, but miraculous, and inspiring. In effect, only 'alternative' history provides us with the meaningful connection that archeology manages to uncover. The official historiography is not based

on material facts. Ancient esoteric groups in Russia and the Middle East have knowledge of such 'alternative' history. We will do a brief presentation of it here, to make the picture of what we are talking about somewhat clearer. Especially the point as to why man is religious in the first place.

Mankind did not originate on Earth, but in the constellation of Lyra. The consciousness of the soul manifested directly in the physical universe there. When it stabilized to a sufficient degree in the human body, they dispersed throughout the cosmos, and gradually degenerated because they did not develop creativity; they only used knowledge they had from the past. In their voyages they reached as far as the Earth, and their deterioration continued, followed by constant conflicts. When, after one of these conflicts, Atlantis sank, they came to the conclusion that they could no longer go on like this; their doom seemed imminent if they did not do something to prevent it. They used their genetics to create modern man, us; they removed all traces of their past (not everything) and planted false leads so that we are not able to reconstruct our true history (remains of prehistoric people we find), they wiped out the dinosaurs so they did not bother people, and set into motion the wheel of civilization of modern man. They installed psychoenergy centres (*chakras*) to attach consciousness firmly to actions, where each *chakra* corresponds to a certain state of consciousness, certain actions, the use of energy, in order to make sure that people do not think one thing and do another without consequence.

We were created in this world with the purpose of returning the human race and human soul to the original divine consciousness, with the purpose of properly experiencing the Omega point and properly encompassing the Alpha.

That is why we are religious.

In order for this gigantic plan to be executed, the first people withdrew from the Earth when they laid the foundations for this new civilization of ours.

Their withdrawal lasted for centuries. As they retreated, they left clear guidelines for spiritual and material development in the future.

This is what history looks like from the Alpha point.

Negative forces, who were in charge of leading the world through the experience of total negativity, by stretching out the Omega point to the extreme, have devised a number of ways to conceal the true history of mankind. However, in modern times this ancient knowledge is revealed more than ever before - although the negative forces, due to their inertia, still persist in their task as though we were still in the middle ages. Their influence on education is still monumental, which means that this depiction of the so-called alternative history will not go down smoothly, especially to those who have acquired their degree in the illusions of Omega point. We had to bring it forth here because it is still less fantastic than many of the assumptions religions are based on, which are institutions protected by law although they base their dogma on the belief that the dead will rise from their graves, virgins give birth to children, snakes talk, etc. In reality, there is abundant evidence for this kind of history, it is only a question of when it will be presented to the public.

[15] We will illustrate with one example only. In the pyramid of Khufu there is a royal chamber with sarcophagus. It has been measured (with a laser) that the walls of the chamber are perfectly flat and parallel, with a deviation of one tenth of a millimeter. This is also true of the walls of sarcophagus. Something like this cannot be engineered using primitive technology, much less placed in the middle of huge blocks weighing tens of tons.

[16] Etruscans were a branch of the ancient Slav nation who called themselves Rasenna. Modern historiography does not confirm this fact since they are more involved in concealing rather than revealing historical background. However, Italian historians and archaeologists prove the unity of the Etruscans with the culture of Vinca, the ancestors of the Serbs. This is proved by their common letter and genetics.

[17] As an answer to the question where the Vatican, more accurately the Jesuits, managed to obtain knowledge on social engineering, with which they were able to plan the creation of peoples and languages centuries ahead; we have to be reminded of the fact that the existence of superior technology in ancient history is a fact. Without being aware of this fact, it is hard to make heads or tails of history. Besides, geneticists have already established that human DNA could not have originated by natural means through evolution. They simply worked out that the cosmos is not old enough for DNA to be formed by naturally following the process of spontaneous evolution. Somebody used intelligent design to create it. That 'somebody' must have had, apart from this obvious knowledge of the creation of our body, additional knowl-

edge of social engineering. On covering up ancient technology, Michael A. Cremo's books (*Forbidden Archeology*) come in handy.

[18] If this sounds too harsh, a good idea would be to get yourself acquainted with the history of the Roman church; for example, how many times the citizens of Rome had to banish the Pope because of orgies and crimes in Vatican, after which the Pope had to come back to Rome by force and hire elite Swiss household troops to protect him from the citizens of Rome. Martin Luther initiated church reform when he came to the Vatican and felt disgusted after witnessing their practices.

[19] Today there are very few psychiatrists who point to the problem of possession on the part of the outer influences, such as Dr Morris Netherton, Dr. W. Baldwin, Dr Elisabeth Fiore, Irene Hickman. A more detailed account is: CE-VI: Close Encounters of the Possession Kind by William J. Baldwin.

[20] On the details of their rule you can get informed in the works of David Icke, especially in the book *The Biggest Secret*. An additional quality read is provided by Jordan Maxwell, Stewart Swerdlow (*Blue Blood, True Blood; Conflict & Creation*) and Antony C. Sutton. However, none of them offer the reason and meaning behind all the conspiracies like this book does.

[21] Ideas for many of the games we have in this world came from our souls, who brought them along to serve as a reminder for the principles of divine consciousness. Billiards is an example of such a game; it shows spontaneous

motion to the point that events are brought to some level of awareness, then is neutralized. Roulette follows the golden section pattern (numbers 3, 6, 9) and shows primary rhythms of vibrations of the quantum field, aether or akasha. A child's game of hide and seek manifests the rudimentary principle of the oblivion of awareness of oneself during the incarnation of soul into the body, and its recurrent discovery; it is the way one divine consciousness, divided across a myriad of our souls, plays hide and seek with itself. The traditional Serbian folk dance 'kolo' represents the cyclic movement of planets, space, and time.

[22] See books by Dr. Michael Newton ('*Journey of Souls: Case Studies of Life Between Lives*' and '*Destiny of Souls: New Case Studies of Life Between Lives*'), Raymond Moody: '*Life After Life*', 1977 and '*The Light Beyond*', 1988.

[23] It does not exist any more, it was destroyed by Islam. G.I. Gurdjieff partially put the broken fragments together in an attempt to reconstruct it, and brought it to the West.

[24] According to a testimony of a former Jesuit, Dr Alberto Romero Rivera, the Vatican created Islam to eliminate ancient knowledge (Sufism) amongst the old peoples in the Middle East, as well as Arabs who refused to accept Christianity. The Roman Church organized and financed the first Muslim conquests. There are many proofs for this in the Vatican. However, Islam has grown big and broke from its roots in the Vatican in the meantime. According to one statement by Shah Reza Pahlavi, there is evidence that dates back to the times of Muhammad that

the Roman Church took part in creating Islam. The evidence is scattered across Saudi Arabia and Iran, kept away from public scrutiny.

[25] In the book 'A Lexicon of Freemasonry', from 1860., Albert G. Mackey uses these words to define the notions of Freemasons, who are taught that the common gavel is one of the working tools of an Entered Apprentice. It is used by operative masons to break off corners of rough ashlars and thus fit them better to the builder's use. This is not adapted to give polish or ornamentation to the stone, and hence it should symbolize only the training of new Freemason is designed to give limited skill and moral training, and to teach that labour is the lot of man, and that "qualities of heart and head are of limited value if the hand be not prompt to execute the design of the master." Its meaning has been extended to include the symbolism of the chisel, to show the enlightening and ennobling effects of training and education. The gavel represents the force of conscience. This is our willpower, through which we govern our actions and free ourselves from debasing influences. It requires repeated exercise of our willpower to subdue our passions. Willpower is common to all and it is fittingly symbolized by the "common" gavel, but just as the gavel is of no worth unless it is used, so is our willpower.

[26] Heraclitus, Fragment, I, 89: 'To those who are awake, there is one world in common, but of those who are asleep, each is withdrawn to a private world of his own.'

²⁷ "What strange beings we are! That sitting in hell at the bottom of the dark, we are afraid of our own immortality." - Rumi

²⁸ There are people who have experienced clinical death but remember none of this, or experienced it as in a nightmare. They are people who, for karmic reasons, are not allowed to experience the truth; they are meant to remain in their illusions for a while longer, maybe to work on their maturity; they are still not ready, and they must find the answers themselves.

²⁹ This is a metaphor from *Tao Te Ching*. It explains that the physical body is only a means of expressing divine consciousness, and is not the only reality that exists. In other words, nature appears as rough and cruel on life, but only because we do not see the whole picture, all of the dimensions of phenomena and higher causes.

³⁰ This is certainly not your way; do not try this at home, do not tempt fate by trying to mimic what you have read here. A better idea would be to recognize all the ways in which consciousness of the soul tries to get in touch with you, all the ways it has saved your life up till now and you failed to notice, or you chose to assign to some materialistic conviction or explanation. They were hardly miracles, like in my case, more like simple life solutions - maybe through people around you as mediators. Maybe a word proved to be very meaningful for you, a gesture of love and understanding, an ordinary event or synchronicity that did not strike you as odd at the time. The soul prefers subtle forms of expression, like a poet who weaves poetry with the phenomena surrounding him, rather than per-

forming miracles brutally, by telekinesis or dematerialization. This is only needed for the very stupid and stubborn, like I was.

[31] Royal Raymond Rife used frequencies to treat even the hardest of diseases during the middle of the twentieth century. His discovery was seized from him by the pharmaceutical industry, which subsequently destroyed his career. Allopathic medicine is not involved in physiological regulation, although it is a crucial issue for healing organisms. This is the way an organism heals itself, because every disease is brought about by a disruption in cell regulation. Cells regulate their function and exchange information with the body through their membrane, which is perfectly sensitive to electromagnetic vibrations. The tiniest signal affects the cell membrane, and light facilitates this process. Our cells glow in the dark, as does our DNA. Hormones convey information to cells using light signals. The biochemical processes of our body are based on electromagnetism.

[32] The functioning of solar yoga is visible in the fact that there are believers with such dark minds (as a result of false religiousness) that condemn sungazing as a Satanic practice; they consider it a form of Lucifer worship because they identify sunlight with Lucifer. Verily, Satan enjoys having such followers who renounce sunlight of their own free will. It is not only believers who show affection toward Satan's darkness. There are ordinary people whose mind is eclipsed with modern science to the point that they believe sunlight to be harmful, who even put sunglasses on small children.

[33] Naturally, not all of the abstinents resurrect, but only those who work on themselves to achieve this goal. Without the fulfillment of this energy requirement, they will not make it.

[34] This explains why Jesus was allegedly born on 25th December, when the new cycle of circling commences. Jesus is the embodiment of the solar principle in its entirety. Do not hope you will be able to achieve this by drinking DMT during a ritual with a shaman. You will have to become aware of your whole being and understand the essence of tantra in practice, with which you will preserve your energy for at least a year to make sure it does not get wasted on lower centres, but only moves upwards. Energy automatically moves upwards if it does not get used in the lower chakras. The thing is so simple and banal that you will be laughing out loud once you resurrect. You will be singing like in the final scene of the movie *Monty Python's Life of Brian*.

[35] In order to understand the esoteric meaning of sayings and New Testament stories you would do well to get yourself acquainted with the works of G. I. Gurdjieff's disciples, Maurice Nicoll and Rebecca Nottingham. And by all means, become acquainted with astrotheology.

[36] See the book by Mircea Eliade: *The Sacred and the Profane: The Nature of Religion*, Harper Torchbooks, New York, 1961.

[37] More on this topic can be found in Fulcanelli's work: *Le Mystère des Cathédrales* (*The Mystery of the Cathedrals*), 1926.

[38] A more detailed account on the discovery of these methodically arranged magnetic lines of the Earth can be found in the works of: Ivan P. Sanderson, Nikolai Goncharov, Vyacheslav Morozov and Valery Makarov, Bruce Cathie, William Becker i Bethe Hagens, R. Buckminster Fuller. The official term for their final Earth grid is *Unified Vector Geometry (UVG) 120 Polyhedron*, also known as the "Earth star".

[39] R.A. Schwaller de Lubicz: *The Temple in Man. Sacred Architecture and the Perfect Man.*

[40] If you are a more advanced reader, grab hold of the book by Bruce Lipton: *The Biology of Belief – Unleashing the Power of Consciousness*, 2005.

[41] Consciousness of the soul in Russians is as huge as their country. It renders them most capable for the greatest feats for the well-being of mankind, for the most ingenious achievements. However, it is as unaware of itself as of the true nature of this world. That makes it equally problematic, for both itself and civilization, spinning out of control and sometimes being destructive. Often its inability to understand the functioning of this world is drowned in alcohol. Prior to the Bolshevik revolution, orchestrated by western Freemasons and Zionists, Russia was bristling with pseudo-Christian sects of the darkest kind, which based their agenda on resistance toward any mention of civilization development. The Bolshevik revolution was the worst evil for the Russian people, but if it had not been for it, they would have been in an even worse situation, and because of them the whole world

too. Bolsheviks and a communist dictatorship grounded their consciousness to this world, it implemented the materialization of the consciousness of the soul in the most brutal way possible. There is a question of whether such a cruel way was necessary, but, unfortunately, a fine tuner for mass global processes is nowhere to be found.

[42] Maybe to some people, these comparisons of the cultures of poor countries and nations seem derogatory. The issue here is about modifying mentality by means of religiousness, something that religions have taught us for centuries. The results of such teachings are apparent everywhere you go. These results are what the whole thing is about.

[43] We could remind ourselves here of the characters in the popular TV show Twin Peaks, Lucy Brennan (Kimmy Robertson) and Deputy Andy Brennan (Harry Goaz), and wonder if David Lynch portrayed their characters deliberately as clumsy caricatures to be able to emphasize the alienated, pragmatic world where honesty and goodness are uncommon, or merely to mock the kind-hearted and sincere people they are.

[44] Such a program of coaching Albert Pike put forth in his work: 'Morals and dogma' in 1872. In his letter to Giuseppe Mazzini he described with great precision the First and the Second World Wars, together with the Third which will be waged against the Muslim population, with Orthodox Jews as collateral damage. He has been the leading programmer of American Masons to this day.

[45] Giordano Bruno was burned at the stake in 1600, simply because he dared claim in his work 'Cause, *Principle and Unity*' the following: 'The universe is, therefore, one, infinite and immobile. I say that the absolute possibility is one, that the act is one; the form, or soul, is one, the matter, or body, is one, the thing is one, being is one. The maximum, and the optimum, is one: it cannot be comprehended and is therefore indeterminable and not limitable, and hence infinite and limitless, and consequently immobile. It has no local movement since there is nothing outside of it to which it can be moved, given that it is the whole. It does not engender itself because there is no other being that it could anticipate or desire, since it possesses all beings. It is not corrupted because there is no other thing into which it could change itself, given that it is everything. It cannot diminish or grow because it is an infinity to or from which nothing can be added or subtracted, since the infinite has no measurable parts. It is not alterable in terms of disposition, since it possesses no outside to which it might be subject and by which it might be affected. Moreover, since it comprehends all contraries in its being in unity and harmony, and since it can have no propensity for another and new being, or even for one manner of being and then for another, it cannot be subject to change according to any quality whatsoever, nor can it admit any contrary or different thing that can alter it, because in it everything is concordant. It is not matter, because it is not configured or configurable, nor is itit is limited or limitable. It is not form, because it neither informs nor figures anything else, given that it is all, that it is maximum, that it is one, that it is universal. It is neither measurable nor a measure. It does not contain itself, since it is not greater than itself. It

is not contained, since it is not less than itself. It is not equal to itself, because it is not one thing and another, but one and the same thing. Being one and the same, it does not have distinct beings; because it does not have distinct beings, it has no distinct parts; because it has no distinct parts, it is not composite. It is limit such that it is not limit, form such that it is not form, matter such that it is not matter, soul such that it is not soul: for it is all indifferently, and hence is one; the universe is one.'

[46] It was not until the fourth century A.D. that the crossIt was not until the fourth century A.D. that the cross was invented as a symbol of Christianity. Before that, the main symbol of Christians was the astrological sign of Pisces (fish), and the tree.

[47] This difference is best recognized in the words found in the First Epistle of John 4.12-13: 'No one has ever seen God; but if we love one another God lives in us and his love is made complete in us. This is how we know that we live in him and he in us. He has given us his Spirit.' There is not a trace of the heavenly tyrant and mass murderer from Pentateuch of Moses.

[48] The ruler of ancient Egypt was called the Son of God. The modern interpreters of hieroglyphics imposed the title Pharaoh.

[49] The Sanskrit word *nirvana* has the root *va(na)*, which means to 'blow' and prefix *ni(r)* which means 'without, outside'. Prefix *nir* positioned before a noun points to the lack of something the latter word denotes. Usually the word *nirvana* gets translated as 'ceasing, numbness'. The

Pali word *nibbana* is associated with the verb *nibati* ("to cool by blowing") and is often translated as extinguishing, like putting out a candle by blowing it. This term means to put out a fire, cooling, calming down. 'Cooling' refers here to the state of being 'cooled off' from the 'fever' of greed, hatred and ignorance, three great evils in Buddhism.

[50] On all traps of mental projections such as these, see J. Krishnamurti's book: '*The First and Last Freedom*'. On the end of the metaphysics of personality, it speaks of the very notion of vedanta, which means 'the end of knowledge', but Christianity also, which after resurrection sees only transcendence.

[51] The framework of Buddha's teaching regarding the 'middle way' is based on overcoming two deviations: material survival (*uccheda-vado*) which ends in material destruction; and idealistic belief in the eternity of nonmaterial ('heavenly') survival (*sassata-vado*). The middle way leads to a whole personality and higher mind, to wakefulness.

[52] Buddha actually criticizes polytheism. He once said: "When they hear the speech of the awakened (Buddha), the gods flee in fear."

[53] To avoid confusion: the Catholic church and Freemasonry are in complete unity, they only falsely present themselves to the public as being different, even conflicted. The Jesuit general is chief of all the Freemasons.

[54] Nikola Tesla was perfectly aware of this when he wrote: "Aristotle taught that there was an immovable 'entelechy' in the universe that moves everything and thought was its main attribute. I am also convinced that the whole universe is unified in both material and spiritual sense. Out there in the universe there is a nucleus that gives us all the power, all the inspiration; it draws us to itself eternally, I feel its mightiness and values it transmits throughout the universe; thus keeping it in harmony. I have not breached the secret of that core, still I am aware of its existence, and when wanting to give it any material attribute I imagine LIGHT, and when trying to conceive it spiritually I imagine BEAUTY and COMPASSION. The one who carries that belief inside feels strong, finds joy in his work, for he experiences himself as a single tone in the universal harmony."

He also said: "The day science begins to study non-physical phenomena, it will make more progress in one decade than in all the previous centuries of its existence."

[55] The strong anthropic principle (SAP) John D. Barrow: *The Anthropic Cosmological Principle*, 1986.

Printed in Great Britain
by Amazon

25225626R00202